Answers to suicide

presented by
THE SAMARITANS

to Chad Varah on the occasion of
the twenty-fifth anniversary
of their founding

Constable London

First published in Great Britain 1978
by Constable and Company Limited
10 Orange Street London WC2 7EG

Copyright © 1978 by The Samaritans

Paperback ISBN 0 09 462530 1

Set in Monotype Bembo 12pt
Printed in Great Britain by
Ebenezer Baylis and Son Limited
The Trinity Press, Worcester, and London

062015

November 2nd, 1978, is the twenty-fifth anniversary of the founding of The Samaritans. Since its beginnings at St Stephen Walbrook in the City of London (still the home of the London Branch), the movement has not only spread throughout the British Isles but is now represented in many parts of the world. Its development has been built on the loving spirit of thousands of men and women from different origins and cultures, but with the common aim of befriending those who are suicidal or in despair. Without them, the growth of the movement would not have been possible. But the founding of the movement was due to the inspiration of one man, the Rev Chad Varah, for whom the anniversary on November 2nd represents a quarter of a century of untiring commitment and devotion to the needs of those whom The Samaritans exist to serve, and for whom they are now accessible across five continents.

This book is dedicated to Chad Varah by The Samaritans, as a tribute to his sustained and sustaining vision, and to his achievement. In answering what he has defined as twenty of the most important questions raised by the work of The Samaritans, the book seeks to make a valuable and lasting contribution to the tasks of the future, for that is the kind of practical tribute Chad would prefer. But it is also an expression of the gratitude of Samaritans for the privilege of *being* Samaritans; and of their love for Chad, who made it possible.

Contents

Twenty questions

Contents

Definitions of suicide follow each article

Definitions of befriending follow each article

Contents

Twenty questions

1. What is the essential nature of befriending?

SALLY CASPER, BA*   (USA)

The first time I sat through the night with a suicidal friend I was too frightened to worry about saying the wrong thing. In fact, I don't remember saying anything much at all. What I remember is holding her in my arms, her heart pounding—both our hearts pounding—until morning, which was a long time coming.

Later the same year a girl I had known since childhood telephoned the night before I was to leave for a summer job in another state. 'I don't want you to do anything,' she said, 'just let me talk'. She talked for a couple of hours, blaming herself for past failures, disappointments, hurts; hating herself for being the way she was, for wasting her life, for inflicting her pain on others. She saw suicide as the only way out.

I didn't know what to do or say, so I followed her instructions and did nothing, just let her talk. I tried to let her know that I loved her and valued her and didn't want to lose her, but I doubt she even heard me. I wondered if I should go to her, postpone my trip, fix her up with a nice 'shrink'; but since she hadn't asked me to, and didn't seem to expect it, I let it be, and went off the next morning as planned, feeling worried and sad and helpless and inadequate.

Neither of my two friends committed suicide. One did, on her own, see a psychotherapist for a while. The other had some unexpected good luck which completely changed the picture. Presumably they were glad to have survived their suicidal impulse; we never mentioned it again. However, the experience

---

* Sally Casper is Co-Director and executive secretary of The Samaritans of Boston, and elected Representative of North America on the Intercontinental Committee of Befrienders International (The Samaritans Worldwide outside the British Isles).

taught me early that a suicidal crisis could come to any of us. No one is immune.

I knew, vaguely, that some cities in the United States had suicide prevention and crisis intervention centres, but I didn't know how they worked. The name 'suicide prevention' sounded so intimidating and clinical, disapproving of suicide and possibly coercive. I couldn't quite imagine sending a friend there, much less calling myself. However, I felt it might be useful to take their training course for volunteers, like learning first aid; if I ever had to help a suicidal friend again I would know how the experts would handle it.

When I moved to Boston in the fall of 1973 and read in the *Globe* that Monica Dickens was starting the first American branch of The Samaritans, I jumped at the opportunity to join a preparation course for prospective volunteers. Never having heard of The Samaritans before, I expected some kind of esoteric, paraprofessional training. Instead, I never did find out how 'the experts' dealt with suicidal people, because The Samaritans did not presume to be experts. They saw themselves as 'befrienders', and did basically what I had done for my two friends: listen, care, be there.

This is the essential nature of Samaritan befriending: to respond to a suicidal person as a friend, on an equal level, and treat him or her exactly as we ourselves would want to be treated—with unconditional, uncritical acceptance and respect.

The well-publicized 24-hour availability by telephone, visit or letter, the option of anonymity, and guaranteed confidentiality all aim to make it as easy and unthreatening as possible for a suicidal person to contact The Samaritans. Still, the client has the psychological disadvantage; there is no way around the fact that it is much safer and more comfortable to be offering help than to be asking for it. Our befriending must minimize this disadvantage.

The people who come to us are often very vulnerable and sensitive to rejection. They may feel 'I'm all alone, nobody cares, life is not worth living, I'm not fit to live, it is all my own fault, I wish I were dead'. Everything in the befriender's voice, manner and attitude must convey, 'You are not alone, I am here, I care about you, I don't want you to die, you are worthwhile'. Be-friending, in its simplest, purest form, is love; and it is this love that heals, that restores the client's dignity, confidence and self-esteem.

Although befriending is offered on an equal level, one fellow human-being to another, 'equal' does not mean same, and it does not mean mutual. Someone once told me that if I wanted to have my back scratched I should go to someone who wanted to scratch backs, not to someone who wanted his back scratched too. The Samaritans match up those who need someone to talk to with those who are willing to listen. The listener is not superior to the talker. There is no virtue inherent in either role; they are equal, though not the same.

Although I often hear Samaritans say that they get more out of befriending than the clients do, it is not a mutual relationship. Befriending is offered for the benefit of the client, and is limited to the duration and extent of the client's need—not the volunteer's. Depressed people may be temporarily incapable of holding up their end of a mutual friendship; family and friends get bored, impatient, fed up. Samaritan befriending offers a one-sided, temporarily dependent friendship to people who might not be chosen as friends apart from their need. The lack of mutuality allows the client the luxury of being completely self-absorbed; and the Samaritan gives his full undivided attention without expecting equal time in return.

It is a therapeutic, not a social, relationship. Although the Samaritan works within rules and restrictions and supervision, the client has no obligations, no strings attached, no contributions or gratitude required. The client is offered simple, uncomplicated support, and remains free to make his own decisions, reject help, break contact—even take his own life without fear of unwanted interference.

While this lack of mutuality frees the client, it can be hard on the volunteer. Sometimes befriending is a tedious, thankless job and we feel worried and sad and helpless and inadequate. The clients didn't ask us to join The Samaritans, and they are not obliged to make us feel worthwhile. We have to rely on our colleagues for

5

the fellowship and support—all those mutual things—that keep us going.

I got jeered at by my fellow Samaritans last Christmas Eve for grumbling that 'People are not at their best when they call us'. Well, they aren't. Last Christmas Eve they were very hard to love. They were mostly drunk, rude, whining, self-pitying—you know, not at their best. And I was crabby, tired, impatient, self-pitying—not at my best. We all have nights like that, when suicide starts to seem like a good idea.

One night the telephone rang as I was just dozing off on an overnight shift. I heard my sleepy voice answer, 'Samaritans, can you help me?' There was a startled pause on both ends, and then we both laughed. 'You first,' I said, and we assumed our respective roles of talker and listener, befriended and befriender: equal, but not the same, and not mutual—although the possibility is there.

Definition of suicide
Suicide: the legal term for self-inflicted death.

s. c.

2. What kinds of potential suicide is befriending best adapted for?

SARAH DASTOOR, MBBS, DPM, FIPS*   (INDIA)

Autonomous man exists in a socio-cultural milieu and lives by his reflexes and his biological body which constantly adapts to a changing environment. Beyond this, he also lives by faith, a sense of purpose and the will to survive no matter what the odds. And the contingencies of survival are many. I vividly recall prisoners under a death sentence, sent from the Andaman Islands (then a penal settlement) to Rangoon for treatment of advanced cancer, pleading to be cured. The majority of men prefer life under the worst possible conditions to death. Yet there are those who for the most apparently insignificant reasons end their lives. 'If I do not feel I exist, why should I not kill myself?' sums up their attitude.

Is it a crisis of belief in one's potential to keep alive or a turning of one's back on struggle, viewing life as a hopeless endeavour with no rewarding goals? On what past experience, either rewarding or punishing, does one build one's set of values? Or is it that the potential suicide is seeking freedom from aversive controls? History has recorded man's struggle for freedom—an eternal quest. Nations have waged wars to win this freedom. The opposite is also true: that man has subjugated himself to all types of indignities be they imposed by governments, religious practices or cultural patterns. Is the suicide's act a bid for freedom with a hope of a better hereafter?

Viewed in general terms, in practically all human beings considered normal—and the line between normal and abnormal is a narrow one indeed—there is both a conscious and unconscious

* Dr Dastoor is Director of, and Psychiatric Consultant to, The Samaritans of Bombay.

instinct to live and to die: a Freudian concept disputed by present-day thinkers but still a viable one.

Apart from those who consciously attempt suicide because of adverse life circumstances, there are many who are unconsciously self-destructive. Here, there are no dramatic attempts at suicide: the sufferers are people who are unable to meet the challenge of life in coping with a hostile environment, and escape into drug addiction, alcoholism, accident proneness or depressions, or lapse into chronic physical (psychosomatic) and mental illness. These people do not attempt suicide in the accepted sense but have the potentiality for suicide and lead lives of quiet desperation. Also there are those with arrested personality development, due to faulty early foundations, who are also prone to suicide: once a suicide is attempted, the possibility of a second attempt cannot be ignored.

Suicide attempts are a call for help and a drawing of attention **to despair**. Timely befriending is life-saving, for the attempt is a last-ditch stand with a hope of rescue behind it—'that I may live, that someone should know' is the hidden message.

Befriending as understood in the Samaritan context is a commandment and a tenet. It says, be a friend, be close at hand, don't probe or question, don't censor, don't be revolted at what you hear, and understand at all times in a spirit of support, protection, and informed love, empathy and a sharing of the burden of another person: in brief it is an answering of the emotional needs. This is saying much—the befriender has a demanding job on hand. All befriending rests on communication of meanings between two people and the sharing of an emotional experience: therefore it is a two-way relationship. The one cannot give unless the other takes. Thus the person who is befriended must seek help, feel the need for it and be in a position to understand and share the befriender's spoken and unspoken communication. An attitude of acceptance and trust must develop during the transactions between befriender and befriended. Why should befriending be the province only of a lay volunteer? Anybody in any walk of life, professional or non-professional, if so inclined, if so believing, can use the concept.

People who are best adapted and not so well adapted for being befriended

Endangered people who are in crises
The person who feels endangered enough will accept befriending and benefit by it. The Taungup Pass where thousands of evacuees crossed the border from Burma to India either on foot or in bullock-carts escaping the Japanese invasion, was a scene of much befriending. Each one felt uprooted and insecure. Caste and creed consciousness and personal scruples were laid aside. Sharing food with a coolie or cart-driver, living cheek-by-jowl with one and all were accepted with gratitude. The nearness of human beings who silently shared the same fate was the befriending experience of a lifetime. One particular instance comes to mind. An elderly woman jumped out of a cart and ran towards the valley in an attempt to end her life. A stranger sensing the danger leapt from a moving cart and restrained her, talking her out of her decision. Later she described the episode as a madness from which she was saved. She further added that 'because it was a stranger who cared that I should live, I changed my mind. It was the least I could do for him'. Ready availability of timely help was the deciding factor. Befriending deals with crisis intervention, as this example shows.

In considering the strict textbook categories one may commit a serious error of generalization. If you say schizophrenics cannot be befriended you will err. If you say the paranoid with his doubts and suspicions is a bad subject, you will again be mistaken. If you say only the neurotic and not the psychotic can be befriended, this is not necessarily always true. They are all potentially suicidal and despairing people. Let us not be solely concerned with textbook classifications. To label a human being is to reduce him to an inanimate object, robbing him of his dignity as a person.

Situations of stress where people feel threatened and anxious are numerous. To mention a few—chronic unemployment, losses due to death and economic crises, failures and frustrations, skewed family relationships, migration problems and physical illness. There are traditional periods in life, such as adolescence, menopause, marriage, when man's vulnerability to crisis overwhelms his usual defences and his well-tried methods of problem-solving give way. None of us can go through life without experiencing feelings of depression and anxiety. The capacity to meet stress varies. If stress is overpowering and sufficiently prolonged it will tend to break down the coping behaviour of most people. Some will show symptoms of an anxiety state and others will react with a depression. If anxiety and depression are as mild as what is normally felt by people under stress, then befriending will help, but if anxiety and depression are severe and accompanied by other symptoms both physical and mental then only psychiatric treatment is effective—though befriending may help to lead the sufferer to treatment.

Anxiety states can be mild or severe and cover a wide range of symptoms and personality configurations. People with neurotic anxieties are full of guilt and irrational fears, feelings of inadequacy and a low self-esteem, with a possibility of suicide in a small minority. These inadequacies tend to dominate inter-personal relationships, work, family and sex life adversely, with resulting poor functioning and an inability to take action which will enable the person to solve his problems. At this juncture individual or group befriending minimizes his isolation and feelings of helplessness and assists a better adjustment.

One does not come across pure forms of neuroses. There are always admixtures, hence the success of befriending the neurotic depends on characterological differences and dominance or absence of certain traits. For example, a highly narcissistic person who has a glorified self-image and is insensitive to the feelings of others may find it difficult to be befriended, when hurt pride makes him depressed and suicide-prone. The self-effacing, dependent types with inferiority feelings will do well with a friendly ego-support—the befriender. It may be stated here that severe anxiety states with physical symptoms, hysterical obsessive-compulsive and hypochondriacal conditions cannot be dealt with by befriending in their acute stages.

Thus it is evident that anxiety and depression accompanying

stress conditions, and mild anxiety states with incapacity to relate to people at home and at work, benefit by individual befriending or group therapy. It must be remembered that there are scores of people who cannot avail themselves of specialist treatment and who are in constant despair, with ideas of suicide—hence an experienced befriender would be of great help.

Depression
There are many types of depression and they vary in degree from mild to severe. The serious forms—the endogenous types—are the result of hereditary factors and disturbed chemical balances. Though not all endogenous depressives end their lives, the potentiality for suicide must be borne in mind for approximately one-third of such clients. At the stage when subjects are deeply depressed and withdrawn and with no capacity for *rapport*, befriending is not possible and physical methods of treatment are life-saving. If left entirely to the befriender, it would endanger life and amount to gross, inexcusable neglect. Befrienders should be alert for the signs of an imminent suicidal risk, so that a timely referral to the proper channels is possible.

After a client has recovered from acute symptoms of depression and between cycles of depression, the befriender's supportive role is crucial in not only helping him but acting as a liaison between the client, therapist and relatives, who have by now gone through an anxious period and are also ready for help. There is no reason why a volunteer worker cannot be trained to recognize early symptoms of relapse, such as a paucity of emotional response, loss of interest, increasing moodiness and irritability, an unwillingness to communicate and a general slowing down of function. These are easy enough to spot. In an over-populated city where suicide is on the increase, where hospitals can barely cope with the rush of clients, where private consultants' fees are beyond the majority and where psychiatrists rely heavily on physical measures and tend to be callous and impersonal in their approach, a well-selected and effectively supervised corps of befrienders can make a major contribution to the city's mental health.

A severely disturbed professor, intent on suicide, was be-friended by a colleague. Inordinate self-pride and a secretive, obsessive personality forbade him even to accept the fact of an emotional breakdown, let alone submit to treatment. This colleague played an important role in helping him to change his mind and finally accept treatment. The befriender was instructed to spot early signs of recurrence and report for a follow-up. As an observer and befriender she was invaluable. A small talk with the psychiatrist was enough to make her wise as to her role.

In masked depression the problem is basically one of recognizing the fact of depression—because the patient does not complain of a depressive mood or of any gross difficulties of adjusting to the environment. This depression is substituted by physical symptoms whose origins are felt by the patient to be somatic rather than psychic—hence he is never likely to accept psychiatric help or befriending and may commit suicide. Besides a befriender is not in a position to deal with depth psychology.

Loneliness is a condition where a person suffers from the lack of a personal relationship as seen in immigrants, foreign students, people who are cut off from others. 'Belonging' is an emotional need: the wish to belong to a family, society or group. People herd together in big cities to end a feeling of loneliness, driven by a protective herd instinct. It is more a problem in western cultures than in India, where individualism and self-determination are not prized so highly and where the joint family system with all its drawbacks and group-living still prevails. Befriending the lonely can be rewarding provided they can accept the befriending relationship.

Bereavement. Grief is a normal reaction to the loss of a loved person and in the course of time works through progressive stages to normality. If great guilt feelings are present, then the person may not be able to resolve grief and will enter into a reactive depression which can, if severe, lead to a suicide attempt. Often volunteers show hesitancy in working with grieving clients as they themselves feel upset and are at a loss how to befriend. Befriending can offer great support to the bereaved by encouraging them to recall painful memories and finish what Freud called 'griefwork' to a better adaptation.

The concept of alienation
In recent studies the concept of alienation has been much stressed. Under this heading are included—sexual deviations, problems of identity, alienation of adolescents, loneliness and psychotic illnesses such as schizophrenia. These people lack depth of feeling and have difficulty in relating—that is, they are unable to get involved with other people for fear of rejection; hence they need to be exposed to a befriending situation.

Sexual deviants are people who have been unable to form relationships, feel unloved and display a considerable carry-over of early immaturity. They are in great need of compassionate befriending, particularly when they belong to a culture where normality in sex relations is rigidly specified, where society is not permissive or where great guilt and a sense of crime is attached to deviancy.

Not all types of sexual deviancy are associated with criminal behaviour. Let us consider the story of Silas. He was the youngest of ten children with a tender, overprotective and indulgent mother. His father was dominant, aggressive and hated the boy for being a timid, soft child. Silas grew up hating his father and often wished to kill him. He provoked his father and courted punishment at his hands. It is understandable that at adolescence he went through a crisis of identity. Maleness was attractive but he could never 'be' a male. Femininity for himself was a safer station to halt at. He roamed the world failing everywhere, hurting himself, and seeking an identity, until he decided 'I am a woman. I need a man.' But this was no solution as he continued to feel unloved. At work, where there were men, he felt amorous and could not concentrate. Where there were women, he felt unnerved as he thought they were ridiculing him. He attempted suicide thrice—who was Silas to turn to? His family was responsible for shaping his homosexuality and his terrible sense of alienation—the feeling of 'I am an outcast'. He was befriended during and between his panic states. He was able to express his hostility in illustrated letters which were openly pornographic. He tested the befriender's endurance, friendliness and tolerance towards his condition. When he found he was never rejected, he regained the confidence to search for employment and in general to face the world. Finally he wrote, 'Thank you for curing me. I have started work in a studio. I trust it will not be necessary to see you any more. I boasted at the interview and got a job. Imagine, Rs.500 - a month. I have never earned so much before. Probably I will be able to bring up a show for The Samaritans. Thanks and sincerely yours—Silas.'

Silas felt cured. No one attempted to 'cure' or change his deeply engrained homosexuality to heterosexuality. He was able to stand on his feet and face the world, accepting himself. And when he was in the grip of a panic he knew whom to approach to find relief.

Social pressures invariably bear down heavily and do not make allowances for the individual to pursue his own preferences in an atmosphere of freedom. In a country where diametrically opposite viewpoints are held regarding sexual practices, ranging from total abstinence (Brahmachari) to phallic worship (Lingam worship) and permissive sexuality (Tantric practices), the individual is faced with a confusion of ideas productive of much anxiety and guilt. The common practice of masturbation often causes crippling anxiety, physical symptoms and psychic impotence for which people commonly seek help. Here group befriending under supervision has been known to be of much help in correcting wrong ideas.

Psychotics are incomprehensible to most people. They are estranged and alienated from the outside world and are unable to experience reality as the majority see it. On the face of it, schizophrenics are unbefriendable. Of course, the totally disorganized and demented chronic cases cannot be involved in any befriending relationship. But less hopeless cases, who had attempted suicide, were befriended, not for just one year but for four to six years, by social workers and doctors as well as by lay volunteers. They were exposed to human influence and participated in a human experience. They freely chose to attend and they did so fairly regularly.

Of these two have made a recovery which could be pronounced a dramatic 'cure' and the rest have made a social recovery. They continue to feel sheltered and befriended.

Factors in the social environment which do not promote befriending

A passing reference to socio-cultural attitudes of the client and his family, which may interfere with befriending in those best adapted to being befriended, is necessary in order to understand the difficulties and failures of befriending. Whether befriending will have an impact on the client will be largely determined by the socio-cultural set-up and attitudes of the family. In India (and some other countries) the closely knit family with conservative standards directs what a member must experience and think and how he must behave. In a joint family with multiple cross-currents of ideas, new ideas are rejected by deeply encrusted prohibitions. 'A befriender, in our family—an outsider giving love and support? We provide food, clothes, entertainment and even love.' Yes, all this, except an understanding of his emotional needs. There is a compulsiveness built around a highly idealized family image. A client coming from such a family was symptom-free after a battery of drugs and electric treatment but felt isolated, rejected and the odd-man-out. Soon she began to feel that she had brought disgrace on the family name and made an exit with an overdose of the same sleeping pills which were generously fed to her by the family psychiatrist. Her suicide note read: 'I killed myself to serve my mother—that she may live. Anyway who cares whether I live or die'.

The presumption that the next of kin know the circumstances under which the attempt at suicide has been made and are hence in a better position to help out is prevalent. Unbearable conscious and unconscious guilt feelings and the fear of exposure of the role played by the family, leading up to the suicidal act, will not permit the emotionally distressed client to be befriended by a lay volunteer. Every family has to face repercussions of a single member's emotional disturbances, and the skeleton in the cupboard must of necessity remain there in silence. It is a strongly rooted belief that only a medical man (psychiatrist), or a holy man with magical powers to exorcise the devil, is in a position to deliver the goods and to give an 'instant cure'. That marriage is a solution to all emotional disturbances is widely held; hence the fear that the chances of matrimony would be jeopardized if a client were exposed to an outside agency. There is a strong feeling that only a doctor can be trusted to maintain confidentiality.

Thus the befriender meets with social resistances which may or may not be apparent but subtly influence the whole befriending process.

Dr Rashmi Mayur, Director of the Urban Development Institute, speaking on the 'Telephone System in India and world communication revolution', has called India's phone system 'the worst', and has cited the problems as mismanagement, misallocation of resources and human error.* Bombay telephone services are inadequate, inefficient and expensive to maintain and install. The allotment sometimes takes years and the cost is prohibitive for the common man. A man contemplating suicide is unlikely to have a phone and cannot use a public one since it is usually in a noisy and exposed place. Hence our befriending service by telephone cannot be on a mass scale as in the UK, and befriending has of necessity to be almost entirely of the face-to-face kind. Our volunteer workers need to be instructed intensively to meet the challenges of our requirements, viz., the resistance of the client and the lack of anonymity. In spite of drawbacks and deficiencies, the befriending spirit prevails in all fields of Samaritan work, whether befriending over the phone, in a clinical setting, a one-to-one befriending situation or befriending in a group. The latter has become very popular with clients and the results are encouraging.

In concluding we must remember
Most people who are potentially suicidal or who make an attempt are not mentally ill, but are in the grip of a social crisis. A recent study on suicide behaviour has cited family conflict in 51%, and

* *Times of India*, 19th January, 1978.

work problems in 22% of all cases of attempted suicide. A Birmingham study cites personality difficulties in 70% and domestic stress in 40% of all attempted suicides. Thus the scope of befriending could be extended to the family who are also under stress.

Befriending must be accepted as a therapeutic force and professional and lay public must become more fully aware of the nature of crisis intervention.

Those who can be helped are people who feel endangered and are under stress, the depressed, anxious, lonely, dependent, fearful, bereaved, certain sexual deviants and even the alienated.

Those who cannot be befriended are the deteriorated, disorganized and chronic psychotics, psychopaths, alienated and estranged young people, chronic alcoholics and drug addicts and certain personality types.

Modern-day psychiatrists do *not* work in isolation. They collaborate with workers in other disciplines outside their professional circles.

Not all emergencies need the help of a psychiatrist, who is not equipped to serve the needs of a community of potential suicides. Conversely, emergencies cannot all be the sole province of a befriender.

Psychiatric labels are only 'descriptions' of irresponsibility, loneliness, lovelessness, insecurity and a hundred other emotional turmoils. Befrienders should be made to appreciate the fact that they are not dealing with labelled entities but with emotionally distressed people. Hence befrienders should be of two types— those that man an emergency service and work for crisis intervention, and others who are better trained, more knowledgeable and supervised to help clients in the early stages and after recovery from an emotional breakdown.

There is convincing proof that people after a breakdown need befriending more than anything else in order to prevent a relapse. It has been observed that those who have recovered and are symptom-free have lost the confidence that they will remain well, that people won't ridicule them, that they will be trusted and accepted as normal by their families and friends.

The twenty questions

In a country like India, where there is a paucity of half-way homes, rehabilitation centres and such like social welfare institutions for the mentally disturbed, there is a crying need for befriending of a different nature, in which para-medical services may be suitably involved.

The Samaritan befrienders are a therapeutic community—well trained and disciplined.

But for the Grace of God and the power of Eros, man would exercise his potentiality for suicide to a much greater extent. Does the unconscious in man not seek annihilation?

Definition of suicide
I vengeful, killer, hate-inspired—so I die;
I guilty, sinner, trapped—escaping life;
I hoping rebirth, forgiveness divine—live again.

S. D.

3. To what extent can befriending get through to the psychotic?

MICHAEL HARARI, MRCPsych., DPM*
with an example by SUSAN FLINT†   (UK)

Historical background

Our handling of psychosis down the ages presents an extraordinary hotch-potch. Broadly speaking, this hotch-potch can be divided into two: approaches to the psychotic on a human level (which is of course where befriending comes in) versus a policy of spare not the rod and spoil not the patient. (This latter policy was itself the result of a hotch-potch. There were well-intentioned misconceptions. There was panic in the face of the unknown. And there was the opposite sort of panic: at recognizing, writ large, what one dimly perceived in oneself.)

To set the scene for current developments, let us pick a few examples out of the historian's hat.

Spare not the rod and spoil not the patient

The practice of trephining, still being advocated in the middle ages, dates back to neolithic times: make a sizeable hole in your patient's head, and this will let out the evil spirits.

Following the publication in 1487 of *The Witches' Hammer* (*Malleus Maleficarum*) we Europeans spent some two centuries burning the mentally ill at the stake. (Estimates of the number of women involved vary from scores of thousands upwards; a considerable proportion were undoubtedly hallucinating schizophrenics and psychotic depressives with delusions of guilt.)

In eighteenth-century London it was a popular Sunday pastime

* Dr Harari is Psychiatric Consultant to the London Branch.
† Susan Flint is a Leader and Tutor at the London Branch.

to gawp at the men and women of Bedlam. And the mental hospitals of the Age of Enlightenment were something to gawp at. Disturbed patients were chained up, defecating and urinating *in situ*. Treatment included beating, blood-letting, purging, vomiting and the 'fools' bridge'—a walk-the-plank device which plunged patients into icy water. Some of these methods were a hangover from the time-honoured belief that if you made life uncomfortable enough for the evil spirits provoking the madness, they would leave their abode in the patient and migrate elsewhere.

Finally, let us not forget that a well-tried remedy for attempted suicide was still being used in the United Kingdom up to a century ago: death by hanging.

Not much room for befriending here.

Approaches to the psychotic on a human level
The ancient Egyptians devised a régime of trips on the Nile, music, dancing, painting—curiously like what we would now call milieu therapy in a well-run psychiatric unit. (Or like a befriender winkling a client out from the isolation of his psychosis and reintroducing him to the world: a bus trip, a concert, a disco, the National Gallery.)

Music was also used as psychiatric treatment by the followers of Pythagoras (influenced, no doubt, by their belief in the music of the spheres). Compare Samuel 1.16.23: 'And it came to pass when the evil spirit from God was upon Saul, that David took an harp, and played with his hand: so Saul was refreshed, and was well, and the evil spirit departed from him.' (Modern equivalent: befriender invites client to listen to his hi-fi.)

The Mohammedans were traditionally friendly in their approach to insanity, being inclined to believe (like the author of the Book of Samuel) that it was inspired from on high. (Modern equivalent: befriender values psychotic client as a fellow worker in the business of living, undergoing special tribulation and needing special care; perhaps, with Laing, seeing a meaningfulness in the client's whole psychotic reaction.)

How do you get through to a psychotic in fetters? By taking them off. Pinel was accused of insanity when he unchained fifty male patients at the Bicêtre hospital in Paris in 1796. His response was to unchain the women at the Salpêtrière.

From unchaining patients to unlocking wards is a logical development (which took about a hundred and fifty years). So if I have a psychotic breakdown tomorrow, I shall have cause to feel grateful to Pinel for the fact that, with any luck, I shall be admitted to an open ward. I shall also have cause for gratitude to the pioneers of the therapeutic community (men like Maxwell Jones and Denis Martin) when I find that, again with any luck, I am not left to vegetate nor sat on, but attempts are made to get through to me from every quarter. (E.g., I can expect to be involved, while still as nutty as a fruitcake, in group therapy, in the running of the ward.)

An extension of this open-door policy is the current emphasis on the care and rehabilitation of psychotic patients in the community whenever possible. This means (a) that there are likely to be more psychotics in the community to befriend; and (b) that befriending psychotics is right in the mainstream of present-day psychiatric thinking.

Opportunities and difficulties
Compared with a quarter-century's accumulated experience of befriending in general, our experience of befriending psychotics is still relatively limited. Drawing on the knowledge that we do have, and supplementing with what we know from other disciplines, we can map out the following territory and guidelines.

1. When there is a suspicion that a client who makes contact may be psychotic, if there is a cat's chance in hell of coaxing him to accept medical aid, the ideal is a psychiatric assessment forthwith (whether by a psychiatrist or sympathetic GP). In an ideal world again, this should precede any decision on befriending. In practice, befriending may well be needed before the client can face the spooky idea of going to a doctor at all.

2. If the client is in an acute psychotic state, then he is unbefriendable (and needs to be in hospital). Psychotics in this plight are less likely to seek us out in the first place; if they do, or are brought in, it is a question of pulling out all the stops to get them

21

to an emergency clinic. (Rule-of-thumb examples of an acute psychotic state: [a] 'A raving lunatic'. [b] Depression to the point of severe retardation, a deal of weight loss, monstrous guilt—'My wickedness caused the outbreak of cholera in P'ing P'ong'.)

3. If the client is not in an acute psychotic state, then the chances are good that rapport can be established; in which case befriending can be every bit as valuable as for any of the non-psychotic troubles we see. But the befriender may have to stretch his ideas. He may need to adjust to a longer time scale and slower tempo (see under 5 below). He may have to hang on to his wits in a magical world (e.g., share the client affably with the client's own 'voices'—there may in fact be a whole party going on, rather than a dialogue between client and befriender). And the befriender may have to accept, in some clients, a degree of irreducible handicap (e.g., a permanent delusory system, or a blunting of emotional potential).

4. Memorandum to ourselves, when we're grappling with difficulties like these: more psychotics are more accessible more of the time than we think. We know from an authoritative source, namely from those who have made the voyage into psychosis and out again, that even depressive stupor, even schizophrenic catatonia, are not what they seem. These states may look like Lot's wife after being turned into a pillar of salt; but many sufferers are receiving loud and clear every word spoken, though quite unable to respond by so much as a murmur or a twitch.

The psychotics we befriend are well on the hither side of torpor or catatonia; so we can comfort ourselves when we feel we're knocking against an invisible glass partition, and go on knocking.

5. Time scale and tempo have been touched on.

Elisabeth Shoenberg, a colleague of Denis Martin, gives a pertinent account of an experiment in group therapy. The group had a surrealistic flavour: all of its half dozen members were mute. (They were schizophrenic women who had been despaired of; passive, doubly incontinent.)

The group met daily. For five weeks Dr Shoenberg talked into silence; not trying to be 'therapeutic', but speaking to these women about everyday things, telling them what she had been doing herself.

Then one of them asked a question. Gradually, they all began to talk. Over the months there were outings in Dr Shoenberg's car, visits to her home for tea. Some seven months after the first silent meeting, three of the women were ready to leave hospital. This remarkable venture would obviously have been sabotaged by inflexible ideas about time and pace. ('Give them twenty sessions; if they haven't spoken by then, forget it, it's not cost-effective.')

6. Delusions ('I know the Freemasons are after me') and hallucinations ('I can hear a voice commenting on everything I do') need not preclude communication.

'Lord help us, it's the devil himself,' said a middle-aged lady on catching sight of me. But for want of a better audience, Mephistopheles would do for a gossip about her husband and caravan.

Arguing with delusions and hallucinations is usually a waste of breath. On the other hand it can be unhelpful to agree with them: the befriender is called upon, among his other roles, to be the ambassador of external reality. What can be valuable, and a real point of contact, is to share these adventures of the client on the basis of: 'I respect this as your experience of the world, even though I don't experience it that way myself. I can feel how terrifying/weird/depressing/interesting it must be.'

Delusions and hallucinations can of course be interpreted analytically—but this is outside our job as befrienders.

7. Some psychotics can be, and have been, successfully treated with little reliance on medication. This is fascinating work. We have however to bear in mind our ignorance: we do not yet know what proportion of psychotics, and what exact categories and degrees of psychosis, are going to respond to this régime. As of now, in our everyday world, most psychotics (like most diabetics) need the help of their tablets and injections, whatever else they need. Many are reluctant to persevere. (The schizophrenic: 'They're trying to poison me.' The hypomaniac: 'I've

never felt better in my life, I don't need the stuff.' The depressive: 'I'm not worth treating.')

Befrienders have a contribution to make here (not necessarily by nagging!). It's a two-way process: befriending can facilitate medication, and medication can facilitate befriending.

Baron Pietro Pisani, eighteenth–nineteenth century, lost his son. This triggered a depression lasting many years. He later became superintendent of the asylum at Palermo. Framing new regulations, Pisani wrote: 'In spite of their mental disorders, patients respond to a frank and sincere approach; and are able to experience feelings of confidence, benevolence, friendship and pride.'

Example (by Susan Flint)
Elaine was brought in by a friend at work, who felt she needed help.

The friend departed, and Elaine sat. We both sat, in silence— for about twenty minutes. Suddenly she dashed out of the Centre, leaving one bewildered volunteer feeling acutely inadequate.

A while later she was back. Another silence, and another hurried exit; which was all for that day.

Next day she was back again. She looked absolutely terrified. With gentle questioning, something disjointed emerged about an aunt who had died. Out she dashed again. Back, and a bit more about the aunt. But still no name, no address, no age (mid-twenties?) and nothing about her immediate family. Out again, and back for a longer period.

It was only gradually we discovered that Elaine was hallucinating. She was hearing the voice of her dead aunt (it usually came from outside the window). The voice was telling her to kill herself.

Elaine was persuaded to see a doctor, and I went with her. But when we arrived she reverted to her frightened silence.

Arrangements were then made for her to see a psychiatrist, and again I went with her. There was a lengthy wait at the clinic, which was problematical: Elaine kept rushing out of the building.

The psychiatrist advised an immediate admission and found a

bed for her. It was on the way to hospital that Elaine told me her name; she also gave me a phone number, so that I could contact her parents. The hospital staff were so concerned about her that she was put in a closed ward. I had my misgivings about this, and was not too surprised when she phoned to say she'd discharged herself.

She came back to the centre and we talked further. She began to tell me about her home, her parents, the aunt. A family doctor was mentioned, who could be consulted. And she would see another psychiatrist, provided this was a woman.

With the GP's help a lady psychiatrist was located. Once again there was the silence, the panic, the rushing out—but we managed it. This psychiatrist, like the first, advised treatment in hospital; but now we approached the admission much more slowly.

A friendship was being built up. Elaine would still stare into space, and one never quite knew what she might be hearing. Between whiles our meetings were becoming much more productive.

Eventually she went into hospital, this time on an open ward, where she had some group therapy and a course of medication. She kept in close touch by telephone, and went home at weekends. On a visit to the hospital I had the opportunity of meeting her parents.

After about two months Elaine was discharged, perhaps a little better. But there were still the blank looks; and there were the bottles of aspirin. She would hand them over, having decided not to take them. I formed a whole collection. (There were also sporadic calls from hospitals, when she had taken a few too many.) But she was keeping her psychiatric outpatient appointments. And we were beginning to get round to the problem areas in her sexual development.

We jogged along, sometimes talking three or four times a week, sometimes once a fortnight. Then she told me she'd met a man in a pub; she had talked to him about me, and he wanted to meet me. We duly met up: he was kind, gentle, thoughtful.

They spent a lot of time together and Elaine began to look much happier. At this point her fear of sex erupted. She sought counselling for her difficulties at the Family Planning Association; sometimes she needed me to go with her to boost her morale.

As if she hadn't been through enough already, she now started having blackouts, and had to go into hospital for investigations. Epilepsy was diagnosed. Her boyfriend could not have been more supportive. They became engaged, and set a date for the wedding a year ahead, as Elaine wanted to make sure the epilepsy was controlled.

She still has her moments of doubt—whether she's 'normal', whether she should be marrying at all. Her treatment at the Family Planning Association continues; she no longer needs me to escort her, but she drops in for support. When the difficulties of treatment are intense, a gift of bath salts seems to help.

The wedding approaches.

My first meeting with Elaine was some five years ago. She has taught me a great deal. I shall always feel glad to have known her.

Definition of suicide
Suicide is when you can't cope with yourself.

S. F.

4. How can befrienders (Samaritans) be protected from useless manipulation by the psychopathic?

DR DOMINIQUE ALESSANDRI*   (FRANCE)

The statement of a young volunteer after a year's experience in The Samaritans seems to be a good introduction to this question.

'I came here thinking that we ought to do everything possible to help those who ask for it—now I see clearly that there are some people for whom we can do nothing more.'

This was by no means the remark of a discouraged person—her faith and enthusiasm for the actions of The Samaritans remain undiminished. At first glance this seems to present a contradiction; yet it does not. For the Samaritan of the Gospel performed two very distinct acts:

First, he brought immediate assistance to a man in need.

Secondly, and much more importantly, he gave him the possibility of setting out again in life, freely and with dignity.

This is the story of an action which is completely exemplary: an anonymous act (the choice of a Samaritan is free of any religious or moral conviction), disinterested, efficient, and limited in time. This action in no way left the recipient dependent on the Samaritan but, on the contrary, free to return to live among other men. In addition, the action did not inconvenience the Samaritan in any way. He possessed the material means (time and money) to bring this help without neglecting his own occupations—this, too, is not without importance. And it is this special meaning of the Samaritan's help that the parable emphasizes.

Two essential questions now arise that define the limits of this help.

* Dr Alessandri, who is a psychiatrist, is a member of the Groupement d'Etudes et de Prévention du Suicide; she is also a member of Befrienders International.

Will the Samaritan's help have this liberating power for the person to whom it is granted, or will it be only temporarily effective, leaving the recipient in a state of dependence on his helpers and society?

Can the Samaritan's help be effective without carrying a prejudice (either moral or material) towards the organization, which would endanger its capacity to help other clients?

In the case of people given the rough, general label of 'psychopaths', these questions have a very special relevance. Psychopaths, or 'immature personalities', comprise all categories of individuals whose emotions have remained blocked at an infantile stage. The extent of this blockage, as well as the stage at which it occurs, varies, as do their disorders and degrees of psychopathy.

If we limit ourselves to plain psychopathy, the business of enumerating, describing and classifying psychopathic disorders is of only very limited interest for Samaritans. There would even be a certain degree of danger for Samaritans in believing that one can, by reading descriptive and theoretical work, learn to 'label a client' and anticipate the surprises and dangers that he has in reserve. By so doing, The Samaritans' spontaneity—one of the most important qualities in their response—risks being weakened.

It seems infinitely more appropriate during the volunteers' training to prepare them to face these dangers when they present themselves in practice. Two distinct aspects of this topic should therefore be considered. The first would summarize the most obvious and frequent traps laid by these psychopaths, according to the characteristics of their personality. The second, and the most essential, would be to get The Samaritans to ask themselves why they fall into certain traps, and to consider both the need for and the means of avoiding them.

Certain characteristics often found in psychopaths
An enormous emotional greed: their demands for help constitute 'the proof that they are loved', but no sooner is this proof of love obtained, than it is rejected—deemed insufficient. And so their demands will be renewed. They can be materialistic (money, social aid), or emotional (a desire to monopolize attention, a

desire for pity, a desire to challenge through aggressive behaviour, then see just how much they can be loved despite this). These demands and challenges can only become more and more incessant and abusive. With this 'emotional greed' is associated an incapacity to love of surprising magnitude. What they are looking for is to seduce, to attract pity, to manipulate. Other people are for them only the instruments of their desires. Aggressiveness always lies behind their demands. The more one has, in acceding to their demands, given them the hope that they can always be satisfied, the less able they are to tolerate frustration. Here we must point out a danger for Samaritans. If they allow this kind of hope to develop in a psychopath, a perilous 'return to reality' is to be feared the day they refuse to go further in befriending him. Faced with frustration, the psychopath's aggressive nature will be released, often in an impulsive and destructive manner, be it against himself (in impulsive suicide or some sort of auto-destructive act), or against a Samaritan or the entire organization.

It seems that in most cases the psychopath is incapable of overcoming his drive or controlling his behaviour. In extreme cases, criminal acts are committed without the psychopath feeling in any way responsible. He does not know 'what came over him'!

The psychopath, in an attempt to obtain something, or in an act of revenge, will also take more elaborate measures such as various forms of blackmail, of which the most delicate—the threat to commit suicide—should be noted by Samaritans. In dangling the threat of suicide, the psychopath tries simultaneously to obtain what he wants and specifically attack The Samaritans. While trying to burden them with the responsibility for his death, he will try to spread uneasiness, remorse and scandal within The Samaritans. This blackmail is sometimes followed by impulsive suicide. However, usually it concludes with a simple attempt or fake attempt. But what would one get involved in if one gave in to this blackmail? The manipulator is going to obtain what he wants, and that will defuse the conflict for the moment. But it will begin all over again, and each time for motives which become more and more frivolous. Thus one becomes involved in a particularly dangerous relationship, destined to failure. If such a case presents itself to Samaritans, it seems important, from the moment a response is to be made, to think of future consequences, after having, of course, weighed the suicidal risk.

Besides the true delinquents and criminals whom one will be dealing with among these psychopaths, there will be all sorts of 'social cases' among The Samaritans' clientèle: people incapable of holding down jobs, unable to take care of a family, accumulating debts, continuously having problems with neighbours, minor delinquency, alcoholics, drug addicts, sexual deviants, and so on.

The stories told by these people of their sad lot can be very upsetting for those who listen. It seems that throughout their lives disaster has followed them, they are rejected by everyone, catastrophe accumulates along their path. The Samaritans must learn to control their own feelings in response to such touching stories. They must realize that it would be unwise, out of excessive emotion, to take any decision without expert advice.

Sometimes there is a really urgent need for social aid, and this cannot, in these cases, be systematically refused.

But if one is clear-headed enough to control these emotions, impose firm limits to their demands, and not, under any circumstances, allow the assistance given to be detrimental to the needs of other clients, the risks that one takes can be greatly reduced. Furthermore, when having any dealings with a psychopath, it is of the utmost importance that The Samaritans stick together, and that all the members concerned are aware of what is acceptable and what is not, in each case. The psychopath has a particular flair for discovering even the smallest weakness in the cohesion of a group. He will *always* try to get from those in the group who seem more hesitant (in general the most inexperienced) what he has been unable to obtain from the others. If he succeeds in this, he will not only achieve his ends but, in so doing, will cause one or more Samaritans to infringe the discipline of the organization and have to be penalized. His hope is thus to stir up trouble within the group.

It seems worth while to underline the cunning (and sometimes downright perverted) aspect of certain cleverer psychopaths. These cunning psychopaths find a great pleasure in hurting, scandalizing, and spreading discord. This pleasure will be even more intense if the object of attack is a source of respect to others. This is what makes The Samaritans a perfect target. If the psychopath cannot spread dissension among The Samaritans, he can try to discredit the organization by slandering the work of the group, by the use of violence against one branch of the organization, or by trying to push Samaritans to the use of force themselves. Having achieved this, he will claim that The Samaritans are not at all what they claim to be . . . He can try to make the group spend large sums of money (for example by making frequent reversed-charge calls), or to monopolize their time endlessly (by repeated telephone calls)—in short, to sabotage the organization by every means at his disposal. These cases are extreme and fortunately rare, but can be a cause of real damage to the organization. The best attitude to adopt to counter this behaviour and render it harmless seems to be one of strict neutrality. The least show of irritability on the part of Samaritans can feed the destructive force within these psychopaths. But equally dangerous would be lack of firmness or useless tolerance of their attacks. From this it is clear what a delicate matter it is to choose the right attitude. Those volunteers who are less experienced must learn to refuse to deal with these problems and to refer them to those with more experience (Director, sic).

The means at the disposal of The Samaritans
During their training, the new volunteers have an assortment of methods at their disposal. They can listen to potted case histories which expose problems already encountered with psychopaths. In this way they can get an idea of what it is all about, how these critical situations arise, and the consequences of the errors already committed. They can also learn how necessary it is to prepare oneself to avoid these situations. Above all, the various types of 'role-play' have an immense advantage by giving them an opportunity to play an active part. If during one of these role-plays the volunteer falls effectively into one of these traps, the

question of why the trap worked should immediately be raised. Rarely (except in the case of a very skilful liar) is it the client's fault. Usually the volunteer will at this time have certain questions to ask himself:

What is his idea about his role as a Samaritan? Does he perhaps think that he must be able to do everything to help all the clients, and that the greater the effort the Samaritan's course of action demands, the better it must be?

Is it his sensitivity which led him to perceive too keenly the need of the client for more pity or interest, and caused him to lose his own capacity to evaluate the situation calmly?

Does he have a certain naïveté which renders him incapable of even conceiving of the existence of the means used by psychopaths arising out of their total lack of scruple and regard for others?

Does he panic in the face of blackmail?

Does he lack the training to reflect on the long-term consequences of the help given, and have too short-sighted a view of the interest of the client?

Is it a fact that he likes to feel needed? This is a very natural feeling for a person beginning Samaritan work, since something was required to give him the impulse to offer himself. If he can recognize the existence of this tendency in himself, without guilt, that can contribute one of the most essential stages in his development.

Does he suffer from an inability to say 'no' firmly but without aggressiveness? This can certainly be acquired only with experience and through total conviction.

Many other questions can be asked as the role-playing exercise becomes more and more developed and detailed. For the volunteer to learn to question himself in a positive manner—that is to say with the aim of understanding the problem better, without systematically accusing or torturing himself—can be a difficult task. A totally new and different way of thinking is sometimes necessary. To a new volunteer this exercise might seem unnecessarily painful, even frightening. Nevertheless, if he directs himself in this manner and if he is also helped by those who are experienced and of goodwill, he will quickly see the benefits that result from such instruction. He will soon see that his case is far from unique, and that many others—perhaps all—will have the same problems and that, by discussing them, they can often be effectively overcome.

For certain volunteers, their reluctance to question themselves in the preparation classes may come from an exaggerated fear of seeming inadequate in the eyes of others. But to refuse to face this questioning can only aggravate the fear, isolate the person from the group, and exaggerate the difficulties of the task. Thus the instruction of these anxious applicants requires that those who help them use great tact, take sufficient time before setting them to work, and encourage them more actively to develop a sense of self-confidence. If, on the other hand, others do not see the necessity to question themselves in this manner, this could be the result of a sense of false confidence. These applicants consider that they have already done enough self-questioning to meet success-fully all the circumstances which might arise. Sometimes it is especially difficult and delicate to integrate these applicants into the team, and in this case it is more a question of slowing down their initiative without shaking their convictions too much. It is, perhaps, reasonable to allow them to face a real situation and make mistakes. After this, those who have made mistakes, and who are honest enough to admit it, can have a fruitful discussion with those Samaritans assigned to help them. These should not judge severely but, on the contrary, by being friendly and positive, should integrate them into the team without risk of further error. In certain cases, unfortunately, it seems from experience impossible to integrate new applicants successfully into the team, and their exclusion from The Samaritans should be considered.

Practice has shown (and we have also just seen) how important group discipline is within The Samaritans, particularly where psychopaths are concerned. Learning to work as a team instils a natural reflex of delegating responsibilities to the most competent, whenever this is judged necessary, or at least asking for advice without hesitation. Perhaps it is a training-ground for a certain modesty? It also teaches a respect for discipline: volunteers should under no circumstances undertake, without warning, any hasty action which contravenes the common mind of the group, even if they think themselves more capable of judging the problem than others. This is not to say, of course, that each member must obey blindly without having his personal opinion. When there is disagreement, discussion and debate should be encouraged. But this must precede any action, so that, when action is taken, it will be in a coherent manner, making it impossible for the psychopath to find occasion to sow discord amongst The Samaritans.

Of course, all volunteers may make mistakes with psychopaths, letting themselves be manipulated and abused. In such cases the Directors and the sics have an essential function.

It would be highly regrettable for a volunteer who has realized his mistake, especially when dealing with a particularly tricky psychopath who has disillusioned him, if he became discouraged and lost confidence in the efficacy of Samaritan work. It would be equally regrettable if he became exaggeratedly suspicious in the hope of defending himself from a repetition of this experience. He should seek an interview with someone more experienced than himself, as this can sort things out and restore his confidence. But after many experiences, sometimes unhappy, isn't the development of a good sense of humour the best protection of the volunteer? Once he has gone beyond this stage of disillusionment, he realizes that he cannot do everything, or succeed with every client, but that what he does is 'not so bad'.

Definition of suicide
Suicide is the act of killing oneself by taking death as a means and as an end. This act may be either totally conscious and voluntary in a mentally sane person, or conditioned by the existence of some kind of mental disease and/or carried out in a diminished state of awareness. But sometimes it is difficult to distinguish suicide from sacrifice or accident.

D. A.

5. What kinds of client require their befriending to be supplemented by counselling?

BRIGITTE DE BETHMANN, BA*   (FRANCE)

Clients who need counselling plus befriending are among those who want to or need to explore their own feelings in greater depth. This applies to many young callers and those with sex problems. You could describe counselling as a less intensive form of psychotherapy.

How counselling works

Counselling is a healing process which is achieved through the encounter of two people: the client and the counsellor. While the befriender 'goes along' with the client in his crisis and stress, offering his presence and support, the counsellor helps the client to look at his feelings and clarify them by talking them out. This implies the gradual building up of a relationship in mutual trust, in order to work towards the restoration of balance and self-esteem.

What matters in counselling is the quality of the rapport between the two people—the client has suffered a lot of emotional and relational upsets. The fact that he is able to experience a 'real' relationship where he can express all kinds of feelings, even anger and resentment, without being rejected, but on the contrary where he is understood and loved, will help him to get a more realistic and positive idea of what he is and what he is capable of.

Thus counselling is a therapeutic process which aims to give the client greater independence. It enables him to be more integrated and more aware of his responsibilities towards himself and others.

The counsellor helps the client to build a stronger ego—the

* Brigitte de Bethmann represents France on the European Committee of Befrienders International. She has worked as a counsellor at the London Branch.

befriender helps him to 'practise' what he has actively found out with the counsellor as he is more concerned with helping the client to find his way out in social life.

In the Samaritan set-up, counselling is available in some branches in what is called 'special interviewing' sessions, once or twice a week and continuing for several weeks or months, given by some Directors or Consultants (not necessarily medical or psychiatric).

The client is helped to find his own way out, and often undergoes a lot of pain and anger at facing his feelings. The counsellor's role is that of an 'active mirror' as he enables the client to put his feelings in perspective. Gentle questions and feed-back—a sort of recapitulation of what the client has expressed—make him realize that he has been understood and also help him to understand his own feelings. This is essential as the client is often deeply anxious, and has a tendency to underestimate himself and consequently is on the look-out for 'negative feelings' in himself or others. He is convinced and will try to convince the counsellor that he is no good and that no one loves him. The counsellor will have to cope with the anger and pain of the client by meeting them with a constant, calm attitude, always expressing encouragement and keeping an eye on any positive movements of the client, even 'magnifying' them, in order to help him realize there are things worth loving about him. These feelings of rejection, worthlessness and inadequacy can only be worked out through a real and deep respect for the client who will gradually learn to feel accepted, understood and loved and will eventually accept himself as he is.

As he feels more secure with the counsellor, he will open up, allowing himself to look more deeply at his feelings, but having felt or been deprived of love and having been hurt, he remains very vulnerable. This is why, when the client is able to experience more positive feelings, the counsellor must be very careful not to hurt him in any way—a look, a smile, a sigh, can easily be misinterpreted and experienced as rejection.

Though the client may feel more confident as time passes, he may still feel dispirited and come to the interview full of anger and resentment, or totally upset at not being able to live outside what he has experienced with the counsellor. This is to be expected as years of negative feelings do not melt like ice, and it is necessary to talk these feelings out over and over again until he feels more confident that he is loved and able to love. But as time goes by it is quite likely that the client will no longer need to have pointed out where things went wrong. He will be able to realize it by himself. As he gains insight into his own self he only needs further encouragement to carry on experiencing in the newly discovered field of possible meetings with real people. Before, he was too anxious about what was wrong with himself, far too self-conscious and inhibited to be aware of what other people were really like— they were regarded as dangerous, as only rejection could be expected from them. But the feeling of rejection which was an obstacle to communication was also a defence. It has now lost its power. He feels stronger in himself and now he stands in his own right. So do other people—he now needs to learn to relate to others in a less tense and hurtful manner. He must be helped not to look in others for what will hurt him, for if he kept on relating in an aggressive manner he would prevent others from loving him. He is strong enough to realize that all human relationships are based on 'love and hate' and that he will not necessarily be rejected because of what he is. He may now work at acquiring a new system of references.

At this stage, the client may still feel the need for a few more interviews in order to talk about his new experiences and encounters, but it is quite likely that counselling will come to a natural end when he realizes he can cope by himself.

It may also be that, though he feels more secure and more confident, he feels deeper therapy is necessary to fight some persisting anxiety. The request for such advice does not mean counselling has failed, it can simply mean that counselling has been the first step in the course of a consolidating and rehabilitating process and that it is up to others to take over from there. As The Samaritans are often fortunate to know professional therapists, they can make the necessary arrangements if the client so wishes.

Who benefits, and who doesn't

It is necessary to bear in mind that some people will not respond to counselling. Intelligent people, even very bright people, if they are deprived of any moral conscience—i.e., a sense of responsibility—are to be ruled out. Psychopathic personalities will not gain insight into their own feelings. They are not capable of any reflective, constructive attitude as they act on the spur of the moment. Any attempt at counselling with them would be a waste of time and energy both for the client and the counsellor.

When dealing with depressed people, it is essential first to recognize depression, and to help the client get medical treatment when this is needed, if he has not already done so. It would prove impossible to help him get insight into his situation if he feels emotionally dead and is far too vulnerable to bear the stress of looking at his feelings. It would more surely lead him to end it all than to any kind of recovery—but supportive befriending is highly recommended here, however little response one may get from the client.

Nor should one attempt counselling with mentally ill people. They can be supported by a warm, friendly befriending, but they would be too withdrawn or aggressive to be able to work out their inner feelings, and afraid of things getting out of control.

It would appear from what has been said earlier that everyone who feels rejected might be a candidate for counselling, but one must be careful. Some people, though they complain they are rejected, do take pleasure at being so. They are usually masochists and it would be pointless to try to help them overcome their feelings, as they find too many advantages in being unloved. Here one should suggest psychiatric help. On the other hand, other people who do feel unloved as a result of unfortunate situations may benefit from counselling, provided they genuinely feel the need to work their feelings out.

The lonely person who feels cut off from his fellow human-beings and experiences a particularly distressing kind of isolation, linked to his inner conflicts, will respond to support and encouragement and is likely to gain insight into his situation. He will welcome talking his feelings out so that he can get to the root of what is preventing him from entertaining ordinary relationships.

The client who had to struggle his way through a disrupted family situation, and as a result cannot enjoy the life-long advantages of early loving, is probably our main and most likely client to benefit from counselling. He has suffered a lot of traumas in early childhood and adolescence, resulting in a lack of self-confidence and bouts of dispiritedness. Whilst counselling will not make up for the lack of support from loving parents, the secure climate of an accepting and loving encounter may help him to restore damaged self-confidence.

Adolescents

More and more frequent clients of The Samaritans are young people in their middle or late teens, who have got in touch because they are fed up and just do not see much point in life. It has been said we live in an age of disillusion and general chaos, a transitional age. Be that as it may, younger people who have not yet reached maturity—obviously—are particularly vulnerable to any external changes, and may express their feelings in different ways or directions. They tend to get together in groups, and take part in different activities. Though isolation in a crowd is a well-known phenomenon—we do come across this type of loneliness in The Samaritans—they are still a privileged lot. They experience some kind of exchange. Whether it is satisfactory or not, they are not altogether alone.

But what about the 17-year-old girl who has no one to turn to? She lives with her parents. Both work hard and have little time to spare for her, and though she gets on with them, she does not feel close to them and anyway would enjoy a life of her own with friends and interesting activities. She does work and could save up to rent a flat, but it is not so easy, and she would like to share it with flat-mates, if she knew any. At the office, people are nice, but they all seem to have a life of their own and though the occasional chat occurs, people go home after work and that is all there is in the way of exchange. And life goes on, day after day, the same old routine, with one or two magazines as a background to her daydreams. She reads about rich, happy, successful women who enjoy an easy-going life of endless evenings out with very attractive men and numerous friends . . . And for her, all the time, the same feeling of wasting her life.

You might say if life is that boring and uneventful why doesn't she join a local club? It may seem the obvious, simple thing to do to those who feel self-confident and have enough energy to make the effort to go and enjoy themselves, but if you feel shy, un-attractive, stupid, it is not so likely that you will go to that place where they are enjoying themselves but where 'I'll have to stay in the corner because no one will notice me'.

Too many people go on experiencing that feeling of 'being different' just because they have no opportunity to talk. Befriend-ing will help them to feel loved and supported, but they also need to talk their feelings out in a more structured way. They will benefit from a regular meeting with the same person at a set time and place. They will explore what prevents them from feeling loved. They will learn to trust the counsellor and talk about their relationships with their parents, their school-life, their hopes and disillusions, their anxieties about life and the future, all that goes on in a 17-year-old's mind. It is a great relief when they realize they can express their guilt and anger.

They may feel guilty about leaving their parents or angry or dispirited because of an unsatisfactory relationship with them or other people around. The counsellor may be the only person to whom they can freely talk. Gradually they gain insight into their situation and see their relationship 'in perspective'. Step by step they find their own ground and proceed to more conscious and responsible independence.

Here the counsellor must watch over-protective, maternal feelings and attitudes, which would only be met with a 'here you are again' and the client withdrawing or hiding behind irony or contempt. And he might never come again. Young people do not want professional or parental advice, just open clear friendly reassurance and encouragement. What matters is to communicate the feeling that you care for them and understand them. This is why the counsellor must not be over-anxious: if he really respects the client in his own integrity and empathizes with him, this feeling will come through.

The difficult time of adolescence seems like a period of hardships (and joys too) and of many changes. It extends over several years—some would say from 12/13 to 19/25. It seems to be prolonged nowadays with the raising of the school leaving age and the extension of student life. As a consequence, young people are often kept in a state of semi-dependence—they are not given the opportunities to face up to the realities and responsibilities of life—they are dispirited and anxious, they feel helpless and empty. If on top of the difficulties inherent in their age and situation, the circumstances of their personal life have been or are unhappy, they often resort to counselling as a means of helping themselves find their identity and autonomy. It enables them to experience some kind of 'non-directive guidance' in their self-questioning and questioning of the world. By gaining insight into their own personalities, their anxiety, aggression, or feeling of helplessness may find a creative outcome.

In dealing with adolescents, it is essential to take into account the 'pains of adolescence' with its contradictions and ambivalences, its moments of elation and despair, etc. . . . It is all the more difficult, as it is hard for an adolescent to verbalize his feelings. One must be specially attentive to non-verbal elements—and be really available and attentive. Too often adults are afraid of adolescents because they find them difficult to understand, and so they have a tendency to show repressive attitudes which in turn lead to the adolescent withdrawing. He feels isolated and misunderstood, fighting hard with self-questioning anxieties, 'Who am I?' 'Who am I becoming?' and will welcome someone to share them and explore them with.

Conclusion
It would appear that the most likely candidates for counselling are those who basically have a sound personality but who have suffered emotional and relational upsets, with a resulting lack of self-confidence and feeling of rejection. By entertaining a relationship with someone who supports them and helps them to come

to terms with their own feelings, they become more confident in themselves. Also, encouraged by this very relationship, they gradually come to feel they can enjoy relationships outside a set interview. But it takes time, and this is why we feel both counselling and befriending can be complementary and experienced simultaneously. For as there would be no satisfactory social life without supportive counselling, an emotional rehabilitation would be pointless without further social encounters helped by the befriender until the client is strong enough to cope by himself.

Definition of suicide
Suicide: the ultimate comment on what life was for me.

I. J.

6. What kinds of patient profit most from psychiatry or psychotherapy, with befriending used only to break down resistance to these?

ERWIN RINGEL, MD*   (AUSTRIA)

Effective suicide prevention certainly has to be initiated by consultants working as a team, ideally in either a suicide prevention clinic or a crisis intervention centre. However, without public support, their efforts are in vain. There is plenty of neighbourly concern just waiting to be directed—those in distress must not be left in the lurch, but rather referred to the various specialized agencies, before it is too late, and, after a suicide attempt, as well as in other situations, after-care is to be encouraged. I consider the 'befriending' of the English Samaritans, which shows positive results, to be the best method of this kind.

Which of those with a propensity to suicide should be put in touch with the psychiatrist or the psychotherapist? If at all possible, all of them. This is because a suicide tendency nearly always originates in a (acute or chronic) psycho-pathological condition which ought to be diagnostically clarified and a psychiatrist is trained to do just that. An important point here is that the correct diagnosis must result in correct and specific therapy and this varies tremendously from one diagnosis to another. As a result of many years' experience I believe the picture in the table overleaf to be fairly accurate for Austria (and it won't be very different in other countries).

There is not room here to go in to all the therapeutic problems which occur. However, I'd like to dwell, if I may, on one topic which is still too little known and which is not taken seriously

* Professor Dr Erwin Ringel is the Founder and Honorary Life President of the International Association for Suicide Prevention.

Psychiatric diagnoses in cases of suicide and suicide attempt (in % of the total).

	Suicide	Suicide attempt
Melancholia (— endogenous depression)	28%	15%
Schizophrenic pattern	4%	4%
Organic dementia	2%	3%
Neurosis	26%	30%
Neurotic reaction	2%	30%
Pathological reaction due to age	26%	5%
Psychopathy	12%	11%
Debility	—	2%

enough—neurotic disfigurement of life which so often ends in suicide, and I believe that apart from the psychotic cases (endogenous depression, schizophrenia), it is the underlying factor in the majority of non-psychotic suicides.

One needs to draw attention continually to the fact that there is a type of neurotic behaviour pattern which tends *specifically* to suicide, in other words a suicide-inclined neurosis. The symptoms of this neurosis are:

1. Neurotic life-style in childhood
In these cases the family situation does not provide the conditions necessary for the normal development of an individual into a vitally dynamic and optimistic personality. In spite of a great deal of research, it is not possible to identify a single typical childhood situation behind this suicide-inclined neurosis; there are in fact a great many possibilities, typically perhaps relating to trauma intensity and to its long-lasting effects.

Erikson, indeed the most significant psycho-analyst of our time, was able to show that in the oral phase the decision has to be made between innate trust (in the case of positive development) and innate mistrust (in the case of negative development). In the anal phase the choice is between autonomy, shame and doubt, and finally in the Oedipus stage, between initiative and inhibition arising from guilt feelings. One repeatedly finds all three of these negative behaviour patterns in the suicide-inclined neurosis. Thus it seems highly likely (according to Erikson's concept) that these people have been thoroughly traumatized and neurotisized. Talking to this type of patient, one gets the impression that the victim's destiny has not really supplied him with the wherewithal to recover in one phase from the adversities of the preceding one. (This is normally possible to a certain degree.) What actually happens is that new traumas intensify the existing negative consequences.

Another prevalent fact in these cases is that the foremost symptoms of neurotic behaviour patterns in childhood invariably typify an inhibited and demoralized child, anxiously insecure and often incapable of relating to people. At this time, too, the foundations are laid for a future negation of life. There is no better expression for this stage than the one Zwingmann established when he spoke of the dangers of 'suffocation of enjoyment of life'. According to the findings of depth psychology, lack of self-confidence is always linked with egocentricity—understandably the need for reassurance here becomes an absolute necessity, in order to increase the feeling of self-esteem. But this makes all human relationships follow an unnatural pattern, because of course the other party is 'used' to an unnatural extent—this being a means to an end (self-assurance). Such a relationship is doomed to failure from the very outset, and this culminates in isolation.

2. The outlined pattern persists beyond childhood
The vital point here however is that one will look in vain for the symptoms which characterize the classical neurosis presentation. However in this case hysterical, phobic, anancastic,* neurasthenic or psychosomatic mechanisms are lacking; if these appear, the tendency to suicide seems to have lessened. But even more important, this changes the basic presentation in that one can no longer speak of a suicide-inclined neurosis: because in a suicide-inclined neurosis pattern, it is precisely those usual defence

* Anancastic = any form of repetitious, recurrent, orderly, stereotyped behaviour or thinking which if left unfinished will lead to an increase in anxiety and tension.

mechanisms (and along with them the standard neurotic symptoms) which are lacking.

3. In place of the classic neurotic symptoms which are lacking here, a pronounced neurotic lifestyle dominates

This is based on the following three neurotic factors:

(a) a fundamentally demoralized and neurotic attitude to life,
(b) particular behaviour patterns which are repeated time after time,
(c) neurotic transfer of emotion.

They jointly lead to a succession of similar, if not identical, experiences and situations arising therefrom. This fits in with the tendency of the neurotic to re-live his original pathogenic situation during the course of his later life. As a result of the consequent applications of these neurotic mechanisms, a chain of disappointments and failures ensues. So one can talk about neurotic suicidal tendencies or even a neurosis about suicidal tendencies. Every neurosis nurtures a tendency towards self-mutilation and towards a neurotic disfigurement of life. So one might describe the neurosis which actually does culminate in suicide as the neurosis with the most imposing secondary conflicts. On the one hand, the defence mechanisms—except the reversive aggressive one—are lacking; on the other hand, a steady deterioration of the living situation sets in as a result of despondency and a persistently repeated behaviour pattern. This situation will lead initially to neurotic depression (every type of depression signifies inhibited aggression directed towards the Ego). If further dilemmas occur, i.e., if the underlying conflicts are not resolved, suicide will result. Here particularly intense neurotic suicidal tendencies prevail, which, it should be pointed out, emphasize these neurotic suicidal tendencies as being the critical detail of this type of neurosis, including the very term itself.

Its further development proceeds in three stages:

a. Stunted growth and loss of expansive ability

Diminishing intrinsic trust leads to insecure despondency. This frame of mind means that a lot of things will not even be attempted, but pushed to one side as it were; thus a whole host of possibilities are immediately eliminated. For instance this kind of person often cannot learn either to swim or to dance: this is almost always a distress symptom which should be taken notice of, even though of course in itself it should in no way be considered a part of a pre-suicidal phase. The ultimate sad fact is that for the people in question, much of what life offers just does not exist any more—this situation results in an inevitable restriction of life space.

b. Stagnation

The fixation to rigid identical patterns of behaviour produces a more or less circular formation, always coming back to the same point; the capacity for change and thus for evolution is lacking. The person gets the relentlessly painful impression that everything is wrong, that he is one of life's misfits, that he cannot experience anything really new, because the same situations (and negative ones, at that) keep on recurring. Is it any wonder that the initial insecurity and distress are now considerably intensified? In our worst nightmares, we cannot get away, keep going round in circles, repeatedly arrive back at the starting point; this repetition of experience leads easily to feelings of hopelessness that then are well on the way towards suicide. It cannot be a coincidence that songs like 'Sad Sunday' have proved to be particularly instrumental in leading to suicide; apart from morose content and suitably sentimental tunes, the repetitive monotony and the continual recurrence of certain melodies and rhythms play a crucial part in inducing restrictive feelings. Meanwhile the victims of this situation—and this is perhaps the worst thing about it—are incapable of learning from the damage they have sustained. They cannot carry out the necessary changes to their behaviour pattern to enable them to be more successful in the future. In the words of a poet: 'Those who do not understand their past are condemned to experience it all over again in the future.' This far-reaching resignation concerning their own possibilities can be seen as a further component in development towards suicide.

c. Regression

In the place of the active principle which has been lost, the passive one becomes more and more prominent—regression. Just like children, these people expect everything from others. They no longer love but want to be loved (want to 'let themselves be loved'). They make no contribution to the life of the community, but expect to be supported and kept alive by others. An intensified dependence on the outside world prevails, but at the same time they are tremendously sensitive and vulnerable. It is then only too easy for a feeling of being misunderstood to occur—or one of being deserted. This in turn produces bitterness and inner withdrawal. One patient described it thus: 'I wait until someone complies with my need for love, but when this happens I would like to be the one to make the active choice and therefore I make no approaches back. Still I'll never take the initiative because I'm afraid of failing.' The wavering between longing and inadequacy as far as achieving a goal is concerned, can hardly be expressed in more moving terms. Anyone would understand that this type of behaviour pattern leads to growing isolation and despair.

When one examines this neurotic development towards suicide, which I have only been able to outline briefly here, there can be no doubt that it manifests and reveals itself in the form of particularly characteristic and striking symptoms. In all these cases, therefore, it is hardly possible to claim afterwards that one 'didn't notice anything'. Here Menninger's statement is fitting: 'one is suicidal long before one commits suicide'—one could extend this to say that particularly in the case of a neurotic development towards suicide, modern findings indicate that it is well within the realms of possibility to discover a 'maturing suicide' in good time. In the last century, a suicide victim left instead of a farewell letter a poem he composed just before his death and which was first published by Pelmann. Loosely translated from the German, it reads as follows:

My thoughts are getting narrower and narrower,
my vision blinder and blinder,
my terrible plight
unfurls more and more each day.
With no strength, I drag myself through life,
bereft of all will to live,
having no one who understands
or believes the weight of my misery.
Yet my death will show you
that I had one foot in the grave
for many, many years
until in the end it suddenly engulfed me.

This verse not only repeats in a shattering, concentrated, poetic form the different stages of the suicide-inclined neurosis, but it also embodies in classical form that psychic awareness, which the author first discovered in 1949, in people with a propensity to suicide and which he accordingly termed 'the pre-suicidal syndrome'. We will spend a little time on this syndrome because its manifestation can signify suicide risk. The syndrome consists of:

1. Restriction,
2. Inhibited aggression directed towards oneself, and
3. Suicidal fantasies.

1. Restriction

a. Restriction of personal choices (circumstantial restriction)
Normally human existence is characterized by a certain number of patterns of behaviour and development. In a pre-suicidal state, the feeling of being in possession of these possibilities is completely lost. In their place is a sensation of being hampered and surrounded, of being pushed and shoved into increasingly smaller areas. As far as the circumstantial restriction is concerned, let us review it as follows:

(i) the result of the *adversities of life* (e.g., severe bodily injuries),

49

(ii) the result of one's own *behaviour pattern* (typical example of our century: Hitler's last days spent in the air-raid shelter in the State Chancellery),

(iii) straightforward *personal delusion* (subjective feelings of restriction, although in point of fact no restriction exists).

This differentiation is extremely important: external restriction alone cannot lead to suicide—only the person's reply to it affords the choice. In other words, the risk grows in relation to the psychic disturbance of the person concerned. However, if the circumstantial restriction relates to one's own behaviour or even to delusion, then the personality is psychically disturbed. The probability also increases that this circumstantial restriction is linked with dynamic reaction which appears as a result of psychic disturbance and which presents the foundation of the pre-suicidal syndrome.

b. Dynamic restriction

Here we have to accept the depressing fact that the dynamics of the personality develop in only one direction, while growth in all other directions becomes stunted. Thus the feeling of a pressing compulsion in one direction occurs which finally leads to suicide. Dynamic restriction must under no circumstances be confused with loss of dynamic. When the latter occurs (e.g. in terminal cancer), suicide is impossible anyway. This is because, without a doubt, dynamics are required to commit suicide.

The detailed phenomena surrounding dynamic restriction can be summarized as follows:

(i) *Rigid pattern* of powers of perception and associations: The person concerned behaves as if he were wearing spectacles through which everything is seen in a distorted manner. By these means, the personality eventually becomes dominated by patterns of thought sequences and content, which constantly remain the same.

(ii) *Rigid behaviour patterns:* In this part of dynamic restriction, we are dealing with a diminution of the reaction choices available to the personality, which has lost the numerous shades of behaviour usually existing. A rigid behaviour pattern—often the sequence is so automatic that one gets the impression of conditioning along the lines of stipulated reflexes—characterizes the presentation.

(iii) *Affective restriction:* This means that *one* affective pattern, amongst many others which are possible in principle, comes more and more to the foreground of the behaviour and finally dominates, whereupon one has to consider above all (but by no means exclusively) a depressive or an anxious state.

(iv) *Restriction of defence mechanisms:* In the pre-suicidal state there occurs a marked diminution of the Ego-defence mechanism, which we studied in relation to the suicide-inclined neurosis. The situation becomes serious when the defence mechanism 'aggression directed towards the self' comes more in to the foreground. The alarm level is reached when this reigns alone and all other defence mechanisms have been extinguished. The presence of other defence mechanisms diminishes the suicide risk, in fact hopefully also the risk of tendencies thereto. (Consider for example the large number of defence mechanisms prevalent in hysteria—logically with this disturbance, there is more likelihood of suicide attempt than of actual suicide.)

To recapitulate then, an individual posture of the personality takes place in dynamic restriction until the personality in question finally feels itself driven and forced towards suicide by this one overwhelming tendency. In this case, the German synonym for suicide *Freitod* (free death) is not applicable; in other words, the dynamic and in particular the affective restriction reaches its peak at the moment of suicide. In this age of space travel, let us use a comparison: one needs a tremendous driving force (equivalent to that capable of overpowering earth's gravity) in order to switch off the instinct of self-preservation. Only a heightened degree of dynamic restriction, and never simple rational delusion, can release this driving force. In answer to the question posed by a doctor as to whether his patient wanted to kill himself, the patient replied: 'Who on earth wants to? It's something one does against one's will.'

c. Diminution of ability to relate to others
This can manifest itself in several ways:

(i) *Depreciation of available relationships* through loss of desire for ties and lacking, indeed often completely missing, abilities to share. (Both are results of dynamic restriction.)

(ii) *Numerical reduction* in personal relationships, until finally one clings on to one person on whom one is completely dependant.

(iii) *Total isolation*. The most tragic example is that of old people, whose death is often not noticed for days on end. They are completely alone, no one notices they have gone, no one mourns for them.

d. Restriction of values
Characteristics of pre-suicidal experience of value are:

(i) *Diminished sense of values*, depreciation of several aspects of life.

(ii) *Predominantly subjective judgement of values*, which have little bearing on general opinion (thus feelings of isolation occur).

(iii) *Lack of practical realization of values*.

In this context, I feel that I ought to say something about the roles played by religious and philosophical systems in pre-suicidal development.

When someone is faced with the adversities of life, his religious and philosophical attitudes have a great deal of bearing on how he will deal with the situation. Now, we've already seen that the circumstantial reaction alone can rarely lead to suicide, but that it can do so if coupled with the other types of restriction outlined above, which are caused by a personality disturbance. Thus, only when the structure of the personality is also affected is there a serious risk of suicide; but, if the structure of the personality is affected, then a depreciation of values follows. This is in fact a subjective valuation and a deficient active realization of values, and means that within the framework of a pre-suicidal development, either religious or philosophical ideas arise. These tally with the prevailing pessimism and tendency towards self-mutilation, or at least they are not a hindrance. When the personality seems to accept philosophical and religious anti-suicide values, however, the result can be a devaluing of self and undermining of self-esteem. Thus at the decisive moment, the personality is too weak to defend itself against suicide. It is a tragic fact that ideologies which are basically conducive to averting suicide, fail just at the very moment when they are most needed. This is because the general sense of values and consequently religious belief can be infected by the pre-suicidal restriction of the personality.

2. Inhibited and destructive aggression directed towards the self

The fact that suicide is a manifestation of aggressive impulses directed towards the self, is one of the brilliant discoveries of Freud. The emergence of unusually intense aggression potential and at the same time massive inhibition when it comes to releasing this same aggression towards the outside world, are the first rungs down the ladder towards suicide. The inhibition of aggression can fundamentally be put down to the following factors:

a. A specific psychic personality structure characterized by a particularly stringent and rigid Superego, which is common above all to neurosis.

b. Psychic disturbances which, from the psychopathological point of view, lead to physical (mainly motor) inhibitions as well as to mental ones. Naturally, the need arises from this situation to get rid of emotions outwardly. The classical example of this type of condition is endogenous depression.

c. Inability to relate to others. It was Horney who insisted that such relationships do at least serve to work off aggressions against each other.

The aggression inhibition is the decisive pre-requisite for the exertion of aggression against the self. This process relates particularly to the physical law of preservation of energy; accumulated strength has to find an outlet—the only one left in the acute stages is the self. This reversal of aggression is particularly stimulated by guilt feelings, both conscious and subconscious.

3. Suicide fantasies

Here we must differentiate between active (deliberate) and passive fantasies. The latter close in unintentionally, indeed uninvited. They often take the form of compulsive thoughts which gradually become dominant.

There are cases where the pre-suicidal fantasies appear to start off harmlessly with the conception that one 'could do it if this or that went wrong'. But what seems at first to be an off-loading mechanism, can later become a serious threat to life: To be precise, this happens at the point where this type of fantasy turns into passively compulsive suicide fantasies. The subject matter of these fantasies can be divided into three stages: The first one, which is still relatively harmless, is fantasising about 'being dead'. The concept of actually killing oneself, which is the second stage, is a greater risk. The third: a danger situation is reached when the fantasy concerns itself with the actual method of carrying the deed through and concentrates in minute detail on the method to be employed.

If we refer back to the fateful combination of the pre-suicidal syndrome in three stages, we can see how things come to a head as a result of a vicious circle. Just to mention a few examples— isolation will diminish the possibilities of offloading aggression and also increase anxieties; restriction of powers of perception and of association will stimulate suicide fantasies; prevalence of suicidal fantasies (which in their turn release anxieties) and prevailing dynamic restriction easily lead to the supposition that circumstantial restriction may also exist.

After this portrayal of the pre-suicidal syndrome, let us return to the suicide-inclined neurosis! If it is discovered in good time, it is easily possible to treat the disturbance and thus to give the lifestyle a positive direction. But unfortunately the very discovery of these neuroses can cause the person concerned considerable problems. If someone suffers from fear of locked rooms, from compulsive washing or from conversion hysteria, it won't take him long to realize that he is ill and needs the doctor. But in the case of a neurosis which expresses itself in a neurotic lifestyle, it is pretty easy for the person concerned to regard himself as a victim of coincidences, unfortunate circumstances, tricks of fate, etc. Would any of these sufferers examine their own neurotic arrangement, thereby, to quote Alfred Adler, 'boxing their own ears'?

So, in all these cases, one needs to be twice as aware and to do everything to make sure that psychotherapeutic treatment is started in good time. (To express it somewhat over-dramatically, it is harder to get the patient to the therapy threshold than to take him through the door.) If a man meets nothing but failure, his misfortune becomes a personal characteristic (adapting Napoleon's words to suit), or when he continually repeats the same experiences . . . these are symptoms which are cause for alarm. Let us take a few patients' remarks to highlight the situation: 'Luck is a foreign word to me.' 'I'm a complete and utter misfit.' 'Fate has thrown me into the gutter of life.' 'My life is only running on a pilot light.' 'I get everything beautifully organized, but in such a way that it cannot work.' 'All my disappointments have been fulfilled.'

The last two quotes illustrate a transference to insight and the fact that in all these cases, a secret 'guide' is waiting to be looked for and found in the self, could be said to indicate a certain readiness for therapy. To instil the principle, 'It's you who does it all' is the initial aim of this type of treatment and this insight can facilitate matters, particularly if the logical conclusion is drawn that the patient is not necessarily destined to a defenceless and horrific existence for the rest of his life. Of course, and this must be clearly emphasized, the said thought process must ensue only with the help of the psychotherapist, who is able to render unconscious fixations conscious and therefore facilitate a change. Particular consideration should be given to the following five points, which are relevant to all psychotherapy:

c

1. The significance of the ties to the therapist

Here more than with any other type of psychotherapy, a particularly intensive and really effective doctor-patient relationship is necessary. Experience has taught us that one cannot lose a psychogenic patient with a propensity to suicide (in other words a non-psychotic patient) once such a relationship has been established. But of course if the preliminary step is taken to eliminate the decisive restriction of ability to relate, then there is a basic gap in the pre-suicidal restriction surrounding the patient. Naturally, this relationship follows the transfer rules and it must be assumed that ambivalence will prevail, at least on the patient's side. It is vital that the therapist understands this transfer situation and that he, together with the patient, establishes a plan, which would among other things alleviate the particularly marked strain on the patient in the beginning, as far as the doctor-patient relationship is concerned. (The obvious concern on the part of the doctor to keep the patient alive indicates a plus, because it leads the patient away from isolation. On the other hand, it can also be a minus, because it can tempt the patient to take advantage of this interest, thereby putting a great deal of strain on the doctor.)

2. Aggression—working it off

We have already referred to the disastrous part played by inhibition of aggression and also by the direction of inhibited aggression towards the self. It should further be noted that suicide risk decreases in direct proportion to the patient's opening-up in therapy sessions, because this enables him to offload some of his piled-up aggressions. Experience has taught us that this type of reaction tends towards a diminution of suicide tendencies, at least for the time being. In the long run, of course, it is a question of discovering and breaking down the reasons behind the aggression. Apart from that, increasing activity (see next point) produces indirect offloading of aggression towards the outside world. As long as unconscious motivation towards self-punishment is relevant in this aggression, it is extremely important to reveal the subconscious guilt feelings, in order to carry out the actual and much-needed analysis of the possibilities.

3. Encouragement towards success

The question here is one of initiating a positive chain of developments: not only distress but encouragement, too, can release the personal dynamics, in the sense that each success is the basis of and the requirement for the next step forward. The beginning is difficult of course and there is a suitable maxim: 'Start off with small steps'. The aim of the therapy is to present the patient with soluble tasks and, by careful planning, to encourage conquest. Excessive demands must be avoided at all costs—the 'all or nothing principle' prevails in neurotic patients and must be overcome. This is inclined to give them exaggeratedly lofty ideas, the realization of which is quite out of the question. As a result, they just cannot aspire to anything and give up trying. A certain amount of humility must be learnt in order to climb slowly up the ladder to success. In conclusion, one might say that, based on complete trust in the therapist, an active procedure system needs to be introduced into the therapy in order to overcome passivity (an alternative expression for regression). The following results may occur gradually: expansion of life space, improvement in current human relationships, and establishment of new ones, new ranges of values, increasing open-mindedness, elimination of 'constricted mood', atmosphere of confidence. Obviously, the odd setback cannot be avoided, but a great deal has already been achieved when the tormenting feeling of repetition ('the same thing keeps on happening') is overcome, as a result of new tendencies and behaviour patterns. The word 'new' must be the pole-star of the therapy; the former uniformity of experience, with its resulting feeling of being-pushed-in-a-negative-direction must be overcome. All these successes are naturally only possible after a thorough analysis of the origins of the earlier false behaviour and at the same time, active training of new behaviour patterns, under the supervision of the therapist.

4. Directing fantasy positively

Suicide impulses as an expression of a psychic disturbance can only be directly, rationally overcome with great difficulty. (Here ideological persuasion attempts of a problematic type remain—and in any case, they have little to do with medical psychotherapy.) But instead, they can be directed indirectly by occupying them with fantasies which arise out of the psychic recovery pattern and which bear positive future possibilities. It is also usual to extend the vacuum which first permitted suicide fantasies into attractive future plans, and finally to overcome the vacuum. Experience teaches us that it is very comforting when a patient with a propensity towards suicide begins of his own accord to talk about what he will do in the near or immediate future. From this point of view, it seems therapeutically necessary to stimulate the fantasy, to occupy it with as many details as possible about the future lifestyle.

5. A positive lifestyle

The aim of the treatment after analysis and of the training of new behaviour patterns towards success experiences will be a positive lifestyle, rather as a patient put it to his therapist: 'Help me to become the man who can realize his own character, using the versatile possibilities which at the moment are just going to waste'. For this reason, it is advisable to carry on the contact with the patient as long as possible, and in particular to allow him to go back to the therapist when new difficulties occur.

Finally, I would like to say that a great many patients with a propensity towards suicide can profit from psychotherapy, and this means even during acute crisis. However, people with a neurotic development leading to suicide need it the most, and because of ignorance they have had it by far the least so far. That is why I felt it was so important to talk about this particular topic now.

Even though these people, as I have illustrated, lie well beyond the bounds of basic human sympathy, that certainly should not mean that they should be made to suffer alone: psychotherapy can only proceed successfully if it is possible to relax the patients in an atmosphere conducive to such therapy.

(Translated by Veronica Weisweiller)

Definition of suicide
Suicide is the intentional tendency to take one's own life.   E. R.

7. What kinds of patient ought to be befriended during
or after psychiatric treatment?

JOZEF PH. HES, MD*   (ISRAEL)

Professional versus non-professional help
During recent years many doctors have found that professional
help based on training and experience is not always enough. In
cases of diabetes, for example, it is not enough to diagnose the
disease and to institute treatment. Many patients feel better after
treatment and stop taking the medication, a step leading to the
recurrence of the disease. Others believe that one should not
stick so rigorously to the doctor's instructions: they inject
themselves with insulin but do not eat in due time and as result
of that they lose consciousness and slip into a coma.

Or to take another example: a woman with breast cancer has
to undergo surgery and is scared that after amputation of her
breast her marital and sexual life will suffer.

In both examples non-professional help from sufferers of
diabetes and from women after mastectomy come to the aid of
the patient (and of the physician) and fulfil their invaluable role
of assisting a human-being coping with fate.

What about non-professionals and the psychiatric patient?
Here the roles are reversed. For many centuries mental patients
were treated by non-professionals such as monks, nuns, exorcists.
Medical-professional-psychiatric help is of a rather recent nature.
Scientific psychiatry started only in the nineteenth century. Due,
particularly, to the popularization of psychoanalysis, people
gained the idea that only professional psychoanalysts could really

* Dr Hes is Director of Psychiatric Services at the Municipal Governmental
Medical Center, Ichilov Hospital, Tel-Aviv/Jaffa. He is the Founder and
Chairman of The Samaritans of Tel-Aviv.

cure the mentally ill. However, psychoanalysis could not live up to these exaggerated expectations.

The new drugs against psychosis and depression which appeared in the 'fifties and 'sixties of this century likewise gave rise to exaggerated expectations. The fact is that, when it is a question of prolonged mental illness, in roughly two-thirds of the cases neither psychoanalysis nor drug therapy succeed in rehabilitating the patient into the community.

Which patients should be befriended?
In the light of my introductory remarks it is obvious that many chronic patients are abandoned and neglected by the official and established helpers, because the psychoanalytic, psychotherapeutic and drug treatment approaches have failed. In the field of therapeutic failures many opportunities for help are available. Sometimes these patients are taken care of in foster families, such as in the Belgian village of Gheel. Similar systems are in operation in Holland, Scandinavian countries, Great Britain, the United States and elsewhere. However, among chronic mental patients, there are many who are not sick enough to be hospitalized or to be accepted in a foster family, but who are leading lives characterized by an almost complete isolation and barrenness. This isolation results from two sources: the patient has personal inhibitions which prevent him from making contacts and, secondly, the environment is often repelled by the patient's strange and/or offensive behaviour.

These patients are often extremely dependent and helpless even in circumstances where normal children easily know their way. Even more helpless are they in complicated situations in regard to money, taxes, employment and so forth.

Why do these patients need befriending?
Because befriending is exactly what is missing in the lives of the chronic mental patient or, in other words, the person whose social competence is lacking or defective.

Let us analyse for a while the meaning of the word 'friend': in the English language it originates from the Anglo-Saxon word 'freon', 'freogen', which means *love*. A friend therefore is 'a loving one'. In my own language, Hebrew, the emphasis is on connexion: a 'haver' is someone who is connected with you, and many 'haberim' form a 'hebra', i.e., a society.

I think in befriending we find both components, namely, the loving care and the connexion to society: society extends its loving care to a person in need.

In contrast to the established and official helpers such as psychiatrists, psychiatric out-patient clinics, socio-therapeutic services, which are geared to patients coming *to them*, befrienders reach out and extend their loving care to people who are not capable of going to the doctors and clinics.

In this context I would say that professional helpers presume —unjustifiably—the presence of social competence in patients. Or better formulated: professional helpers know that their chronic patients are lacking in social competence but do not change their services to accord with that knowledge. As a result patients who suffer from chronic mental illness become more and more isolated. It follows that befrienders complement the official services, they fill the gap in the network of established helpers.

Should befrienders operate during or after therapy?

From the above it is understandable that as long as a patient is in active treatment there do not seem to be too many opportunities for befrienders except in the case of acute suicidal crises. These crises are characterized by the patients' ambivalence to treatment: on one hand they are desperate, they do not want to live any more; on the other hand they call SOS helplines or The Samaritans and ask for help. But the kind of help needed, once again, is not provided by the established agencies, which work during office hours and are closed at weekends and during holidays.

Also, in this case, befrienders complement existing services and extend help where professional helpers fail.

To conclude, I would like to say that professionals and non-professionals need each other in order to realize their sacred objective: Love thy neighbour.

The twenty questions

Definition of suicide
Fruit of illogical action resulting from 'funnel' thinking, which prevents a person from perceiving alternatives to self-destruction.

J. H.

8. What kinds of potential suicides are unlikely to ring
   or visit the Samaritans? What can be done to help
   them?

JEROME A. MOTTO, MD★   (USA)

A statement often made to persons considering suicide is, 'I'd like
to help you as much as I can, but I can't do that if you're not
here'. Such an observation usually follows an offer of assistance
that is not accepted, leaving the would-be helper feeling helpless
and saddened by the prospect of being unable to deter an untimely
death. Yet a large proportion of despairing and suicidal persons—
perhaps 40%, though the true figure is unknown—find it difficult
either to request or accept help, posing a dilemma to those who
are concerned about their well-being.

Established resources offer assistance on their own terms to
those who are able to accept it, that is, the person (or someone
acting for him or her) must initiate contact by a telephone call or
a visit to the agency. Those who do so may be offered an invaluable human resource, while others of uncertain number are
'not here' and thus create the vague discomfort that needless
suffering might be alleviated or tragedy averted if those unknown
individuals could be reached in some way.

Characteristics of the non-caller
One kind of person unlikely to call on The Samaritans when in

★ Professor Motto is Professor of Psychiatry at the University of California
School of Medicine, San Francisco. He is a former President of the American
Association of Suicidology, and former Secretary-General of the International
Association for Suicide Prevention (IASP).

The work reported here was supported by US Public Health Service grant
MH-25080, from the National Institute of Mental Health, Mental Health
Services Development Branch.

need includes those individuals who find it difficult to turn for help to their own family, friends, colleagues or professional resources. The most frequent deterrent for this group is the sense of shame, guilt, or inadequacy learned by these persons during earlier years to be attached to any lack of self-sufficiency, especially of an emotional nature. Even when reassured to the contrary, such persons see a turning to others as 'wallowing in self-pity', 'whining', or 'narcissistic', and experience being helped as evidence of weakness, rendering them an object of contempt and unworthy of the love and esteem of others. Cultures glorifying rugged individualism contribute to this distortion, which the *I Ching* recognizes with the observation that 'to seek help in a difficult situation is not a disgrace but a sign of inner clarity'.*

Another kind of person unlikely to approach The Samaritans includes those who are intensely suspicious and distrustful of other people and their motives, avoiding any self-disclosure for fear of a nameless threat to their person or possessions. Still other individuals nurture a public image (and sometimes a self-image as well) which is based on a fantasy of invulnerable stability, such as certain members of the military, the judiciary, legislators, ministers, physicians and police. Included in this group are many persons from all walks of life who are extremely hard-working, conscientious, meticulous individuals who tend to set high and uncompromising standards for their own performance.

We can also recognize the patterns of those who experience such severe anxiety when approaching close to others that they are unable to initiate contact, adolescents threatened by loss of peer esteem, elderly persons fiercely protecting their independence and autonomy, and those who are prone to feelings of persecution.

Some who decline help, of course, such as you and I, do so because they are remarkably strong persons who may suffer severe stresses but are confident that their strengths will sustain them through any crisis. Such persons demur, when offered assistance, in deference to those who 'really' need the benefit of the proferred help, or at least who 'need help more than I do'.

* *I Ching* trs. Wilhelm Baynes (London, Routledge & Kegan Paul, 1961).

We also recognize that many persons who need help with problems of living go directly to mental health professionals, and assume that additional sources of assistance are superfluous. In a given case this might be a correct assumption, though in some instances—at least in the USA—the person's therapist may believe that added sources of help would hinder the therapeutic process by draining off anxiety that requires careful study, or by diluting the relationship with the therapist in a way that reduces therapeutic potential. Thus not contacting The Samaritans may be largely the decision of a colleague in the helping field.

There are undoubtedly other kinds of obstacles, appearing as shyness ('I've always been so self-conscious I couldn't talk to strangers'), élitism ('If I look for help I want to find the best person in the field'), cynicism ('No one really cares about my problems, let alone some amateur do-gooders'), or expressed in other ways as numerous as the persons involved. Any combination of the characteristics noted may be found in a given instance, providing the usual spectrum of patterns associated with a given behaviour. Some persons are hindered by practical problems such as physical debility or handicap, inability to afford a telephone, the limitations of being in an institution or, in the absence of access to the usual news media, even being unaware of The Samaritans' existence.

Whatever the reason for not using the proffered help, in most cases we are left with the dilemma of providing a beneficial influence for someone who cordially declines to participate in a programme requiring mutual effort. This formidable task can loom even larger when the person feels embittered, isolated and hopeless, and in spite of anything we say can only perceive us as not caring or even listening.

What can be done?
We are all aware of the power of communication and it is to this that we can turn. Ruesch has pointed out that in the past, social patterns have been such that 'continuity and consistency in human contact resulted in the establishment of a sense of belonging and responsibility, and it favoured the development of controls

from within'.* He had emphasized earlier the need to 'introduce continuity into the life of the patient, in order to let him taste the pleasure of communication, which becomes the driving force of all rehabilitative procedures'.† We may find little argument about the potential influence of communication, but how do we engage with someone who is unwilling to participate?

A first step we have explored is to identify what in public health terms would be a 'population at risk', specifically, persons known to be suffering from a significant depressive or suicidal state. We located them in the psychiatric and general hospitals of San Francisco by identifying those persons admitted because of depression or suicidal manifestations, numbering 3,006 over a five-year period. We introduced ourselves as having a special interest in the problem of depression and self-destructive impulses, and became acquainted with these persons and their situation. Whether we were 'medical' staff apparently made little difference to most patients. They were generally willing—at times eager— to discuss their problems, and seemed grateful for the time and interest devoted to them, which usually totalled two to three hours over a three to five day period.

The next step was to identify those who declined a treatment programme after discharge from the hospital. We defined 'declined' as participating in post-discharge treatment, if at all, for less than 30 days. Those who met this criterion, totalling 995, were considered resistant to accepting help, categorized 'no-treatment' individuals, and divided randomly into two subgroups, designated 'contact' and 'no contact'.

A programme was designed to provide a beneficial influence on the 'contact' subgroup, based on the following hypotheses:

1. The forces that bind us willingly to life are primarily those exerted by our relationships with other people, whether they are intimately involved in our lives or influence us by other psychological processes.

* Ruesch, J., 'General Theory of Communication', in Arieti, S. (Ed.), *American Handbook of Psychiatry* (New York, Basic Books, 1959).

† Ruesch, J., 'Psychotherapy and Communication', in *Progress in Psychotherapy* (New York, Grane & Stratton, 1956).

2. Self-destructive behaviour can be considered a final effort to obtain relief from intense pain. The behaviour becomes manifest when the person experiencing such pain feels isolated from others and perceives his situation as hopeless.

3. A person's sense of isolation will be reduced if he experiences regular and long-term contact with another person who is openly concerned about the former's well-being.

4. The contact must be initiated by the concerned person and must put no demands or expectations on the other, in order to be experienced as a sincere expression of unconditional concern.

5. Such a programme of contact will exert a suicide prevention influence on those high-risk persons who decline to enter an established helping system, or do so only in the most extreme circumstances.

A corollary of this set of hypotheses is that the person initiating and maintaining the contact need not be a health-related professional.

The programme consists of a regular sequence of communications from the member of our staff who had become acquainted with the depressed or suicidal person in the hospital. This is initially in the form of a telephone call or, most often, a short letter. The message is simply an expression of awareness that the person is there, concern that the person's life situation is reasonably satisfactory, or at least bearable, and inviting a response if they wish to send one. An effort is made to personalize these notes in order to avoid a 'form letter' impression. They are always individually typed. Though every note is worded differently, the basic message always contains the same elements, for example:

Dear ——————,

This is just a note to assure you of our continuing interest in how you are getting along. We hope things are going well for you, and would be happy to hear from you if you feel inclined to write.

Sincerely,

If the person does correspond with us, the subsequent contact note includes the content of the response in formulating the basic message, thus 'personalizing' it.

A brief contact like this is not calculated to have a significant effect by itself. Rather it is the cumulative effect of repeated expressions of this kind for a number of months or years that we postulate as having potential psychological force. The time required will differ with different persons to generate what Frank* calls a sense of 'connectedness to others', and Kaiser† refers to as a 'delusion of fusion' with others, which we perceive as exerting the stabilizing, suicide-prevention influence.

The schedule we use for these contracts is monthly for four months, then bi-monthly for eight months, and finally every three months for four more years—a total of twenty-four contacts over a period of five years. This is an arbitrary sequence, geared to long-term risks, that could well be altered. The optimal pattern would probably be one that reflects the unique needs of each individual involved.

What demonstrable effects can be achieved?
We have found that the suicide rate in our contact group is about one half that in the rest of the help-declining high-risk population when compared at yearly intervals for four years (0·6–1·0% per year versus 1·2–2·0% per year). In the fifth year after discharge the difference narrows to a 30% lower rate for the contact subjects (0·7% versus 1·0%) which may be a chance fluctuation but raises the question whether the influence producing the differences is a time limited one. A number of statistical considerations pertinent to these comparisons have been discussed elsewhere.‡ §

* Frank, J., 'Therapeutic Factors in Psychotherapy', *Amer. J. Psychotherapy* 15: 350–61, 1971.

† Kaiser, H., *Effective Psychotherapy* (Fierman L., Ed) (New York: The Free Press, 1965).

‡ Motto, J., 'Suicide Prevention for High Risk Persons Who Refuse Treatment', *Life-Threatening Behavior* 6 (4): 223–30, 1976.

§ Motto, J., 'Suicidal Persons Who Decline Treatment: A Long-Term Program', Paper presented at 8th International Congress for Suicide Prevention and Crisis Intervention, Helsinki, Finland, 20th June, 1977.

The most encouraging evidence for us has been the responses received from those whom we invited to make it a two-way interchange. About one out of four of our contact subjects have replied to our notes, with about one-third of those entering a fairly regular correspondence. It bears repeating that the goal of the contact is not to prompt a reply, but to nurture a feeling of relatedness that can be strengthened with time and repetition. The psychological impact should be heightened by the persistent renewal of the message regardless of the response to any specific contact.

After an initial period of cautious distrust ('Is this letter a routine inquiry?') many persons came to regard the contact programme as a convenient resource for a variety of practical matters, such as legal issues, medical records, insurance, references, and—most important—a non-threatening source of assistance if the person's life situation again began to become unbearable. The assistance was in the form of facilitating re-entry into the health care system when they felt unable to take that step on their own. While citing 'not knowing what to do' or 'embarrassment' ('I told them I'd come to the clinic, but never went back') as reasons to delay, there was generally little objection to our offer to contact the clinic staff and arrange for them to be seen. Using our relationship with the person as an intermediate step to obtain help again when needed may have contributed to the reduced suicide rate as much as our hypothesized emotional support.

The most frequent responses (about 40% of them) are matter-of-fact statements of the person's situation:
'I am not seeing anyone for assistance—I am assisting myself.'

'Thanks for the note. Life is going fairly well but it has its ups and downs. Will be expecting future correspondence.'

'I have been divorced. Now remarried and very happy except I can't seem to find a good job. But I'll make it.'

'I'm doing OK. I have been moving and didn't pick up my mail for a while, so this has been delayed. My new address is ———.'

'My wife and I are separated. I am trying very hard to make up for things I have done wrong. It seems as if I just cannot get right.

I have a very demanding job and don't know what's going to happen.'

'To me I seem to be the same as before. I'm working and going to school.'

'My thoughts are confused and I have long periods of depression and anxiety.'

'I'm doing fairly well, not the best.'

'What can I say? My husband left, I've moved with three small children three times in two months. I'm terribly depressed and unsure of my future. I don't like myself at all.'

Many responders (about 60%) also include in their remarks some acknowledgement of the message we are trying to convey in our contact letters:

'Thank you for your continued interest. My work is demanding but rewarding, and it's hard to believe two years have passed.'

'. . . I'm grateful that there are those who really care. I am still unable to work, but I cling to the hope that I will once again be a useful, productive member of society.'

'. . . I have been married for about a year, and have a very good job which I enjoy. Thank you again for your concern.'

'Thanks for your continued interest in me. I weathered the rough times of early this year and am now doing well. I have to come to terms with getting older and living alone.'

'Many thanks for your interest in my welfare. I don't sleep too well, but otherwise I am fine. I hope you are well too!'

'Again, thank you for your continued interest. When I fail my expectations I must learn to accept it and try again, but it is a difficult task for me to accept.'

'Thank you for your concern and interest and I regret I've not written before now. I sometimes wonder at all that has happened. I have a job I like and look forward to the future . . .'

'I appreciate your concern. I'm doing OK but don't know about the future. I think what happened was a spiritual experience.'

'My job makes me travel and move a lot so the mail is all mixed up. I'll keep you informed of my correct address. Again, I appreciate your continuing concern, and hope to hear from you.'

'Appreciate your continuing concern. Slowly but surely I am getting used to the life style here. I am giving you my home address, not only for your files but if you happen to see —— you might mention where I can be reached . . .'

'Thank you for expressing concern for me. For the first time since my breakdown I feel I should be talking with someone, as I'm having some radical changes in my thinking.'

'Thank you for your continued reminders—letting me know about your caring—that's pretty neat. I'm doing so well maybe you could discontinue these notes. Not that I mind, but you must have others that need it more.'

'You asked if I wanted to drop you a note but I've written you a book.'

Some responses (about 5%) request assistance with living problems:
'Could you get the Veterans' Administration to send me back home?'

'My biggest problem is finding a job. Could you locate something for me?'

'Would you send me a prescription for my medicine?'

'I'm really down and don't know what to do. Would you call me and talk to me?'

'Maybe if you contact my husband and talk with him, you can get him to take me back.'

'I've been drinking a lot and realize that there is no continued help available. There is really little hope for me. Please feel free to call me. I appreciate your interest.'

'I am not employed, and wonder if you would write a letter so I could get welfare benefits.'

'I need help. I'm broke and don't know where to go.'

'Would you recommend some place to get help other than ——?'

'I don't need any help but my husband does. Can you help him? We are separated but you can contact him at ——.'

'I really thank you for taking time to drop me this note. I really need help before I croak.'

'My main problem is finding a home for my beautiful cat that my landlord won't allow in the building. Please let me know if you can assist me with this.'

Some responses (about 5%) are from concerned family members:
'I forwarded your letter to my daughter. I hope she answers your inquiry. I so want her to have a fulfilling life.'

'I am ———'s wife. He was alright for a short time, but now every day when I come home from work, I'm afraid he'll do something terrible to himself again.'

'Many thanks for your continued interest in my husband. It pleases him that even though he has done so well, your interest in him has not subsided.'

'I'm ———'s wife, and though I left him I want to thank you for being so kind as to inquire about him from time to time. I was sick too, but recovered. Again my thanks for your attentiveness and concern.'

'I'm ———'s mother. I'm happy that you're interested in my son's welfare, and have been trying to have him write to you. My husband and I are worried. Can you advise me what would help my son in any way?'

'We've been trying to locate ——— for over a year. If he gets in touch with you will you tell him his family in ——— is anxious to have word of him, whether he's alright?'

'——— is not seeing a doctor, has not seen one and has no intention of seeing one. I can't talk her into seeing one and I firmly believe she should be seeing one.'

'We were so relieved to hear from you, as it means ——— must be OK. His father, sister and I hope and pray that his drug problem is behind him. If he needs more treatment and comes to you, please let us know.'

A number of responses (about 5%) are best characterized as chatty reviews of life situations and experiences.
Some of the content becomes quite serious, but it is generally in a friendly, conversational tone as though addressing a pen pal. They make up in volume what they lack in numbers. We will omit examples, as they are not distinctive in any way.

Some of the responses (about 2%) are not so friendly:
'Why don't you guys hire me since you're so interested in my welfare?'
'Please ignore my ridiculous plea for continued help.'
'I am tired of hearing the same typewritten letter. If it's of any importance I'm completely screwed up emotionally. Next time just Xerox it and save your secretary's time.'
'I, ———, am pleased to know that your interest still continues. Life is going well for me at this time. It would lighten my life to hear from you at any time.' [A parody of our contact note]
'You need not send any more letters. Please take me off your mailing list.'

Outspoken expressions of positive feelings are found in about 35% of responses:
'Thanks so much for your faithful interest over the years.'
'I am just hanging on, facing each day with dread. Your interest in my welfare is genuinely appreciated. It suggests to me a possibility of hope.'
'I was so glad to get your note, because it's always nice to know that somebody is concerned, especially since the closest people I live with are not.'
'. . . Whenever I think I won't write any more, getting your note encourages me to keep writing, even though there's no change in my life.'
'I'm deeply touched and grateful for your letter as it seems sometimes that there is no hope at all.'
'You can't imagine how much I appreciate your interest. I keep all your letters.'
'I'm glad to know you think about me. You and my daughter are the only ones who care. You see, I don't trust people.'
'It feels good to get a letter from somebody. Please write again.'
'It is really nice to know that there's someone out there wanting to know how you are even though it is your job.'
'After I threw the last letter out I wished I hadn't a couple of days later, so I was glad to get this one.'

'You are the most persistent son-of-a-bitch I have ever seen, so you must be sincere.'

'My house burned down and I had to move. I feel much better now that I found you again. Please keep in touch.'

'Thank you so very much for being interested. You and others are what keep me alive today.'

'Take good care of yourself, and thanks for being a friend to me.'

'. . . I can hardly believe that I still hear from you after two years. It may be standard procedure, but it makes me feel good that someone cares about me besides myself.'

'Your letter reached me half-way around the world. Quite a surprise. You're really faithful.'

'You will never know what your notes mean to me. I always think someone cares about what happens to me even if my family did kick me out.'

'Thanks for your concern. This is the first time I have written back since the correspondence began about four years ago.'

'I think of the things you have said more than anything else that happened during that nightmare.'

'I'm grateful you are following me up. I am trying to overcome my desire for self-destruction. It is very hard indeed. Again thanks for caring.'

'I cannot express how much your notes have been helping me. I have never answered, but always had you in mind in case I need to contact someone.'

'. . . It's surprising to me how I only *hear* the message "I care" at the time it's said, but much later am able to *listen* to it.'

'I'm not sure why I'm writing you—probably because you care.'

'Thanks very much for your concern—it made me feel that someone was thinking of me in this world of turmoil where everyone just thinks about money.'

Implications of this experience
The excerpts noted above are readily recognizable examples of well-known observations, specifically, that in a despairing state very simple expressions of caring can have considerable emotional

impact, and when such expressions are repeated over an extended period of time they can exert a stabilizing influence. It is important in this context that the expression be unsolicited and freely offered, with no expectation of anything in return, even acknowledgement.

In using this approach the advantages of verbal interchange, whether by telephone or face-to-face, are relinquished in a trade-off for regularity and permanence. Instead of the sense of presence and the audible qualities of warmth, concern, humour and ready response that verbal communication can provide, we accept the palpable quality of words on paper. This permits what verbal contact does not—unlimited repetition of the message, by re-reading, at any time or place. The choice is not a preference but an acceptance of the terms dictated by the person we are concerned about. For example, a worker in a door-to-door survey in San Francisco reported that a somewhat reclusive informant showed her a worn letter from us, confiding that she keeps it in a place where she can re-read it from time to time.

Our correspondents have been drawn from a large metropolitan urban setting. In addition to their psychological resistance to asking for help, many of them do not have a private telephone in their living setting. Many change their address frequently, especially those in the younger age groups. The postal system has served the written contact well, delivering our notes to persons throughout the USA as well as to Canada, Europe and the Middle East. The potential for repeating a caring message to this mobile population could only be realized in written form. The same can be said for elderly persons who live in nursing homes and small hotels, seamen who are in port briefly and irregularly, persons in state hospitals or in jail or prison—all of which are prone to feel isolated and abandoned.

The bonds that are formed can work both ways. Contrary to conventional crisis counselling, when the immediate stress is resolved there is a continuation of the relationship in the form of sharing the ups and downs of every-day living experience. One of the indications that the crisis is past is that the person begins to express concern for the crisis-worker's well-being. On the other hand, though we planned a five-year programme to evaluate the efficacy of this approach, our staff found themselves extending the time for some responders as an expression of their continuing interest in those persons. This can be done very easily, as the time required to maintain such a contact is very small compared with a verbal interchange. Large case loads can be carried for the same reason, making it possible to offer the programme to a very large population.

In a number of instances a period of written communication will lead to an acceptance of a face-to-face counselling or treatment. The original writer could fill that role or refer the person to another resource depending on the circumstances. Thus the written contact may begin as an alternate approach but serve as an intermediate step to a more traditional plan.

The contact approach can be used by telephone as well, and in specific instances may be preferred to writing. Our experience suggests that it is more difficult to maintain over long periods unless the person lives in a special situation, for example, a shut-in who has a telephone that is not shared with family or others. Awkward situations can develop unexpectedly in ways that would not be encouraged with a written note, and the potential for intrusiveness is much greater. Combinations of written and verbal interchange are worth trying out, especially with a relatively stable population.

In summary, to reach at least some of those persons who will neither initiate nor maintain a conventional pattern of relating, it may be possible to offer the beneficial force of befriending by means of the written word. What we are suggesting, in effect, is to create a 'significant other' role in spite of some persons' reluctance to participate actively in bringing that about. They remain free to decline this effort, of course, by indicating that they wish no further correspondence, or by simply ignoring the letters. If they do permit them to continue, even though they do not reply, we can take some comfort from the evidence above that a beneficial effect is being exerted. If all else has been offered and this approach is rejected as well, we can only suggest a philosophical

equanimity on the conviction that we have done what we can d
and have even tried to do some things that are beyond us.

Definition of suicide
Suicide is self-inflicted, self-intentioned death.

J. M.

9. What kind of attention does a person need who has been medically rescued after an act of self-injury?

IVOR H. MILLS, PhD (London), MA, MD (Cambridge), FRCP, HON. FACP★ (UK)

People deliberately perform acts of self-injury and run the risk of killing themselves when the coping mechanism of the brain is completely exhausted. An understanding of how best to help them depends upon an appreciation of the means by which challenges to the coping mechanism may lead on to failure of this mechanism.

In the majority of cases they know that they are faced with problems with which they can no longer cope. So often they say 'I couldn't cope any more'. What they do is an effort to escape from the situation and if in escaping they risk death, they do not care. Almost always there is a final trigger which makes them perform the act, which in most cases is to take an overdose of drugs.

The most critical time to talk to them is just as they are recovering from the effect of the drugs. At that time they are most ready to talk about what has happened. Sometimes, if they sense that there is not a receptive ear, they will refer only to the final trigger which initiated the act. Characteristically, they will have thought about taking the overdose for less than fifteen minutes before they did it. This final trigger is often something which appears too trivial to justify the risk of suicide. Here lies the clue to successful help for the person. If the trigger were accepted as the only challenge to the coping mechanism it would be impossible to understand, let alone help, the individual.

★ Professor Mills is Professor of Medicine at the University of Cambridge. He has carried out extensive research into the relationships between stress, the coping mechanism of the brain and attempted suicide.

At the time when they are most ready to talk one can usually obtain the details of the repeated challenges in recent months—yes, months, not usually just days or weeks. If there have not been repeated episodes demanding exercise of the coping process in the brain, there will have been a longer term continuous, grumbling problem.

The arousal mechanism

Challenges to the brain represent problems to be solved, even if it is only to decide how to go on living with someone who is a continuous strain to live with. In trying to solve these problems the brain gets into a more excited state, ie, the level of arousal is raised. It is then quicker and more efficient in solving single problems. If the challenges represent learning at school or doing mental work to earn one's living, the same elevation of arousal occurs. Major upsets in one's life may lead to sleep disturbance because the high arousal persists from one day to the next. Repeated major disturbances may lead to failure of the brain to cope with them and an underlying depression becomes manifest. Enjoyable mental stimulation may then add more load to the coping process because it also raises arousal level and may then help to lead on to depression. Success leads to a sense of satisfaction but failure causes frustration and may precipitate violence in association with depression.

To help the person who has risked suicide, you must know the nature of the challenges which have had to be coped with. These may be divided into two groups: (a) those which are externally determined, and (b) those which are personally, i.e., internally determined.

Externally determined strains on coping

These will represent factors which occur in the environment in which the person lives or works. Indeed, it is frequently the summation of events at work and home which brings about the exhaustion of coping. Some people seem to be born with very little coping power. They are often referred to as having inadequate personalities. Quite simple difficulties may seem to them to be gigantic. They are constantly at the end of their tether because their coping power is so low. To keep them from recurrent attempts at suicide it is necessary to surround them with metaphorical cushions to lessen the blow when they fall down. Some of them are quite intelligent and it seems so incongruous that they stumble over the smallest problems in life. They are very demanding of attention and expect someone to drop all else they are doing to rush to their aid. Only a secure and quiet life will sustain them and this is by no means easy to arrange.

One of the most demanding of challenges in family life is a broken home. This may be a home broken by parents splitting up and thus leaving children with a continuous strain, especially if they were equally attached to both parents and so pine for the one that they are not living with. Or it may be a break-up between husband and wife or between a man and woman who have lived for some time together but not got married. The one who makes the break frequently has someone else to turn to, whereas the one left behind is likely to feel very insecure. This is especially true if he or she has few friends and no relatives near at hand.

This represents the time when befriending is most needed. They will need someone to help build some security back into their lives. Frequent contact is necessary and sometimes a strong right arm to reinforce the security. It takes some months usually to help to establish someone in a secure life once they have been left. A whole social structure of life is necessary so that the person has the stimulation of meeting friends who can share the burden of comforting and uplifting and giving support. In the case of a mother left with young children, this is particularly important. She may have no baby-sitter to let her go out in the evenings or she may never have made contact with other mothers at the child's school. The withdrawn, shy person is extremely hard to help in this way and yet she most needs the stimulation and support of a number of friends and contacts.

Family strife
This is in some ways a greater strain than the final separation. The

friction in the family, however, may lead to some mental stimulation and may keep the brain sufficiently aroused to mask the underlying depression. The 'attacker' in the argument may feel stimulated by it but the person 'attacked' may be constantly frustrated and end up feeling depressed. The children in such families are often torn between the two parents.

Visiting the homes where such strife goes on may make it settle down. Often they will not argue and fight when an outsider is there. While the person who succumbs is in hospital there is a breathing space and the family given support afterwards may be able to refrain from the arguments and battles and allow peace to return. Not infrequently, the 'attacker', without the stimulation of the arguments, may begin to feel depressed some two or three weeks later when the high arousal level has come down and exposed the previously masked depression.

Helping the children from such strife-torn homes is not always so easy. First of all it is necessary to find out whether the difficulties at home have led to interference with school work. The teacher who is unaware of the home environment may interpret poorer work as just due to laziness and punish the child accordingly. It is essential to try to lower the excitement level all round if the child is to be able to cope with all aspects of life while growing up. Sometimes it is best if the child spends some weeks with a relative or friend. Even then the child may be too depressed to work at school without treatment with antidepressants.

Another aspect of family strife becomes manifest when the father has to work away from home for periods of time. Teenage children may then take advantage of his absence and become unruly. The friction generated and sometimes the retribution when father comes home may lead to breakdown of the child's coping ability. Befriending may play a very important role here in encouraging the child to obey sensible rules and allow peace to be re-established. Once again it may be several months before the child can cope without support. The long time-scale of the recovery from exhaustion of coping is frequently not appreciated and help may be withdrawn too early.

Working mothers

These are nowadays common even when they have young children. With modern devices to facilitate housework, mothers would feel bored and unfulfilled without something to do. However, the mother who comes home after her children arrive from school may not be aware of what is happening in the child's life. When children come home from school there is a short time when they are bubbling over with excitement to recite all the good and bad things which have gone on that day. By an hour later, they will be playing or doing homework and not bother to tell their parents. Thus a child's life may become disturbed without the parents understanding the reasons.

Another aspect of mothers working full time, or the 'twilight shift' from 6 pm to 10 pm after spending all day with toddlers, is that they get tired more easily and have less patience with husbands and children. Friction may be set up at these times and go on to more violent arguments. A mother who takes part in the social life of the works may find this stimulating and enjoyable but she may get worn out by it and end up desperate. After attempting suicide, it is important that she spend some weeks at least under less of a strain. She needs constant attention over this time, not only to recover from the desperation which exhausted her coping power but also to help her through the difficult time when she does not know who knows and who does not that she has risked her own death. Wondering what people will think and say is a very difficult problem when she first comes home.

In a few cases the strains within the family become intolerable. It may be precipitated by a worn out working mother, it may be started by a severely anorexic daughter who not only resists and resents the struggles of the family to make her eat, but also is likely in her disgruntled state to pick arguments and fights with any one of them. The father may then take solace in the local public house and may return in a vicious mood. The children learn to get out of his way and go to bed before he arrives but the mother may be the butt of his verbal abuse or his fist. There is a limit to the battering that a wife can take and not a few attempt suicide in desperation. They need particular care when they leave hospital and sometimes they need help in obtaining appropriate legal restrictions on their husbands. Not infrequently the husband may need help but this is usually medical rather than befriending.

The husband may take the overdose because of the severity of the challenges to his coping ability. In these cases he is rarely a drunkard but is more likely to be an over-working man, exhausting himself for his family and losing a great deal of sleep under the mental strain. As his coping nears his limit, he may strike out regardlessly and later be filled with remorse when he realizes what he has done. He may well need a great deal of help subsequently and perhaps require advice in getting his affairs into a state that will not exhaust him.

Personally determined strains on coping

At first thought it may seem strange that anyone should contrive to get themselves to a point where they could no longer cope with challenges of their own making. Clearly this depends upon the person's personality. The people who do this tend to be those with a determined, driving personality. Often they are perfectionists and drive themselves on and on to achieve the high goals they set themselves. They tend to be ambitious, want to do well in examinations and climb the socio-economic ladder to the top. Whether they achieve all these things or not depends upon their innate ability but frequently they push themselves way beyond what they have any hope of achieving.

Some of these people have been labelled type A behaviour people and they are known to have a higher incidence of coronary thrombosis (heart attack) than the more placid, less driving type B people. The strain of driving themselves to the limit of tolerance may lead to the frustration of failure. At that time they may feel their coping power is exhausted and take an overdose of drugs, trying to escape from their own failure. They are quite difficult to handle afterwards. The overbearing ambition is so difficult to curb. At every turn they are trying to escape from the helpful support of friends and relatives. The frustration of their unsatisfied desires makes them reject the very help they most need.

Self-starvation

Some of the high-driving people are made to develop this characteristic rather than being born like it. This is sometimes true of one group of perfectionists, the women who starve themselves and have anorexia nervosa. This is much commoner than it used to be and is mostly in teenagers and those in their early twenties. In severe cases their lives become stereotyped and they may become obsessed with tidiness. Everything has to be very precisely in place, books with their edges parallel to the edge of the table or shelf on which they lie. Nothing can be left lying about, it must be picked up and put precisely in place. Their handwriting is meticulously neat, on a straight line with every letter identical all over the page.

Their starving usually starts because they are a bit overweight or because of the fashion for girls to be slim. They soon discover that when made to eat by the family they feel less well and are less able to work. In fact starvation excites the brain and raises arousal level. It is this that they come to be dependent on. A mother will sometimes describe how her daughter changed over a year from being a happy, carefree, untidy girl to being a solemn, overworking, excessively tidy but irritable and self-willed person whom she hardly recognised. Some anorexics push themselves to the limit of tolerance and the high arousal of starvation may then fail to mask the underlying depression. Frustration with their failure to achieve what they, and perhaps others, expect of them may lead to self-injury. They are not easy to treat but it has to be by people outside the family because so often the strain on all members of the family brings it to breaking point. Their iron willpower gets them past the normal point of hunger until appetite is totally suppressed. The same iron will defies all but the stoutest heart in getting them over this illness successfully. The severest ones have to be in hospital anyway but many can be treated outside hospital if the family gets enough support. Since 75% start crash dieting in the year they are working for an important examination, it is often very difficult to help them until their examinations are over.

In recent years self-imposed starvation has become much

commoner among married women. These are women usually in their thirties who previously have not been anorexic. Many are on the verge of depression and then discover that not eating causes mental excitement and they then refuse to go back to eating. Since they are sometimes so near to depression it is not surprising that they get desperate at times, especially since friction is set up between them and their husbands because starvation causes total loss of libido.

Sexual problems

Friction between sexual partners is one of the commonest causes of self-injury. Overwork is an important factor in the loss of libido by women or the onset of impotence in men. Loss of libido commonly occurs in married women who take on mentally demanding jobs. She may be a secretary to a busy executive or a woman doing an open-ended job in the commercial world. They feel the mental reward of success, sometimes aided by financial rewards, and go on striving despite the needs of their family. Few husbands can understand the progressive loss of interest in love-making and tend to assume that they have a rival in the office. Friction mounts to arguments and perhaps to open warfare in the home till the woman, in desperation, risks killing herself. An alternative version of the same theme is the precipitation of a crisis when the woman finds that her husband is paying court to another woman.

Teenage love-affairs have been suggested as being of much greater importance nowadays compared to years ago. In fact rows between a boy and a girl rarely lead to attempted suicide unless there are other factors which had been eroding the coping ability for some time before. Indeed, the friction leading to the row or the break-up is often a reflection of the fact that one or other of the couple was under such a strain as to cause the irritability and intolerance of early depression. It is essential in be-friending such youngsters to find out all the other pressures in their lives which may be of more vital importance than the row which was only the trigger.

Stimulating arousal to mask depression

The effect of starvation in stimulating the arousal of the brain and thereby masking depression has already been referred to. The starving girls may not know this at the outset but they certainly use the increased arousal to facilitate greater mental agility. This was first described by those studying professional fasters at the beginning of this century.

All the techniques used to stimulate arousal level carry the potential danger that the constant high arousal will lead to the development of an underlying depression. As a result of frustration or a fall in arousal level the person may then take an overdose of drugs. Alcohol is a well-known agent which, taken in greater amounts than usual, will lower arousal and make the person aware of depression.

The stimulation used to raise arousal level varies greatly. Probably one of the commonest is the intense noise at many discotheques. It has been shown that noise of this intensity can make the brain more efficient if it is already fatigued by loss of sleep. To those not accustomed to the noise it may be painful to be present: deterioration in hearing occurs in those who are constantly exposed to such a noise. The mental excitement produced by this intensity of noise could well mask depression for a time. Eventually this, like so many other artificial mental stimuli, may lead to depression becoming obvious and then a slight trigger could initiate self-injury.

Some of the stimuli used by adolescents and young adults to mask depression are not so innocuous. Challenging authority is a device which some younger people have used. Perhaps the challenge of parental authority is one of the mildest of such stimuli and a number of young people clearly use it. This may take the form of damage to parental property, usually in such a way as not to be caught. It may be more dramatic as with breaking ornaments, doors or windows. It may be particularly used by teenagers when they have no father living with them or he is intermittently working away from home. It may be either the child or the mother who succumbs to the strain, usually when the father returns and inflicts retribution. These teenagers have invariably been under pressures of a variety of sorts and have intermittent depression. Initially they learn by accident that producing excitement (good or bad) masks depression and they then pursue a course of repeated events to raise arousal level. Almost always the depression becomes progressively more severe until it cannot easily be masked. Coping power is then near the point of exhaustion and self-injury is easily triggered.

These situations are quite difficult to handle, partly because the desire to challenge the parent to raise arousal becomes almost an addiction. More particularly they are difficult without the use of antidepressants for the teenager and often the mother as well. Strong support for the child by the befriender will be needed for many months. Discussion of the primary challenges which produced the depression in the first place is essential.

At school, challenging authority can be much more effective in terms of stirring up excitement. There may be only one or two children in a class who start a disturbance but the other children are only too glad to join in the stimulating experience. Clearly the success of this type of activity depends upon the attitude of the teacher. The strictest ones are rarely challenged because the response tends to be so fast that little excitement is caused and it is overwhelmed by the fear of severe punishment. In some classes, however, total chaos can be produced day after day so that practically no work gets done. Eventually punishment by the school and the parents helps to build the underlying depression to the point where it cannot be masked and it is then that the ring-leader may take an overdose of drugs.

Support has to be given for a long time but it is more effective if the depression is treated with antidepressants. The original underlying depression is usually related to problems at home or between boy and girl friends. Family support may be needed to resolve the problem.

Finally, the challenge may be to the law when stealing, damaging property, mugging, fighting and real violence are undoubtedly used by some young people to raise arousal level. Frequently they have had a prolonged time with multiple difficulties in life such as broken homes or intense friction at home, etc. Few of them would

D

be expected to appeal for support by befrienders because the law and the probation service often take care of them. However, other people in the family may well be driven to depression by the child's activities and then attempt suicide. Helping such a family is a difficult and long-term job but there may well be a member of the family who needs it and could benefit by it.

Conclusions

Those who engage in self-injury are desperate at the time they do it. Primarily they wish to escape from circumstances that they feel they cannot possibly cope with. The final trigger may be relatively trivial and after an hour or two the person may see a way to cope and then ask for help. This should not lead one to think that the original act was not genuinely one of desperation. They need to escape from the challenge: they do not necessarily intend to die but they are sufficiently desperate that they will take the risk.

Constant challenges cause initial mental arousal but as coping ability fails, depression sets in. Good excitement and bad excitement are additive in this mechanism. In befriending these people, it is necessary to understand the long course of time over which things build up and the long time it takes to facilitate peace and security until coping powers return completely to normal.

Definition of suicide

Suicide is the death of an individual as a result of his (her) deliberate action from which he (she) could clearly run the risk of death.

I. M.

10. Is there any kind of suicidal person whom no known method can help, other than the impulsive type?

MARIA LUISA RODRÍGUEZ SALA GÓMEZGIL[*]   (MEXICO)

Throughout history, suicide has been studied from different angles in different periods. Using the classic work of Durkheim[†] as a point of departure, doctors have mainly approached the subject in a very scientific manner. Works of a social and psychological nature are less frequent, although in certain countries, especially the United States and in some western European ones, there have been numerous attempts over the last few decades.

In Mexico, the phenomenon of suicide has been studied in an isolated form by psychiatrists, using private cases in clinics. Works of an analytical nature[‡] which have studied different characteristics of suicide on a statistical basis, and which have sought to interpret the act of self-destruction within the framework of Mexican society have used Durkheim as a starting point but have shown a preference for interdisciplinary approach.

The conclusions of our work, expressed in general terms, establish that, although suicide in Mexico does not represent a social and psychological problem of numerical importance (the annual rates are very low—for 1972 it was 2·7:100,000), its characteristics do not differ substantially from those which have been located in other societies, from which we may conclude that theoretical generalizations may be valid for any type of cultural environment —not excluding Mexico.

[*] Sra Sala Gómezgil is a research sociologist at the Institute of Social Research, Universidad Nacional Autónoma de Mexico.

[†] Durkheim, Emile, Le Suicide (1897).

[‡] Sala Gómezgil, Ma Luisa Rodríguez, El Suicidio en Mexico DF and Suicidios y Suicidas en la Sociedad Mexicana (Instituto de Investigaciones Sociales UNAM, Mexico, 1968 and 1974).

The twenty questions

1. Theoretical review

The theories most widely accepted and employed in the study of suicide—as much by those who examine it scientifically as by those who cheerfully devote their lives to offering help to the suicidal—have used the social aspect as a point of departure, and this has been reinforced by doctors and psychologists. This article makes no claim to review and criticize the theoretical conclusions in all their ramifications, but a rapid review is essential to support our contribution.

The first theory is the sociological one, initiated by Emile Durkheim in *Le Suicide* and expanded first by Maurice Halwachs and later by Dublin and Bunzel in the United States, where in recent decades there has been intensive work in this field. The studies of Gibbs and Douglas—to mention only the most outstanding—have enlarged the sociological approach and attempted to fit it to the structural changes in their social environment.

With the advent of psychological and psychiatric studies, two parallel schools of theory have developed: the school of Freud and the neo-Freudians with the work of Menninger, and the school represented by Delmas who considers suicide the result of a phenomenon associated exclusively with illness.

Each of these three points of view plays a greater part in the interpretation of suicide if we relate them to: (a) disorder of the personality; (b) failure of the individual to adjust to his social environment; (c) disorganization of society itself.

(a) Disorder of the personality

By this we mean those emotional disturbances which lead to a feeling that life is not worth the pain of living. The sense of stability is destroyed and the individual's adjustment to society around him breaks down. During the course of his life, an individual learns to adjust to his surroundings; he knows that he belongs to a defined group, that he relies on personal relations with people who value him and help him, and in whom he can confide; he learns that he has to submit to a series of controls which society imposes on him, and that he can co-operate with the said society in a variety of ways. In a word, he adjusts to a complete social organization and feels content and happy.

However, when something happens to an individual which disrupts this adjustment, then his personality crumbles and internal conflicts arise which then exteriorize themselves. But what is that something which disturbs him? Generally it is a question of various kinds of sickness which attack the individual, chronic or severe mental illness. The first are the most frequent and those which lead to suicide and manifest themselves most often in melancholia, the depressive phase of manic depression, psychopathy, acute or chronic paranoia and epilepsy. Among physical illnesses which can lead to a disorder of the personality, the most prevalent are those with incurable conditions such as cancer. But there are also numerous cases of patients suffering from hypochondria—this suicide factor is frequent among women who are going through the menopause. In all these cases the personality of the subject finds itself swamped in feelings and ideas which rob him of his balance. He feels that something is lacking in himself, or that there is no more hope, or that life is becoming intolerable, or that he is suffering continual persecution or perhaps that he is no longer capable of supporting physical pain, or that nothing can restore his health, and consequently he tries to free himself from these states through suicide.

(b)   *The failure of the individual to adjust to his social environment*
'Even when an individual does not suffer from physical or mental illness his personality can become disordered, due to a failure of social adjustment.' Social conditions are reflected in every individual, and when they are not favourable, they can affect the personality in a decisive way. Consequently, many cases of suicide are registered in which there is no suspicion of physical or mental debility, but where there has been a crisis in the social field: loss of employment, a grave economic situation, family quarrels, or deception in love. 'There is no doubt that in these cases the person who commits suicide has done it to escape from a social situation which has become impossible to bear.'* It is clear

* Gillin, J. R., *Social Pathology*.

that once a conflict of social order arises in an individual, his personality becomes disordered, and this prevents him from reorganizing his life and overcoming adverse social conditions, so that he opts for a refuge and solution in death. Nevertheless, people who behave in this way are likely to be affected not only by a failure of social adjustment but also by a psychological state verging on mental illness, since it is unlikely that a human-being whose personality is in perfect mental order is going to deprive himself of his existence merely because of a reversal in his social situation; on the contrary, his gut reaction would be to overcome it.

(c) Disorganization of society

Using the ideas of Gillin, Gibbs and their followers as a basis, we can safely say that in periods of social disruption, suicides increase; rapid social changes which carry implicit rejections of traditions and custom affect the way the members of those societies behave. A great number of young people, adults and the elderly find themselves confused. They fail to stand up to and adjust their personality to the constant changes. Nor can they channel their behaviour as much towards their expectations as towards social requirement. Many of them, impelled by the disorganization of society, become incapable of maintaining their social status and maladapted to their conflicting and changing environment.

In the majority of highly industrialized societies, individualism has developed as one of a number of responses to the change which has broken with traditions. It is in those societies, in those in which financial circumstances change with unaccustomed speed, that the rich of today can become the poor of tomorrow; that a man who feels he is a success can cease to be so in a very short space of time; that the idol of the masses falls to earth as quickly as he was erected. In our environment, such circumstances can attain such an anguishing reality only in the great urban centres—our capital, Mexico City, one might almost say, comes close to it, but even here there are sectors which are strongly rooted in a traditional society, in which family solidarity and respect for norms of behaviour and ethno-religious values preserve its members against personality disorder and its immediate consequence: suicide.

Although we have given only a very brief look at general theoretical analysis, we can permit ourselves a first hypothesis and conclusion: in self-destruction two fundamental factors converge: (a) a state of disorder of the personality—be it expressed in a psychopathic state or in a neurotic crisis—and (b) adverse or conflicting conditions which produce a social maladaptation of the individual to his environment, which is manifested in a loss of social status in one or several of the social roles which the individual plays in the group to which he belongs.

We shall see how combinations of these factors result in suicide and determine to what degree help and rescue are possible—from intents with a minimal potentiality for self-destruction to cases of high lethality (death by self-destruction), and with it we shall try to reply to the anxious title-question of this article.

2. (i) Aspects of personality disorder

We have said that a suicide case, whether attempted or successful, generally presents a disorder in his personality which profoundly affects his behaviour when there is in addition a loss or diminishment of social status.

The disorder can be observed through examining the aspects which help to detect a suicidal person and to quantify his likelihood of success. For this, those who have had experience in suicide prevention provide the specific theoretical bases—not only in relation to current psychiatric principles, but more particularly in relation to the process of identifying a possible suicide case—which help to pinpoint the types of suicide case with little possibility of help. To discover this, Tabachnick and Farberow* suggested finding out: the intrapersonal aspects of the suicide case which are made up from two categories: (i) the strength of the desire for self-destruction, and (ii) the structures of the character which permit the realization of the intention to commit suicide.

* Tabachnik, Norman D., and Farberow, Norman L., 'Validation of the potentiality of self-destruction', in *The Cry for Help* (New York, McGraw-Hill, 1961).

By considering the conscious or unconscious intention of the individual, we can detect its degree of dangerousness, and thus we have concluded that:

1. The more lucid and sensible the person is of the consequences of his self-destructive behaviour, the greater will be the possibility of death.
2. The greater his knowledge of the means that can be utilized, the greater the risk that he will choose an effective method.
3. The fewer the preparations required to carry it out, the greater the degree of risk.
4. The appearance of one or more dynamic factors which reveal or presume the existence of a physical or mental illness, or the increase of those factors in states of neuroses, all indicate a high degree of potential lethality.

The dynamic factors which signal danger are: depression, most especially when it is accompanied by anxiety, tension and agitation, hostility and the feeling of guilt, as well as the necessity of dependence, and the displacement of logical thought by the appearance of fantasies of a destructive nature.

Although there can be present in a person one or more traces of conscious or unconscious intention to destroy himself, these will be of lesser or greater lethality according to the organization and structure of the personality. The greater the lack of adjustment and control in the personality when faced with dynamic and social factors, the greater will be the risk of achieving self-destruction. There are three dichotomized characteristics which contribute to the organization and disorder of the personality: (a) impulsiveness/control; (b) rigidity/flexibility; (c) isolation/relations.

Resuming the explanations of Tabachnik and Farberow, it can be said that:

1. The more impulsive the person is, the greater the risks of self-destruction and the loss of self-control; certain states of

physical change aggravate impulsiveness: alcohol and drugs exercise a powerful effect.

2.   The lack of flexibility and that of adjustment regarding situations of personal or social crisis make it much more difficult to face these situations positively and can easily lead a person to self-destruction.

3.   Isolation with its immediate consequences of lack of support and help, by being deprived of relations, contributes greatly to loneliness and desperation and, with them, a heightening of the risk of suicide.

2. (ii)   Maladaptation to the social environment and social disorganization

The maladaptation of an individual to his social environment, in many instances initiated by the disorganization of the society in which he develops, is manifested in a reduction or loss of social status, which is contained in the system of concepts and values which enable a person to understand his environment. The system is composed of a series of characteristics which have helped the individual to fix his boundaries, his aspirations and his actions, and which are translated into a series of specific indicators which enable the identification of status.

Following the sociological tradition of Durkheim, we meet different theories, which have as their basis the idea of integration/ disintegration of social status as an explanation of suicide. In these, an inverse relation between integration of status and suicide is established, the conclusion being: the greater the disintegration, the greater the probability of self-destruction.

Just as in the theme of disorder of the personality, so it is for social maladaptation: modalities are presented which range from the reduction of status to its total loss, and the differential levels indicate the grades of suicidal lethality. However, not only the levels of reduction should be considered, but the suicidal risk as well—the concept introduced by two eminent authors, Jack P. Gibbs and Walter T. Martin, who consider suicide to be the result of a process which combines both a sequence of facts over a wide space of time and an immediate situation which leads directly and inevitably to the act. From their empirical studies, the authors have extracted three variables of change associated with suicide: change of economic prestige, the relating failure of strong social bonds, and personal crisis. According to them, suicide is produced in the moment that economic prestige is lost—generally through loss of occupation or reduced occupational level; this adds to personality disorder or a state of frustration which can be aggravated by a loosening of social ties or by the disorganization of the social environment. The second factor can, from a distance, appear to be independent of the loss of economic prestige. Nevertheless, in general, the three factors become united: there is a personal crisis, be it as a consequence of the loss of prestige, or even as a motivator of it, and the crisis cannot easily be resolved, through the fact that social relations are lacking.

Let us consider that the loss of social status or its reduction is not only produced by the intervention of the economic factor.

Throughout our studies in Mexico, we have analysed in detail other variables, and have verified that the following can also add to the reduction and loss of status: age, civil status, and educational level, in addition to occupation—already mentioned by the authors whose theory we have just expounded.

Each of these indicators feature within themselves a process generated over a wide stretch of time, in particular age and educational level, but awareness that an age has been reached or anticipation of an educational level which represents a loss of status, can be revealed suddenly and hopelessly. The problems related to occupation—its loss or change for the worse—and the change in civil status (loss of a marital partner through separation or death) happen generally in an immediate and sudden manner, and with it the personal crisis is sharpened.

As regards the maladaptation of the individual to his social environment, be it through loss or diminishment of status, we can establish the following variables:

1. Adolescence and old age are stages of age in which social and physical change are experienced which can contribute to a personal crisis.

2. Old age and divorce produce changes in the individual's social situation with loss or diminishment of social status.

3. Change of occupation, its loss or carrying out a job beyond one's capacity produce perturbation and personal crisis.

The three variables above are the ones which, throughout studies in Mexico and other countries, have registered the greatest number of suicides, principally when they are shown in relation to the total population in similar circumstances or in suicide rates.

3. Who are the suicidal types for whom the possibility of help is most difficult?

Using the theory we have expounded as a basis, it should be relatively straightforward to pinpoint the type of suicide for whom help will most likely result in failure, or whose outcome depends on circumstantial situations which people dedicated to suicide prevention find very difficult to foresee.

For the potential suicide to obtain his self-destruction, the personal factors must combine with social ones in their modality of maladjustment, as much of the personality, as of its adjustment to the social environment; but not only should these two factors be present, but in each one of them the individual will have to have reached those levels which are most dangerous in terms of lethality, or he would show signs of those negative features of the dichotomy which is given in the majority of the indicators.

A potential suicide with scarcely any or no probability at all of help will be a person in whom all the indicators we have mentioned are concentrated. In the proportion in which the number of indicators is reduced, or, in the case of them all being present, the proportion in which a combination of positive and negative characteristics is produced with the former predominating, the probability of help will increase, and with it the risk of consummating self-destruction will be each time less.

The indicators which would need to be present are:

(a) Lucidity and a sensitivity towards the consequences of his self-destructive behaviour.
(b) Effective knowledge of the means used to carry out the act.

(c) The need to carry out few preparations.

(d) Appearance of the factors of (i) depression and anxiety; (ii) tension and agitation; (iii) feelings of guilt; (iv) hostility; (v) dependence.

(e) Characters with the following features: (i) impulsiveness; (ii) lack of flexibility when faced with situations of crisis; (iii) isolation, and incapacity to communicate.

(f) Diminishment or loss of social status by coming up against: (i) critical evolutionary stage in age (adolescence or old age); (ii) break-up of marital relations (divorce or widowhood); and (iii) modification of occupational role (change, loss of occupation, or occupational problems).

Although it is certain that when all these negative indicators come together in the individual, the survival factor is minimal, it is also certain that the increase in services of help and prevention can always be an element which encourages a small chance of pulling through. In particular, the accomplishments of certain organizations, among them The Samaritans, always constitute an element to which even someone very predisposed to self-destruction can resort in a moment of clarity, calm or reflection. Without the existence of people and organizations dedicated to encouraging friendship and collaboration, it is certain that should a person feel suicidal—with only the smallest factor of risk—he could, on finding no helping hand, in a moment when some of the negative characteristics of the dichotomized factors grow worse, be left caught in the act of his own destruction.

From a humane and social point of view, it is worth stressing the urgent necessity of enlarging every class of service engaged in suicide help and prevention. They surely are one of the most valuable contributions in the field of human collaboration. Saving the lives of our fellow men is without any doubt the highest goal to which members of these organizations can aspire.

(Translated by Elfreda Powell)

Definition of suicide
Suicide: alienation's last word. A. T.

11. Is there any way of predicting the likelihood of impulsive suicide?

RICHARD FOX, MB, BS, MRCP, FRCPsych., DPM*   (UK)

Shortly, no. As with every prediction of human behaviour, the best guide is what has gone before. People who have acted impulsively in the past are likely to do so again such that impulsive suicide may be feared in anyone who has abruptly and un-controllably done damage to themselves or, come to that, to property or to other people. The great majority of non-fatal acts of self-injury—parasuicide—are impulsive but as to suicide itself the judgement is harder to make. Careful planning over a period of time with the foreknowledge of the day and time of cessation is rare. Suicidal thoughts with variable degrees of planning may— or of course may not—end with a final impulse. What suddenly came into the mind of the bankrupt businessman to make him drive his Jaguar into *that* telegraph pole, and not another one?

The first rule, when trying to help distressed people, is to assess their attitude towards life and death and careful enquiry in the latter category may ring warning bells in the interviewer. All whose business is to any extent that of human distress must remember to make this assessment in all cases and *learn* how to do it. All too often ignored in training courses even for Mental Health professionals, it is a mandatory part of Samaritan preparation classes and may best be approached from the point, whatever it is, that is troubling the caller—a crisis in the marriage, trouble with the neighbours, crushing insomnia or whatever—by some such question as: 'Has it been that bad that you have ever felt desperate

* Dr Fox is Consultant Psychiatrist at Severalls Hospital, Colchester; Honorary Psychiatric Consultant to The Samaritans; and UK Representative and first Vice-President, The International Association for Suicide Prevention and Crisis Intervention (IASP).

about it?' A hesitant answer must be probed more deeply as: 'Have you sometimes wished you could go to sleep and not have to wake up?' Or more strongly: 'Has it been that bad that you have sometimes wondered whether life is worth going on with?'

Affirmative replies to either of these open the way for more detailed discussion of suicidal risk without, still, mentioning the emotive word 'suicide' with its lingering overtones of legal prohibition and mortal sin and one must distinguish next between suicidal *thoughts*, which probably everyone has at some time of life if they are honest about it, and suicidal *intent*. The greater the planning, the greater the hazard—those who write suicide notes, for example, are more likely to kill themselves first time or succeed later, than those who don't. Where a plan offers a possible second chance—and overdosing is the classic example—the hazard is less than where it virtually does not, as with shooting, jumping and hanging. A person may admit to having been very close to self-injury and only just drawn back, and it is always a wise precaution where this may occur again—as indeed with anyone who seems to present suicidal hazard—to bring out the possibility of impulsive behaviour which would later be regretted, and allow the person to consign to others the safe keeping of the antidepressant medication or, where the risk is high, to be accompanied until such time as psychiatric assessment can be obtained.

In those diagnosed as suffering from schizophrenia, unpredictable behaviour of any kind may occur, including suicide, and there appears nothing that anyone can do to prevent it short of incarceration and even that may not succeed. A really determined suicidal person can asphyxiate with a strip torn off a bed sheet or hang with a coathanger from a doorknob. It is the hazard facing all of us who work with the emotionally distressed that, sooner or later, we are going to have someone who is 'ungrateful' enough to commit suicide, however experienced and skilled we may be. Maybe we should learn what we can and share any fresh understanding with our colleagues but try, above all, not to let our grief, anger or perplexity interfere with the help we give to others, and in particular those friends and relatives of the deceased whose emotions are likely to be so much more disturbed than our own.

Definition of what suicide is not
Self-injuring behaviour comes in many forms which include over-eating, the abuse of alcohol and the taking of too much by way of drugs or too little by way of exercise. There must be few heavy smokers of cigarettes who do not know that their chances of premature death from lung cancer are immensely increased thereby, not to mention from diseases of the heart and arteries and chronic bronchitis. Because these forms of self-injury may lead to death they are sometimes referred to as 'indirect suicide', 'subintentioned suicide', or 'suicide equivalents'.

Much the same arguments apply to deliberate, risk-taking activities like motor-racing, hang-gliding, sailing solo round the world and even mountaineering.

Now, there *are* people who drive very fast in the course of a depressive illness as part of the classic 'gamble' with life and death, not caring very much whether they hit a tree or not; and there are deeply depressed people who drink themselves into oblivion, not caring whether their liver packs up or they die in one of a dozen other ways in which alcohol can be a lethal drug. The over-whelming majority of people who come into the above categories, however, have no desire whatsoever to kill themselves through what they are doing. Risks add zest to life and the average heavy smoker just wants to go on smoking heavily—and for as long as he can. He reckons he could be one of those who get away with it. The use of the word 'suicide' in relation to these activities widens its definition almost beyond meaning, important though all of them are, obviously, from the point of view of research into human behaviour and, in particular, damaging human behaviour.

Which leaves the difficult concept of 'altruistic suicide' propounded by Durkheim in 1897. Captain Oates and the Japanese Kamikaze pilots did not actively wish to die but willingly sacrificed their lives for what they saw as a higher cause— Captain Oates, the survival of his colleagues and the pilots, the survival of their nation. Captain Oates presents problems to absolutist philosophers and theologians because it seems a bit hard to regard him as having been mortally sinful. Of course, he *might* have been trying to find the next cache of supplies and the pilot who failed to eject in order to guide his malfunctioning plane away from a town *might* have expected to survive the inevitable crash. Be that as it may, these very special cases of suicide should, pragmatically, not be regarded as suicide at all so far as research into cause and prevention are concerned.

R. F.

12. What are the danger signs of suicide in pre- and post-pubertal children, which teachers should look out for?

DORIS ODLUM, MA (Oxon), MRCS, LRCP, DPM, FRCPsych, Dip. Ed.* (UK)

Only too often parents and teachers fail to realize that a child is in danger of becoming suicidal. When the child has attempted or succeeded in committing suicide they try to find out the cause and why they failed to realize that the child was in such great distress. Often they then remember that he or she showed symptoms which could have alerted them to the danger, but in many cases neither parents nor teachers realize what these symptoms are or what steps they could have taken to help the child and prevent the tragedy.

It is therefore extremely important that they should be given some information which would enable them to be forewarned and take action.

Some of the cardinal symptoms include a change of mood (this is most important), a change of behaviour, a change in the child's relationships with parents, teachers, friends and school-fellows, a falling back in his school work.

Endogenous depression
If a child who has formerly been outgoing, alert, interested in his work, games and going about with friends and school activities, affectionate with his parents and enjoying life, becomes quiet, withdrawn, apathetic, slow, unable to concentrate or take an interest in his work or play, apparently unresponsive and lacking in affection, there is the strong probability that he is suffering from

* Dr Odlum, who is Honorary Consultant Psychiatrist to the Elizabeth Garrett Anderson Hospital, is Life President of The Samaritans.

a form of mental illness known as endogenous depression. This is an illness of the mind which we now believe to be caused by an imbalance in the chemical substances that control some of the activities of the brain. It is a very common condition and affects people of all ages and both sexes and it is also a very common cause of suicide.

It is not sufficiently realized that children and even more frequently adolescents can suffer from this condition. If detected it can in most cases be successfully treated and the sufferer returns to normal, but if not recognized it can persist for months and even years and the risk of suicide is very great.

This is especially the case because one of the gravest symptoms is that the depressed people believe that it is all their own fault, or due to some weakness or inadequacy in themselves.

They feel unworthy and guilty and are often not willing to accept that it is an illness but believe that they should not have any form of help or should be punished. They also feel that they are a burden on their families and would be better dead in many cases.

Parents and teachers, though they may have noticed these unfavourable changes, may either ignore them or assume that the child is deliberately behaving badly, and scold and put pressure on him to make more effort. Either of these courses is extremely dangerous because it reinforces the child's feelings of guilt and inadequacy and increases his tendency to become suicidal.

Schizophrenia
Schizophrenia is another form of mental illness which may affect even children and it is not uncommon in adolescence and young adults. It takes various forms. In a number of cases the symptoms are not dissimilar in some ways from those of endogenous depression. The child becomes more and more withdrawn and out of touch with what is going on or with the people around him. He may become apathetic and slow and seem unable to comprehend or remember what he is being taught.

In other cases he behaves in what is commonly regarded as a hysterical manner. He becomes over-emotional with rapid changes of mood, in which excitability and over-optimism alternate with depression and despair.

In some cases there are definite delusions or hallucinations. Although parents and teachers may be aware that there is something wrong, they seldom realize that the child is suffering from a mental illness. They usually think that the child is behaving badly and very rarely consult a doctor until the condition has gone from bad to worse or even until the child has attempted suicide.

In schizophrenia suicide attempts are not uncommon and they are usually impulsive and often of a bizarre and distressing nature, such as cutting the wrists or other forms of self-mutilation, or drowning or hanging. Poisoning with sedative tablets is also a method frequently employed.

Drug-taking
A number of adolescents and young adults resort to drugs. These can produce mental changes which in many cases are of a depressive nature. Suicide attempts and successful suicides are a serious risk.

The symptoms of drug-taking, especially of heroin and of LSD, include a general slowing down of all mental processes, apathy, withdrawal from all human relationships, irritability, irresponsibility, unreasonableness, and in consequence a falling off in school work or academic achievement at college or university. These symptoms in the early and possibly preventable stages are seldom appreciated as dangerous and often it is not realized that they are due to drug-taking until the habit has become established.

The reasons that young people start taking drugs are various and often complex. Many school children smoke cannabis as a gesture of defiance and independence. This in a number of cases leads to taking 'hard drugs'. Heroin and LSD are resorted to by older adolescents and young adults who feel frustrated and inadequate, and in some cases are used as a form of excitement to counteract boredom and a feeling of lack of meaning and purpose in their lives.

Unfortunately they become addicted very quickly and once they are 'hooked' the chances of recovery are very poor.

The risk of suicide is greater in the early stages than when they have become too apathetic and lacking in initiative to make any suicide attempt.

If a child or adolescent is emotionally disturbed whether because of mental or physical illness, or by problems in the home or school, or in his relations with other children, an early symptom is a falling back in his school work. This is the symptom most likely to be noticed by teachers. Their first reaction is in most cases to blame the child and often send an unfavourable report to the parents with the misleading words 'could do better'. This also makes the parents think that the child is to blame and they scold him and put more pressure on him.

Sometimes with fatal results.

The emotional disturbance will almost certainly have been building up for some time before anybody notices it and when they do they relatively rarely make any attempt to understand the causes.

Apart from mental illness such as endogenous depression and schizophrenia, the commonest and most serious causes of emotional distress are those which threaten the personal security of the child and lead to a loss of confidence and belief in himself, what in technical terms is called a diminishment of the ego. A child who is neglected or unloved or undervalued by his parents or sent away from home to strangers at an early age is handicapped from the start. In order to develop a sense of security and personal value it is essential that a child should feel that he is loved and wanted and what is even more important, that he can give his love to someone whom he can trust and rely on. Rejection of the love that a child needs and wants to give is a major cause of emotional disturbance. Many small children cling to their homes and parents even when they are unkind to them as they feel more secure than if they are sent away to strangers in an unfamiliar place.

It is often difficult to decide whether a home is so unsatisfactory and damaging to the child physically or emotionally that he is better taken away or whether he is better left in his familiar background. Quarrelling parents and disharmony in the home present one of the greatest stresses for the younger child especially because he is faced with a conflict of loyalties and often fears that his mother will be injured by his father or go away and abandon him. A child may attempt or commit suicide because he cannot face this situation.

On the other hand a child who has been put with foster parents and has formed an attachment to them can be very seriously distressed by being returned to his home. Once a child has formed a loving relationship with anyone it is always dangerous to break it.

Children develop different capacities and aptitudes at different stages and unless they have the opportunity and encouragement to develop them at this crucial time they may fail to a great extent to develop them later on. This is especially true of the capacity to make loving relationships. The unloved or rejected child may never be able to make a satisfactory relationship with anyone.

Problems at school may arise because the child is unable to keep up to the standard of work demanded of him. This can stem from several different causes. The teacher may be inadequate, or the child's intellectual capacity may be insufficient to enable him to understand what is being taught, or he may find a subject particularly difficult, or he may have difficulty in seeing or hearing. Some children find themselves completely out of their depths with arithmetic, others have great difficulty in reading or using words. These seem to be the two subjects which present more stresses to children than any others and any emotional disturbance is often reflected in a falling back in one or other of them.

Unfortunately many parents are over-ambitious for their children and try to force them to attain a higher standard than they are capable of, or expect them to develop capacities before they are able to do so.

The child in such cases is often greatly distressed and feels that he is a failure and is letting his parents down. This is especially true of the conscientious, obsessive child who is a perfectionist and expects to achieve a high, or an unrealistically high standard in everything that he does, or, on the other hand, when the child knows that his capacities are not equal to the standard demanded of him by parents and teachers.

In both cases there can be a risk of suicidal attempts because the child has lost confidence in himself and feels diminished both in his own eyes and those of his parents and teachers. This is also the case where a child is afraid of the teacher or the teacher has a 'down' on the child.

Another cause of severe distress is bullying. As teachers tend to regard this as a slur on their powers of observation and control, they are seldom willing to acknowledge that it occurs and if the child tells his parents about it, which unfortunately he rarely does, owing to the false idea that it is tale-bearing, or a sign of weakness or cowardice on the child's part, they also are inclined to disregard it or even blame the child.

If they do report it to the school the head teacher often refuses to believe it and accuses the child of exaggerating or of bringing it upon himself by annoying the other children. Indeed a child who is suffering from any form of stress either at school or at home very rarely has anyone to whom he can turn or who will even listen to him. Small wonder that he becomes desperate and seeks to escape from an intolerable situation, or feels that he is worthless, or even that by killing himself he will be revenged on the unkind parents and teachers.

Every school should have a parent-teacher association and encourage parents to meet the teachers and discuss their child's progress and well-being with them. Parents and teachers see children from a very different angle and each can learn a great deal from the others about the child's reactions and gain a greater understanding of his problems and difficulties.

Unfortunately unsatisfactory parents are not usually willing to meet the teachers and take no interest in the child's school life or activities. Some form of counselling either by a member of the staff especially suitable, or an outside body such as The Samaritans, can do a great deal to help troubled children. In an increasing number of schools some counselling is available. The child can go of his own free will or may be referred by the teacher, and a certain number of children do make use of it.

There are advantages in having a member of the staff as counsellor. They are easy of access and know the conditions in the school and can find out from the form master or mistress and their observations a great deal about the child's personality and his reactions. Such counselling should of course always be confidential or the child will be afraid to speak of his real problems or of his true feelings. This fear undoubtedly does prevent many children, probably those who need it most, from using school counsellors. In such cases many of them feel more confident in talking with an outsider who will not be in touch with the school or the parents and with whom they have no emotional ties.

The Samaritans in the last few years are seeing an ever greater number of children even from as young as seven or eight years old and an increasing number of adolescents and university students, many of them potentially or even actively suicidal. Since it is now accepted that being in touch with someone who cares, is willing to listen and will respect their point of view is of the greatest help to people of all ages and especially to desperate children and young people who have no one to turn to for help, this is most encouraging.

Adolescents and students are particularly at risk. Adolescence, the period between the years of twelve and eighteen, and especially from fourteen to seventeen, is one of the most critical, probably *the* most critical in the life of any individual. In addition to the physical changes that mark the transition from the child to the adult, there are profound changes both in the intellectual approach and in the emotional development. At the same time the child is undergoing the most strenuous and important part of his scholastic education in preparation for his future career and is having increasing contact with the adult world. The adolescent is inexperienced and often has great difficulty in dealing with the emotional situations that inevitably arise as a result of all these changes. He has to cope with the changing relationships with his parents, his greater need for independence and self-expression, and their natural resistance to this demand, and above all his changing attitudes to the other sex and his first experience of the more adult type of love. Unfortunately this is a much misused word because it includes so many different kinds of emotion and this leads to tragic misunderstandings and conflicts.

As adolescents go through so many and such rapid and extreme changes of mood, it is sometimes difficult for parents and teachers to distinguish between those which are within the normal range and those which are pathological and present danger signs from which they should take warning. Depression of the endogenous kind, and schizophrenia, both occur at this period and in addition a depression which stems from any emotional disturbance, especially those which make the young person feel insecure or undervalued or rejected or a failure. Any or all of these may occur in his relations with the family, the school and friends, especially those with the opposite sex. The first love of adolescence is usually based on fantasy and is often irrational and usually short-lived. But it is so intense that it may seriously disturb the adolescent's emotional balance and even lead to suicide.

An unwanted pregnancy may also lead to suicide, especially if the girl comes from a rigidly orthodox family in whom she feels unable to confide, or who reject her if she seeks their support, or if her boyfriend lets her down.

It is surprising on the other hand how frequently the girl does not tell the boy that she is pregnant or refuses to give his name or involve him in any way.

Parents and teachers and the attitude of the community are greatly to blame for failing to give either boys or girls any adequate preparation or guidance in regard to the emotional problems that they will almost inevitably have to face in regard to their physical and emotional sexual needs, and there has been relatively little improvement in this respect in the last 50 years. This seems extraordinary in view of all the other far-reaching changes of attitude that have taken place, especially the more permissive attitude to sex, which has itself created many serious problems for young people.

Students' problems

First-year college or university students are extremely vulnerable especially if they are leaving home for the first time. Going to a college or university involves adapting themselves to an entirely different kind of environment, meeting people who come from extremely varied backgrounds with different standards and attitudes, changing their method of learning from the school to the university approach, which puts much more responsibility on the student, and above all being separated from their familiar background and required to live in lodgings or in a large impersonal building where they will certainly for a time be isolated and lonely. Weekends with nothing to do and nowhere to go and little money to spend are the most dangerous periods.

Often new students get caught up in an undesirable set whom they find uncongenial and even frightening but from whom they find it extremely difficult to extricate themselves. Sexual entanglements are not unusual and the emotional disturbances that these give rise to often gravely interfere with their work so that they fail to make the grade in their studies. In many instances, indeed the majority, students are on a grant or scholarship and many of their parents have made great sacrifices in order to send them to a university. In others they come from homes with little culture or interest in things of the mind, or are themselves barely up to the standard of a university.

All this may seem to present an unduly gloomy picture but unfortunately there is much evidence that all too many students do suffer from these stresses and there are a distressing number of so called nervous breakdowns and attempted or successful suicides.

There is still a common belief that those who talk about committing suicide never actually do it. This is certainly not true and is a most dangerous fallacy. Though students and children seldom speak of their suicidal thoughts to their parents or teachers, they not infrequently do so to their friends. This can present a very difficult problem for those in whom they confide as they are usually sworn to secrecy.

In cases where the friend feels that the risk is very grave they might well be justified in breaking confidence and alerting parents or teachers. With The Samaritans however the situation is quite different.

The policy of preserving complete confidentiality is undoubtedly the right one; otherwise a great many people who consult them would certainly be afraid to do so and there is no doubt that to feel able to talk to someone who cares and will listen has a powerful therapeutic effect. Therefore it is far better to make it safe for those in distress to try to seek help. In a large number of cases there can be little doubt that this does give them a great deal of relief and may well avert any suicide attempt.

One of the most encouraging things about the changing attitudes of the community today is the appreciation of the fact that all human-beings pass through many emotional stresses especially in childhood and while they are adolescent and young adults, and that they need and can benefit from being able to make contact with others who care and who understand their problems. Nor is it now regarded as a sign of weakness and inadequacy to have these problems or to seek help.

This fundamental change of attitude may well prove to be of the greatest importance and happily it is occurring not only in the United Kingdom but is gaining ground all over the developed and even developing parts of the world.

If we can give our children more help and understanding in regard to their personal emotional problems and help our adolescents and young adults to avoid the many emotional dangers that they so often fall into so that they start their adult life on the right lines, well-adjusted both to themselves and the community, how much personal suffering and social disruption we shall be able to prevent and what a great contribution this would be to the happiness and well-being of mankind.

Definition of suicide
Suicide literally means self-killing. The term is used exclusively to define deliberate self-destruction.

D. O.

13. What are the arguments for and against the claim that The Samaritans are largely responsible for the falling UK suicide rate?

RICHARD FOX, MB, BS, MRCP, FRCPsych, DPM* (UK)

The envelope was full of pound notes, a hundred of them, addressed to The Samaritans of Aberdeen, with a letter. Ten years before exactly the writer had had a flaming row with her husband and become sure that life was not worth going on with. She walked to the banks of the ice-cold river determined on suicide. A bus chanced by with an advertisement on the side—providentially the only bus poster the branch could afford—inviting the suicidal and despairing to contact a certain 'phone number. With nothing to lose she found a 'phone and rang, and soon found herself in the warmth of the Samaritan Centre. She wept, the letter went on, for the best part of two hours, and talked and drank tea, and was eventually taken home. It proved the turning point: she had had no contact with Samaritans since that one contact— the 'once off' situation that is always worrying—but it had proved sufficient and here was a hundred pounds to prove it, and consent to publish her story.

Probably every well-established Branch can tell similar stories if not, indeed, every experienced volunteer: 'But for you I would have overdosed that night, you know', but to prove it in cold, statistical terms, is hard. Mrs. X of Aberdeen might not have jumped or, if she had, someone might have pulled her out. All one can know for *certain* is that some go through suicidal phases and survive while others go through them and do not. Samaritans believe they both relieve distress and prevent suicide, I among them, but scepticism is always necessary. Medical history is littered with treatments such as bleeding and purging, standard

* See page 99.

at the time, but seen with hindsight as doing the poor sufferers, on balance, more harm than good. There is much evidence that suicide, of well-known persons and prominently reported, can be imitative. When the Detroit newspapers went on strike for a year suicide fell. When a public figure in California is reported as a suicide, the number of single-vehicle car fatalities rises. Suicide epidemics have been known for two thousand years. A profound sceptic might argue that Samaritans' insistence on the use of the word 'suicide' in publicity might increase suicidal hazard. In fact, since The Samaritans have become increasingly known and the public have been saturated as never before with feature articles, large ads, posters, radio, television, local talks and every use of publicity one can imagine about suicide, the numbers of suicides have dropped, and dropped strikingly in a way, so far as it is possible to tell, without parallel throughout the world. *Sensational* portrayal of suicide and the reported suicide of prominent people seems to be imitative—the last straw, as it were, for vulnerable people. Low-key mention of suicide with the emphasis on prevention, on wanting to help, seems to be preventive. Not for nothing are Samaritan posters printed in a rather dull, brown colour.

The quest for truth might usefully start with an examination of suicide rates in England and Wales. No disrespect to the Scots but their Procurator Fiscal method of determining the cause of death is so secret as to be the bane of suicide researchers, and the fact that their rate was once so much lower was more than likely due to an excess of 'open' or 'accidental' verdicts.

Since records were first kept in the 1860s a pattern has emerged of low rates of suicide per 100,000 in times of war and of high rates in times of unemployment, unstable governments and economic uncertainty. The lowest pre-Samaritan rate this century was around 9:100,000 in 1941 and the highest around 15:100,000 in 1931. So one can say that people were nearly twice as likely to kill themselves at the height of the slump as they were at the depths of the last war. And so it is with other countries and so it has been in the 'civil war' situation in Northern Ireland. Theories exist for this: the loss of self-esteem arising from being jobless: 'No one wants me' appropriate to losses of all kinds which can lead to despair and, in war, the sense of national unity in the face of overwhelming disaster plus the chance to direct aggression outwards against a distant but menacing enemy instead of inwards against oneself. Suicide has been described as homicide at 180 degrees. To me, the fact that class barriers suddenly seemed less important and that people started talking to each other in trains was an important part of it.

After the war as things returned to 'normal' the suicide rate started its inevitable climb back towards the surprisingly static level of 11 to 12:100,000 reaching a peak at 12·2 in 1963—the year, by odd coincidence, when Samaritans were first nationally organized. Afterwards, unnoticed at first, there was a dip, year by year, of about 200 deaths. I think I was the first to make public note of this at the 1969 London Conference of the International Association for Suicide Prevention. The drop from 1963–8 was 23% and it continued to 1975 when it reached 38%, 7·5:100,000, the lowest level ever recorded and *over two thousand deaths less every year*.

In 1976 there was an increase of just over 100 and in 1977 a modest rise appropriate to the economic situation of the country. But the 1963–75 reduction was one of the most remarkable facts of the postwar social scene. Any student of suicide, scanning the newspapers during this period with rising unemployment, strikes, minority governments, a falling pound and the dissolution of the bonds of Empire (held by some to account for the unexpectedly high suicide rate in Austria) would have predicted a suicide rise during this time. In Japan suicide came down for a time from very high levels as American ideology replaced to a degree the duty of suicide for default to one's Feudal Lord. In Israel their low rate fluctuated according to the state of hostilities but the international picture has otherwise been one of stasis or increase. No one, surely, who recalls the heart-aching 'thirties and the challenging 'forties can doubt which has most in common with the decade from the middle 'sixties? Yet suicide came down.

That the decline was real, rather than some kind of statistical artefact was confirmed by the Registrar General's statisticians in 1974 and it has not been seriously questioned. There seem to be no suicidal deaths hidden in 'open' verdicts more than there have been before and though deaths by accidental overdose have risen there must be a link with the vastly increased amount of prescribed drugs in people's bathroom cabinets and, anyhow, the increment would make but a small dent in the cohort of absent suicides. It was suggested that overdose in the elderly might be returned as some Natural Cause but there is no reason to suppose that doctors certifying death are less rigorous, or that fewer autopsies are carried out in doubtful cases, than in days gone by: probably the reverse. It was suggested that a High Court reversal of a coroner's suicide verdict in 1968 might have made coroners more cautious but the figures do not confirm that, and the general taboos, legal and theological, against suicide have become so eroded that people write books about how they helped their wives commit suicide, and California has enacted a 'living will' whereby people can authorize, in advance, that life-support systems be switched off in the event of serious accident or illness. Thus the social pressures on coroners' courts to avoid suicide verdicts have been relaxed. Paradoxical verdicts there are and always have been, such as the 'accidental' verdict on a woman falling from a tower block because she was seen to grab at a balcony and was hence assumed to have changed her mind, but these perverse verdicts seem consistent enough so as not to influence national suicide rates.

What, then, may have caused the decline? Forget not that suicide is not a discrete entity, a single thing, like carbuncles or appendicitis, but an immensely complex form of human conduct with as many causes as there are distressed people. Students of suicide try to untangle from this morass of distress certain patterns, but one may reasonably presume that not one single, simple, cause underlies such a dramatic change.

The earliest challenge to the Samaritan hypothesis came from the protagonists of natural gas. North-Sea gas or imported bulk methane took over from coal, or 'town', gas and the reduction in suicidal deaths could be accounted for on this basis with a high degree of precision. What the protagonists did not mention, let alone try to explain away, was that other countries going over to 'safe' gas had experienced no such change. Indeed, in Holland, which was the first and most complete country to use North-Sea gas—and a high gas user at that—suicides went up slightly during the change-over and have gone up more since as people have turned to other methods. There should be no surprise about this; the late Professor Erwin Stengel in his book *Suicide and Attempted Suicide*, 1964, the standard textbook in the United Kingdom, noted that detoxifying the gas in Basel as a suicide preventive measure only led to people drowning themselves instead. Which is what any student of Durkheim (1897) would expect in that suicide rates are an index, in a subtle way, of the quality of life in a community. Apart from being a morally rotten way of preventing suicide, removing a method would be bound to lead to substitution. The question hanging over this chapter is whether Samaritans, with their instant 24-hour access and befriending of the lonely, and those who have suffered loss, have altered for the better the quality of life in this country. 'That', an American psychologist said to me, 'is where it's at'.

The coal gas theory seems to have been finally exploded, to use a happy phrase, by the unpublished finding that there was no local relationship between safer gas and a decline in suicide*. What else? Things like the Welfare State exist as well or better in parts of Scandinavia which has a terrible problem with suicide. Intensive care for overdose cases, and substitution of non-lethal sleeping tablets for lethal barbiturates, improved psychiatric treatment et cetera are common to all western countries. There is a point that the highest rates, which are in the elderly, have come down in other countries too, even though this has been more than counterbalanced by a rise in the young which we have not experienced. It looks as though increased community respect for old age and social provisions for it are paying off. However, it is hard to tease out from the fabric of different western societies any 'intervening variable', any special factor, which operates in England and Wales but does not operate in the USA (where

* Sainsbury, 1977.

suicide has gone steadily up from 1968 to '75), Sweden, France, or wherever. Apart, that is, from the unique linked network of suicide prevention centres known as The Samaritans with a common name, publicity technique, selection and preparation of volunteers and general *modus operandi*.

Before examining the Samaritan impact on potential suicides let us examine what is known as the 'medical model' of suicide. Many studies exist to show a relationship between suicide and mental disorder, of which the commonest is, unsurprisingly, depressive illness. This applies whether the diagnosis is made from recorded treatment before death or retrospectively by interviews with survivors after it. The most recent, and most relevant to the local scene, is the retrospective study of 100 consecutive suicides in the southern counties of the United Kingdom by Barraclough and his colleagues.* They found almost all to have shown significant symptoms of depression prior to the suicidal act, but then took the logical leap that suicide = depression = doctors prescribing antidepressant tablets. They were bolstered in this by the finding that most victims had been to their family doctors during the last month and quite a few during the last week, and that the GPs had been singularly inept, in the investigators' judgement, in their choice and dosage of antidepressant drugs. Quite a few had seen psychiatrists too but that is glossed over. The conclusion is that to prevent suicide you train the GP to spot potential suicides and teach him to treat depression.

Without in any way denigrating the role of the GP this needs looking at. First, the top method of self-destruction in both sexes is now overdose, and one of the top groups of drugs used for the purpose are tricyclic antidepressant drugs, which have taken over from the diminishing (thank goodness) amounts of circulating barbiturates. If one is lonely, one gets precious little companionship out of a bottle of pills and all those GP consultations during the month of death *may* have done little more than provide the victim with the means of his own self-destruction. Tricyclics are only available on medical prescription and are of no interest to the subculture that acquire illegal drugs. Secondly, GPs are

* *British Journal of Psychiatry*, 1974, *125*, 355.

(genuinely) very hard-pressed. With maybe 25 coughing people in the waiting-room it is hard to afford the depressed patient more than 'the five-minute interview', indeed, there is a horrendous film in which the Director of a GP research unit says that not only is the five-minute interview inevitable in family doctoring but is actually *preferable*. Happily, I know no other GPs who subscribe to this but clearly the severely distressed person needs *time*. Very few professionals in the mental health field know what it is like to see a depressed person through a suicidal phase following a bereavement, say, two, maybe three hours before handing over to someone else. Samaritans do this all the time. That so many suicides of the 100 had seen doctors while only four had seen Samaritans could mean that Samaritans are not consulted by the suicidal—which is manifestly not so—or that doctors are not very good at preventing suicide. They don't get much practice: the average GP with a list of 2,500 patients can expect to have one death from suicide in four years against about 70 times that number from cardiovascular disease. Finally, so far as the 'medical model' is concerned, no antidepressant therapy has ever, anywhere, been shown to influence suicide rates. Electric shock treatment (ECT) is by common consent the most rapid, effective and predictable method of treatment for those forms of severe, psychotic depression that are most likely to become suicidal but its universal introduction in this country during the 1940s caused not the slightest dent in the gentle upward curve of suicidal death from 1941. At the end of the road, as Carl Rogers has observed, you can only prevent suicide through a personal relationship. There are both ethical and time constraints on all professionals, including doctors, in befriending their patients in the way Samaritan volunteers can do.

What is missing from the 100-suicide study are the factors that led up to the depression in the first place. Pure 'endogenous' depression, arising totally from causes within the person and unrelated to anything happening in life outside is a rarity such that some (wrongly as I believe) doubt that it exists at all. How many of the 100 had broken marriages, had taken to drink, were misusing drugs, had been bereaved, had unrelieved painful illnesses, or had been sacked? The world waits to hear. 'Depression' as an illness is a complex idea which demands from the helper the answer to the question, why *this* person developed *this* symptom at *this* time. Shortly, the person who comes with a problem is by no means always the sickest in the family; he may be 'extruded' by a troubled family as its presenting symptom. Why this symptom—depression—instead of any other manifestation of breakdown such as panic, burst ulcers, nervous asthma or whatever and finally why *now*, instead of last month, or last year. The more one asks oneself these questions the less one sees antidepressants as the answer though I, as an ordinary psychiatrist with part responsibility for an area of half a million people, certainly do use these drugs all the time. And I use ECT, which was to psychiatry what penicillin was to infectious disease. But suicide, as I am convinced, though it overlaps with illnesses treatable by ECT, is an infinitely more complex psycho-socio-physical-economic-political-anthropological-legal-moral and, why not, theological problem than the medical modelists begin to give credit for.

The profoundest student of the suicidal state I believe to be Professor Edwin S. Shneidman of Los Angeles and it is significant that he has forsaken the head-counting and symptom-counting methods of research, for the somewhat discredited individual case study where things like statistical significance are irrelevant. He tape-records interviews with survivors of certain death as, for example, the handful out of the 650-odd who have jumped from the Golden Gate bridge in San Francisco. His most moving case is of a girl taken to his hospital with overdose after a marriage break. She describes how she leaves the psychiatric block and walks in night-clothes through parts of the hospital where she has no business to be and where most of the walls are glass, saying to herself, 'help me, come to me, save me'. No one does, she reaches a balcony and jumps *six stories* to hit the only patch of earth in acres of concrete. She survives, just, with multiple fractures of almost everything to illustrate the point that there are mixed feelings towards life and death (ambivalence) right up to the point of, what is to the person, certain death and that can be a critical period for intervention. A few minutes before may be too soon, a few seconds after may be too late. An outpatient appointment to see a doctor can be worse than useless.

Shneidman, in Boston in May 1977, propounded a 'taxonomy of suicide' which had four phases. The first he described as 'inimicality', where a person finds himself at odds with others, out of step, lonely: perhaps what Durkheim meant with his 'anomie'. The second stage is 'perturbation' which indicates emotional turmoil, whatever diagnostic label conventional psychiatrists may wish to apply. Third is 'constriction' which seems to have everything in common with Professor Erwin Ringel's concept of 'the narrowing-in syndrome', in which human contacts are progressively reduced, together with movement in physical space until the suicidal person is turned in only upon himself. Finally is the desire for 'cessation'—an end to the mortal coil and (supposed) eternal tranquillity. Clearly, there is the possibility of preventive work at the first three levels, medical intervention being perhaps most relevant at perturbation and social/Samaritan at the narrowing-in phase.

To return to the significance of the Samaritan movement in Britain. In 1977 there were 230,000 new callers which is well over one in 200 of the population. We believe this to be accurate from the National Opinion Poll study of 1975 in which some 2,000 people were interviewed at random and 30 admitted to having been to Samaritans (20 said they had been helped). Total contacts were well over a million, and it is probable that at least one family in 40 had contact with Samaritans during the year. That is a lot of people, to contact an organization advertising itself to the suicidal and despairing and, though the 1976 statistical survey of 153,000 new callers is still at an early stage, it looks as though about one in four of them admitted to suicidal thoughts, and one in thirty rang during a suicidal attempt. The NOP study showed that 92% of the population over 16 had heard of The Samaritans and the 'image' of the movement was commendably favourable with over a third willing to contact it if they felt the need and another third undecided. The attitude was more favourable among the young and better educated; even more so among the couple of hundred who had known someone who had been a Samaritan client, and most favourable (though the numbers preclude tests of statistical significance) among actual ex-clients. The messages of being non-religious, confidential and concerned with suicide and distress had been received.

Other countries, which have not recorded a suicide decline, have developed suicide prevention services operating from a publicized, emergency 'phone number. America, and in particular California, has perhaps the most technically sophisticated but costs, resulting from the professional orientation of the service, have perhaps restricted developments. Thus, the largest conurbation in the world in terms of space, Los Angeles—with 8 million people—has one recognized suicide prevention centre, and their overt object is more research than service. Greater London with 7·3 million people, has fourteen Samaritan Branches. This has been achieved because the whole-time employees of Samaritans can be counted on the fingers of one hand and the average Samaritan Branch budget (£3,700) is less than half the salary of a suicide prevention centre director, not to mention his supporting staff. Volunteers play a subordinate role in suicide prevention centres. In Britain the roles are reversed, with 'professionals' like myself, acting only in an advisory capacity. As the years have passed since I came into contact with The Samaritans in 1959, the role of the professional has become less and less important as Samaritans have grown in experience and self-confidence. Samaritan annual conferences now include seminar sessions where any volunteer can offer his or her thoughts on any relevant topic. There is every sign that significant new insights into suicidal states and the prevention thereof will emerge.

The ground-coverage by prevention services on the Samaritan model is as poor in other countries as in America and they tend to be hampered by other things. The American pattern is less acceptable to suicidal people, in some places, by close involvement with the mental health services and even compulsory commitment. In most services no client is met face to face with the offer of ordinary, human befriending wherein the Samaritan stands in for the absent relative or friend. Religion may obtrude, to increase the feelings of guilt which a depressed person is likely to have already.

To change the topic: in 1968 Dr Christopher Bagley published a paper which showed that fifteen towns operating Samaritan services for two years or over prior to 1964 showed a drop in suicide, whereas fifteen towns, similar in various respects but without Samaritan services, showed a rise. The difference was statistically significant. The matter needs to be looked at again in the light of the findings of Barraclough and his colleagues* who matched more towns on more stringent criteria and came up with negative results. 'Knocking' publicity followed which took no account of Anthony Lawton's cogent reanalysis of the Barraclough findings, showing that most of the so-called 'control' towns, without a Samaritan service, had in fact a service within twenty, if not ten miles. The ten best matched pairs showed a distinct trend towards Bagley's findings and eliminating one 'maverick' town would have brought the result to statistical significance but that, of course, one cannot do.

The question of how far The Samaritans exert a preventive effect locally or at a distance remains moot. Since Chad Varah started in 1953 he has received calls from all over the world, let alone all over the country. It was a call from a suicidal widow in a Scottish hotel that made Chad dig out an enquiring letter from a young schoolmaster from that town—David Arthur—who befriended the lady, helped to found a Samaritan Branch there, and went on to become Chairman of The Samaritans for four years up to 1976. One may speculate that the very existence of an organization that says 'we care, come and see us' may be suicide preventive in relation to those who never consult it— maybe even more so than those who do. As a psychiatrist I often ask patients if they had thought of contacting Samaritans. A grubby news clipping may be produced from a wallet with the 'phone number of the local branch and the comment that it had been put there in case . . . a sort of talisman. The very existence of this sort of caring organisation *could* be suicide preventive a hundred, or a thousand, miles from the nearest live Samaritan.

* *The Lancet*, 30.7.77, p. 237.

The special case of Ireland is interesting. Throughout this small island, North a bit more than South, there has been since the troubles broke out in 1969, and before that, a remarkable drive in local communities towards setting up Samaritan Branches. Severe doubts were expressed as to the viability of such Branches both in terms of the volunteers they would get to man the service and the clients who make the service worthwhile. Newry, for example, based on a town of a mere 12,000 has rebuilt its centre after being blown up *three times*—because it happens to be on a central, commercial site. Samaritans here mean much more than just suicide prevention. In a situation where the police, army and politicians have failed and life is much ruled by men of violence and death, Samaritans offer the chance for people of goodwill from all religious communities, or none, to come together and express that goodwill to whoever may seek their help, without regard to race or creed. Blacked-up soldiers in full combat gear have descended on a Northern Ireland Branch demanding to see the files on IRA men whom they have (rightly) suspected to have come as clients in despair at what they had been forced to do. The soldiers went away disappointed. Criticism is easy but if Samaritans were to hand over one mixed-up youngster to the security forces, few others would come, and the holocaust would become the more devastating.

In conclusion one turns to the Helsinki address of Professor Allardt, a Finnish sociologist, whose paper at the IASP meeting in June, 1977 seemed to sum it up. He had analyzed every possible variable within the five Scandinavian countries to try to work out why the Norwegians had such a low rate of suicide compared with Sweden, Finland, Denmark and Iceland. Of every conceivable variable he tested, the only ones that came out with significance were social cohesiveness, family cohesiveness and general friendliness. Could it be that the Norwegians are less suicidal just because they are *nicer* to each other?

Until the antagonists, the medical modelists, come up with a plausible reason for our reduction in suicide, we can reasonably believe that Samaritans should take a modest credit for it.

14. What are the pros and cons of (a) Christians only, (b) professionals only, (c) telephone contact only, with clients?

TADEUSZ KIELANOWSKI, MD[*]   (POLAND)

When we discussed opening the first telephone emergency service in Gdánsk for people under the stress of suicidal and other gloomy thoughts in 1966/67, the organizers evaluated the situation in Poland as follows:

Poland had already overcome moral and material war damage. Growing stability, urbanization and industrialization might induce a rise in suicides, as is the case everywhere in similar situations.

As regards nationality and religion (more than 90% are Roman Catholic), Poland is a very homogeneous country. The health service is practically free for nearly everybody, physicians are numerous and readily available.

There is no unemployment, nor drug addiction, but there are problems of alcoholism and individual conflicts at places of work, and country folk find difficulties in adapting to crowded living conditions in towns. And—as is the case everywhere—marital conflicts, conflicts of parents with growing children, broken love-affairs, sexual difficulties, chronic diseases, and deep mourning and despair caused by the death of loved ones.

In crises of depression, there is very often a feeling of aversion to religion, a tendency to blaspheme, to shift the blame for the adversity on to God, on to members of the family, on to former

[*] Professor Kielanowski, lately Professor of the Academy of Medicine in Gdánsk and Doctor Honoris Causa of the Medical Academies in Lublin and Bialystok, is the founder of Anonimowy Przyjaciel (The Anonymous Friend) in Gdánsk. He is the Additional Representative of Europe on the Intercontinental Committee of Befrienders International.

best friends. At the same time the despairing person is searching for a 'true friend', who is willing and able to listen to his confidences, to all his most secret and personal thoughts and reflections. It is, however, not easy to find somebody who is disposed to be a good listener to an ill-fated person. Professional workers (most physicians and most priests, alas, not excepted) are not the best listeners; professionals are inclined to hurry, to pose questions, to diagnose and to instruct. Instruction and teaching are not what a despairing person is looking for.

This fact led us to organize a telephone emergency service attended by non-professional volunteers, a service modelled on the British Samaritans. We discussed the question with psychiatrists, however, knowing that some forms of depression can be cured with drugs and that so-called 'happy-pills' are used by people suffering from both minor and major sorrows. The psychiatrists of Gdánsk thought that it is first of all a mistake to look for psychiatric help in every case of sorrow and, secondly, there is still in Poland a certain general disinclination to consult psychiatrists. Many people believe the psychiatrist's job is to cure lunatics, and 'when I am unhappy, because my wife is unfaithful, I am not a lunatic'. Happy-pills are worthless and dangerous; real drug treatment is very valuable in selected cases of psychic illness, but psychiatrists, like other physicians, are not of great value in a telephone emergency service.

The Rev Chad Varah came to Gdánsk in 1967 and delivered a lecture, then two organizers of the future Gdánsk service visited Chad Varah in London. The telephone emergency service in Gdánsk, called 'The Anonymous Friend', began its work on 1st October 1967.

Now, ten years later, the staff of The Anonymous Friend have their own experience, which can be summed up as follows:

A despairing person who calls the emergency telephone service does not do so to obtain professional advice. Medical, religious, legal, social and many other counsels are easily obtainable in our country and are generally free. A caller is looking for the possibility of talking to a friendly listener, a friend; of speaking absolutely frankly and being understood. The feeling of being understood and not being disapproved of, the possibility of repeating the conversation with the same friendly listener, and sometimes the possibility of personal contact, induce as a rule the desired calm

That is not to say that we undervalue professional advice, and our listeners ('listeners' are our equivalent of 'Samaritans') have a complete register of names and addresses of institutions our clients might be interested to consult. Furthermore, we have volunteers who are excellent physicians (psychiatrists, sexologists, gynaecologists and others), lawyers, and social workers in very different fields, who are disposed to help our clients in an original, anonymous way. For this purpose we have a special telephone, installed and offered by the management of the Post Office, by which we can connect the client and the specialist (asking him first if he is willing and free at the time), without disclosing the identity or either the client or the specialist. Our listener participates as a third person in the conversation and can disconnect it at any time. The need for such a conversation is not a daily occurrence; most clients, who look for professional advice after having recovered their emotional tranquillity, prefer direct contact with specialists and institutions.

There is nothing to prevent us from changing the pattern of the way The Anonymous Friend operates, if there were another, better pattern in view. But we do not see such a pattern, and so we continue to believe, after ten years of our own experience, that:

The listeners have to be only volunteers: never professional and paid consolers, but only good-hearted people, very carefully selected and trained, men or women, young or old. The standard of education is not a matter of major importance.

Professional advice may sometimes be useful. Listeners may help clients, after having befriended them, to find the right professional advice.

Moral or religious valuation of clients' confessions is inadmissible and could be dangerous.

The possibility of contacting the listener in person must be available to the client. Otherwise the listener could seem unreal ('not a living person, only a voice'). Our experience of ten years' work has proved that personal contacts are not abused, but are of great value in a number of cases.

Definition of suicide
Suicide is the most tragic decision of a man who found nobody to hold out a hand to him.

T. K.

15. Do evangelistic services drive people to suicide?

The Very Rev WALTER HURST, CBE, MA* (NEW ZEALAND)

Since the dawn of reflection suicide has been the last desperate and despairing terminus for people who could see no alternative in life, as life appeared to them in their situation. There have been religious suicides; a dedicated, probably delirious offering of self. There have been suicides of honour: the conquered hero falling on his sword, the German general biting on his poisoned pill. There have been suicides of romance: the jilted lover throwing his life away. Literature abounds with instances of suicide, but whilst it was universally accepted that suicide was a sad end, even criminal, a product of heredity and a disgrace, no one seriously set about preventing suicide until 25 years ago when Chad Varah set his heart, hand and ear to provide facilities whereby a person who was contemplating suicide could dial a number. The response to dialling the number immediately brought the potential suicide into a confidential, anonymous conversation with a friendly voice and an understanding ear. The caller was invited to come to the source of the voice and ear, there to continue the friendship. Responding to the invitation meant making a friend who cared, and who would continue to care until the crisis was passed, and life could be faced again with equanimity and courage. Someone understood and cared.

The person on the brink of suicide is absolutely and utterly alone. A new friend with the right approach can transform the world for the one who is at the end of the road, so that a new and exciting road opens up.

Thus the Samaritans began—a telephone number, a wise and

* The Very Rev Walter Hurst, who is Emeritus Dean of Wellington, founded The Samaritans in New Zealand and was the first Director of the Wellington Branch. He is now the Chairman of Befrienders International, New Zealand.

friendly person answering, and a growing host of similar people willing to listen and befriend without any tags except to look up to the people the rest of the world looks down on, feel what they feel, and endeavour to help them do what they want to do.

While Samaritan Branches were spreading throughout Britain a general concern was being expressed and considered in other parts of the world. In Europe and America groups were forming to make themselves available to those contemplating suicide.

There were two traps into which many of these organizations fell. The first was the assumption that willing volunteers, with a little instruction or training could 'counsel' the despairing, distressed and depressed by talking to them on a telephone. Many groups stopped there though most had some form of emergency force who would go out to urgent cases. The second assumption was that Christians could prevent suicide by proclaiming their personal faith, quoting some biblical passages or inviting the caller to pray with them. This latter approach raises the question: Do evangelical services drive people to suicide?

It is important to understand the balance between the high motives that inspire people to offer their services for suicide prevention—which are in so many cases Christian—and the humble attempt to befriend someone who is suicidal without *preaching* or *evangelizing, moralizing* or *advising*.

Any organization that attempts to help suicidal people by such methods will run the risk of driving their client to suicide so let us examine this statement in some detail. (The term 'client' is used, because some term must be used to define the suicidal person who contacts the organization.)

Preaching refers to the use of religious language in religious terms which are usually quite meaningless to the client. 'All you need to do is accept Jesus'; 'What you must do is become converted'; 'Your only hope is go to Church';'Salvation comes by faith and you must find a faith'. The series is interminable but these examples will suffice. Such instructions have their place in pastoral counselling with someone or some group desiring to discover religion; but the problem of the potential suicide must be dealt with as his or her immediate problem, and the Samaritan endeavours to help sort out and deal with that problem. It is of the utmost danger to create new problems.

Evangelism is the function of changing the mind of a person. This involves a complete change not only of mind—psychologically—but of behaviour, loyalties, values and life-style, in fact physiologically. The normal functions and phenomena of natural living are deeply affected by such a dramatic encounter. Christians will agree that evangelism is a first priority if the world is to become Christian, but during a suicidal crisis any attempt to evangelize could be disastrous. It would be a legitimate use of the word evangelism to apply it to any process of capturing human minds and moulding them, so that people behave according to an agreed religious pattern. One who has decided to commit suicide, but who has dialled the advertised number just in case there is another alternative, is in no condition to leave the immediate problem to take on others, especially religious problems. In fact the sequel to such treatment on the telephone could harden their determination to end it all.

To *moralise* is to denounce and disapprove the suicide's intention and all the mistakes, sins of commission and ommission, that have led to the present situation. As the story unfolds any signs of judgement, horror, pursing of the sanctimonous lips, condemnation or apparent shock will close the client up like a clam. The determination to go ahead with the proposed suicide will be increased.

Giving *advice* is the usual human reaction to the problems of friends and acquaintances. 'If I were you I know what I would do'. The natural answer is, 'What would you do?' After all the good advice has been given, the client is in worse plight than when the conversation began. Even if the advice was superb and an effort made to follow it, the ultimate failure would be rightly laid at the door of the adviser, who had in fact taken on responsibility both for the client's life and most likely for the client's death.

If there are 'evangelical services' that practise such forms of counselling, and of course there are, then it is no speculation, but rather a creditable fact, that they do drive some people to suicide.

Why do they continue, however inspired and well-meaning

their intentions, to wreak havoc with people's lives when with a revised approach and a realistic system their group could be so valuable in preventing suicide? There are probably a host of answers. One could be the fear of or respect for, the originator of the particular group. There are always people who embrace small authority because of a desire to control people. Another reason could be that the Samaritan ideal has not been heard by them, or if heard not understood. Another is that its having been heard, and partly understood, a compromise is adopted that claims to have the best of both services.

There is a polarity between the Samaritan service and an evangelistic service that must be recognized. While both endeavour to change the mind of a potential suicide, the aim of Samaritans is to befriend the client right through the crisis until rehabilitation to coping with life has been achieved. After that, constructive changes can be gradually tried—as exercises and experimentation—still supported by a friend.

Any attempt to evangelize a client in the moment of crisis is virtually increasing the danger of driving the client to fulfil what may have been merely a cry for help—his threat to die.

The thought of suicide is allowed to grow and develop when someone is dissatisfied with life as they know it and live it. The Samaritan aim is to help that person to realize their own worth as an individual, to accept him or her as being worthy of friendship. The transformation aimed at is to change the feeling of 'I'm not OK' to 'I am OK'. I have been accepted by someone as myself. Then in confidence, security and anonymity the whole problem, past experiences, wrong turnings, the desperation of the moment, and the present situation can be talked through and, ideally resolved by the client.

The basic technique of 'evangelism' down the centuries has been to create in people a complete dissatisfaction with themselves, their past life, their behaviour patterns and their inherent selfishness which excludes God. Dissatisfaction is encouraged by fear of the future in a godless condition; and an arousal of guilt. This has proved to be a reasonable and practical approach to the careless, the indifferent, the atheist and the agnostic when the aim of a Christian missioner is to bring people to, and through, a conversion experience. This approach will not do anything for a potential suicide except to hasten and harden the determination to get right out of such a threatening situation—in fact to get on with the planned suicide.

William Sargent in *Battle for the Mind* makes the point: 'Revivalists have long been aware how dangerous it is to use fear-provoking preaching on depressive patients; though useful as a first phase in the conversion of many ordinary persons, mention of hell-fire may aggravate the religious melancholic to the point of suicide'.

Many Christians have responded, at one time in their lives, to the fear-guilt stimulus creatively, and found a new fulfilment in life and living. This cannot be denied; but it is not the only technique. It is possible to introduce the 'Good News' of the Gospel in a sane, sensible, sagacious and convincing way that will appeal to the fundamental spirituality that is part of every human being. Experience has shown that a sequel to befriending a potential suicide, who has at least postponed the plan, is their desire to discuss with a Christian, either clerical or lay, things that are spiritual. In every Samaritan branch there will be people qualified to help in this particular area of counselling. In fact it is the responsibility of the branch to provide this service.

Going back to the inspiration of the name 'Samaritan'; the story of the Good Samaritan is still the basis of the service. The Samaritan went to the victim of the robbers; he dressed his wounds, made him comfortable with his friendship and immediate security, took him to the inn and tended to his needs. He also arranged to call back. This act of befriending saved a life. The Samaritan could have scolded the man for his stupidity in carrying money unescorted; declared the incident a retribution for sins committed; given him a homily on changing his ways; even put a pamphlet in his pocket for future study. His help was practical and exactly what was necessary in the immediate situation. That is the aim, goal and inspiration of the Samaritan Telephone Service.

Let me now relate how the Samaritan Telephone Service came

to New Zealand. In 1964 the partly finished new Cathedral in Wellington was dedicated and opened for worship. During the first six weeks in the life of the Cathedral a constant programme of special happenings went on. Often during that period people were sitting around who were obviously unhappy, worried, depressed and miserable. The idea was formed of inviting a few parishioners to form a roster on duty to talk to them; and that idea, together with a report that on one night eight attempted suicides were admitted to hospital in the city, provided fertile ground for response to a letter from Maurice Russell, vicar of Ipswich and Director of The Samaritans there. The letter was laid on the table at a Bishop's Staff Meeting. It declared that if any city in New Zealand was interested in setting up a Branch of Samaritans he would help. He would arrive in a few months.

I wrote immediately telling him that Wellington would welcome him. We would go ahead with some sort of group with which he could help when he visited the city. A very fortunate cable arrived to say: Do nothing until I get there. I introduced the subject to the Ministers' Fraternal who asked to share in the venture. We set up a working committee and went to work on the lines Maurice suggested in a letter following his cable.

Most happily a member of the London Branch had come to live in Wellington and she had spoken to many organizations about the Samaritan work. The result was that when Maurice Russell came on stage in the Town Hall to tell his story some 450 people sat waiting to listen. The Mayor was in the chair and the size of the audience really fired his enthusiasm. The result of the meeting was that 150 people enrolled to be prepared to become Samaritans. Training sessions commenced and a hasty transformation of the Cathedral Choir robing rooms provided temporary offices that were used for eleven years. Eight of the first Directors were parsons. There were ten who took the responsibility as a team with myself as D.1 and the others in alphabetical order. I have elaborated this beginning to show that this was a Christian, or church organization, but we had been so well grounded in the Samaritan principle that we avoided the trap of seeing ourselves as an evangelical service. All problems regarding the religious angle of what we were in business to do were carefully and willingly ironed out at our regular Directors' meetings. There were a few Samaritan volunteers who felt compelled to 'witness' on every occasion and at every opportunity but their period of membership was short in the extreme.

Contemporaneously with the commencement of Samaritans in Wellington, Life-Line was introduced to Christchurch and Auckland from Sydney, Australia, as a telephone service of the Methodist Church. Over the past five years there have been two conferences in which Samaritans, Life-Line, Under-Stress, Youth-Line and several other independent services have met together. We examined each other's aims, ideals and principles but so far the common meeting ground for unification has not been discovered. In 1977 Befrienders International (N.Z.) was organized. The executive consists of two elected members from each of the five branches. There is an important task ahead of Befrienders International as all the larger cities and towns are sponsoring some sort of Emergency Telephone Service to help those in crisis situations.

Definition of suicide
The decision to commit suicide is more often prompted by a desire to stop living than by a wish to die.

Suicide is a determined alternative to facing a problem that seems to be too big to handle alone.

W. H.

16. How does electroplexy work? In what types of
    depression is it to be preferred to tricyclics or
    monoamine oxidase inhibitors?

CHARLES BAGG, MA (Cantab.), MRCS, LRCP, MRCPsych., DPM*
(UK)

Some broad considerations

At first glance, the technical nature of the two central problems
we are to look at in this chapter may seem so far up in the scientific
clouds, in such a rarefied clinical atmosphere, and so far removed
from the homespun nature of the Samaritan's role of befriending,
as to appear virtually irrelevant or even tedious to anyone other
than medical people or scientists.

In point of fact, matters relating to treatment of depression are
not irrelevant. Nor need they be tedious.

But why, it may be asked, should befrienders in a movement
such as the Samaritans, which rightly exhorts its members to
eschew any appearance of professionalism, benefit from an
understanding of electroplexy?

First of all, the way electroplexy is carried out is usually a
matter of most pressing concern to clients contemplating the
treatment. Although the basic biological factors underlying its
efficacy are the foundation from which its benefits spring—and
in due course their greater clarification should help psychiatrists
towards a deeper understanding of the illness itself—they are
usually less important to the client than the method.

Anxious clients in the grip of psychiatric illnesses may sometimes feel more at ease with their fellow laymen than with
professionals, whose ways of thinking they may believe to be of
a fundamentally different order from their own. Therefore they

* Dr Bagg is Consultant Psychiatrist at St John's Hospital, Aylesbury, and
Psychiatric Consultant to the Chilterns Branch of The Samaritans.

may well ask Samaritans for any comments they can make about details of the supposed 'ordeal' to which they think they will be subjected, perhaps hoping for amplification of earlier information which at first hearing they had not grasped clearly, such as the presence or absence of pain, the treatment's duration, its effects. The information then given may make or mar the client's willingness to accept the treatment. Nevertheless, clients may also express an interest in the science of how the treatment works. And, if only because a reasoned and confident answer is naturally apt to engender a valuable sense of confidence, even though it may necessarily be generalized and perhaps comparatively unilluminating in itself, a few of the ideas about the scientific aspects which have been put forward over the years will also be worth acquiring.

How is electroplexy carried out?
Electroplexy, also called 'electrical treatment', or ECT, has in the past been given several names which are misleading. It has been called 'Shock Treatment'—but does not in fact shock patients in the medical sense. It has been called electroconvulsive therapy (ECT)—but convulsions (violent bodily movements) no longer occur. In essence, a small electric current is applied briefly to the head to cause the brain to discharge a shower of nervous impulses. The treatment consists of having this discharge occur usually twice a week and commonly on about six to eight occasions during the course of treatment. It is given under brief general anaesthesia and the patient feels nothing.

Perhaps the easiest and the most reassuring understanding of the procedure by those to whom it has been recommended can lie in a knowledge of the experiences they should anticipate before the treatment and afterwards, and some awareness of the events taking place during treatment itself.

Before electroplexy is given a physical examination is carried out and, as with any procedure involving a general anaesthetic, food and drink are withheld for six hours before it is given. To dry up bodily secretions and thus facilitate anaesthesia, an injection is given either an hour before the treatment or in the same injection as the anaesthetic. Shortly before the treatment the patient empties the bladder, dentures are removed, the patient lies down and the injection of anaesthetic is given. It causes only momentary and trivial discomfort. Within a few seconds, and again without discomfort, sleep occurs.

Quite shortly afterwards these patients start to regain consciousness, usually within a quarter of an hour. And although at that stage they often feel confused, frequently they then pass into a further sleep for an hour or so, at the end of which time they regain an awareness of their surroundings and general circumstances. On waking a certain amount of headache is often present for a short time; but they can be assured that it is of no significance. Some patients also need further reassurance, sometimes repeatedly, that any amnesia is only a temporary development. But many have already accepted this reassurance without further anxiety.

Often patients ask very anxiously about what will be done while they are asleep. They can be told that as administered by the standard technique the injection given for the anaesthetic is accompanied by the administration, through the same needle, of a preparation which completely softens the strong muscular movements which would otherwise occur, that oxygen is administered through a rubber mask placed over the nose and mouth and a good level of intake is ensured, that moist gauze pads are placed on one or both sides of the temples and that a very small current is then passed into the brain for a second or so, the patient being oblivious to all these procedures. No wires are placed in contact with the skin.

The passage of the beneficial electric current results in very small movements of the muscles of the face and perhaps the fingers and toes, trivial in degree. There is therefore no residual muscular discomfort. As with all procedures in which a brief anaesthetic is given, an element of uncertainty must exist—cases are recorded of deaths from a straightforward dental extraction. Nevertheless with electroplexy seriously untoward occurrences are similarly so rare that as a significant medical procedure it is to be classified as a very safe example.

The main illnesses benefiting from electroplexy
The condition *par excellence* that gains help from electroplexy is
'biological' depression. And when necessary the illness termed
mania, described below, may benefit. But the tremendous
temporary improvement in the symptoms of schizophrenia
sometimes conferred by electroplexy is usually found to be so
short-lived that its place in the treatment of this particular illness,
which fortunately is often susceptible to drugs whose effects are
far more longlasting, has come into question. Nevertheless, used
as an additional measure in those cases failing to respond as
satisfactorily as necessary to these drugs, it is sometimes found to
have a useful part to play.

As a general rule it is only in one form of depression—and
usually this particular form occurs on the basis of one of two
different types of personality—that a satisfactory response to
electroplexy occurs. Happily this type can, as we shall see, often
derive incalculable advantage from the treatment, unless the
depression happens to be mixed with other sorts of psychiatric
illness, whose existence, being insusceptible to electroplexy, will
naturally then limit its beneficial effect on the psychiatric state as
a whole.

Briefly, the type of depression which is likely to benefit from
electroplexy embodies as its early features an insidiously developing state of indecisiveness, a progressive impairment of concentration often reflected in a distressing failure of powers of recall,
and a general slowing of mental and physical processes which
necessitates increasing and painful efforts—ultimately ineffective—
to produce success in even those simple activities which before the
illness were achieved with spontaneity and ease. At the same time
there is characteristically diminishing interest in food, a decline in
sexual warmth and capacity, a feeling of progressive pessimism, a
tormenting sense of inadequacy at times blatantly delusional, and
eventually a feeling of general hopelessness impervious to reasoned
argument. Suicidal episodes, serious and sometimes fatal, may
supervene.

One point about suicide needs special mention. Contrary to
what might be thought, the suicidal risk may sometimes be

greatest at a time when the client appears to be improving. The situation can be dangerously deceptive. The depressive slowing of the mental and physical capacities may deprive the client of the ability to attempt suicide at that stage. But after a certain amount of treatment, or eventually even as a result of spontaneous improvement, the mental concentration and physical energy may have returned to an extent which has restored the capacity for suicide—while the unceasing misery of the illness may not yet have been rendered endurable. Hence during recovery, or in the relatively early stages before suicidal ability has become lost, the risk of suicidal attempt may be overlooked unless this principle is remembered.

If a Samaritan knows that this is the type of depression involved (in contrast to depressions with different features, in which suicidal statements may be made for manipulation), a calm enquiry about suicidal inclinations may be well justified. Every patient with this illness carries a potentiality for suicide.

During the daytime a pattern of progress called diurnal variation is characteristic, at least in the less severe cases. This term refers to a marked tendency for the condition to be at its worst during the first part of the day but to improve as the day proceeds, only to have returned in its full intensity at the beginning of the following day. At nights a characteristic pattern of insomnia also is commonly found. Although sleep may eventually be achieved it is broken by wakeful periods during the night or in the early hours associated with painfully laborious and slow thinking and an incessant turmoil of misery-laden and unconstructive ruminations coloured with a morbid sense of guilt and futility.

The two personalities on the basis of which this crippling and dangerous illness may develop are in general either the 'obsessional' personality (characteristically very tidy, conscientious, self-critical, ponderous, undemonstrative of emotions though inwardly possessing them, with a love of pattern and predictability and a difficulty in adapting personal activities and behaviour to changing circumstances), or the open, warm, ebullient and easily-coping extroverted personality which often leads its possessor to engage in multiple activities. The relationship between the illness and these personalities is merely stated as a guiding principle. It is certainly not found invariably. And it need hardly be added that the possession of either type of personality does not in itself imply that a depressive illness is likely to arise. Very far from it. It is merely to say that in the event of a breakdown happening to occur in either, it would be more likely to be a depressive illness than any other form of psychiatric breakdown.

Although the features of the depression itself are similar, the depressive condition which arises within the setting of the extroverted personality tends to comprise only one phase of the affliction known as manic-depressive psychosis. In other words there may additionally be a past history, and a future possibility, of attacks that are termed mania.

This word does not, as might be wrongly supposed, refer to the state of being a 'maniac'. The latter word, commonly used to denote the concept of 'raving mad' has no existence in psychiatric language. It is purely a lay term—a loose colloquialism of no significance in the present context. The true manifestations of mania consist of features which for the most part are the opposite pole of those found in the form of depression described—euphoric expansiveness instead of the sadness, mental and physical over-activity instead of the slowness, a sense of grandeur rather than of inadequacy, irritability and so on.

Its benefits, limitations and side-effects
The benefits reasonably to be sought through this treatment consist of a total abolition of the symptoms of the illness for which it has been given. In suitable cases electroplexy is often completely effective. Indeed, some of the enormous benefits it may confer on the individual and his family will already be known at first-hand to any reader who has been closely enough involved in the sadness caused by these illnesses; and, from the very unpleasant and sometimes crippling nature of the symptoms described in this chapter, even those with no direct experience will appreciate the great importance of alleviating the sufferings in the client and perhaps also the various misunderstandings they can so easily create in relatives, including children.

The possible limitations and side-effects can also be usefully mentioned, so that if they happen to occur they may be less likely to cause unnecessary anxiety, bringing the treatment into unwarranted clinical disrepute.

In spite of its efficacious influence on an illness in progress, one of the limitations of electroplexy is its inability to prevent the possibility of recurrence of illness. Anybody suffering from any sort of psychiatric breakdown may experience a second attack, possibly years later, if unlucky. The conditions helped by electroplexy are no exception. Nevertheless, recurrences of psychiatric illness do not take place necessarily. Reliable comments about future clinical events clearly cannot be made by Samaritans, therefore. This point has merely been raised so that the treatment will not become the subject of disillusionment by those clients suffering breakdowns who had wrongly assumed that their previous course of electroplexy would automatically produce a lifelong immunity. Through this basically mistaken belief clients may decline to accept a recommendation for a further course, sometimes greatly to their disadvantage.

Another limitation of electroplexy may be the presence of psychiatric features other than those of the illness for which its use is indicated. In these mixed conditions, not unnaturally, only a partial recovery will be achieved—another source of understandable but regrettable doubts sometimes cast on its value by those in ignorance of its basic clinical function. Even so, the beneficial effects on the depressive component itself (if the latter comprises the particular type of depression we are considering) may then enable the sufferer to tackle any psychological difficulties associated with these other elements with a better prospect of success, slow though it may be, than was previously possible.

The side-effect causing the most widespread anxiety appears to be the tendency to forgetfulness which sometimes though by no means invariably occurs during the treatment and for a brief period after its completion. The common use of the word 'amnesia', with its popular and macabre connotation of 'found wandering at large', easily conveys an impression that can be unrealistically alarming. Nevertheless, it is always important that electroplexy should be prescribed by a suitably experienced and responsible clinical psychiatrist and that its use is confined to those illnesses for which it is clinically indicated. In the presence of organic factors such as degeneration of brain cells for example, as may occur in states of senility, the possibility of producing severe memory impairment and general confusion may either render the treatment impossible or indicate the need for particularly close and experienced observation so that the frequency of the treatments and the optimal length of the course can be gauged as satisfactorily as necessary.

Under clinical circumstances there may, though not necessarily, be some loss of memory for isolated incidents which have taken place during a period of up to a few weeks before the treatment; but the bulk of the memory for happenings over this period is usually well maintained. Any such amnesia tends to be at its most marked for the first hour or two on the days on which the treatment is given. There may also be a tendency to a certain amount of forgetfulness for a time after completion of the treatment. Usually, however, this impairment is of short duration, starting to subside within a week or so after the cessation of the course. By the end of only a further two or three weeks, any residual unreliability over memorizing present and future events is likely to have subsided. All these minor inconveniences are usually trivial by comparison with the enormous benefits, sometimes life-saving, available from the treatment.

Lastly, it should be pointed out that the treatment may not seem to work at first. Up to four or five treatments may be needed before suddenly some improvement reveals itself. Also, it occasionally happens that if electroplexy is continued for a short time after full recovery from the depression it may lead to a somewhat overcheerful and overactive state. However, if the treatment is then discontinued, this reaction soon subsides.

How does electroplexy work?

'How does electroplexy work?' carries two meanings. First, 'how does one use it to the best effect and what does one know about clinically adverse possibilities?' These aspects have been touched upon. Secondly, it means 'what are the fundamental molecular physico-chemical and other processes involved?'.

We have a considerable body of tangible evidence about the first meaning. About the second, we have very little. Indeed in relation to this second meaning it must be said quite frankly, at the risk of disappointing the reader, that at the present time we simply do not know how the treatment works.

But there are ideas which are interesting to look at. Electroplexy is by no means alone among beneficial treatments with basic modes of action that are still obscure. Digitalis, a drug that has been in constant use for many years and saves countless lives, is also in this category in which clinical effects are easily observed but where the understanding of the more detailed factors lying behind them is only partial.

Various suggestions, viewing the problem from various angles, have been put forward to explain the action of electroplexy. Some are scarcely, if at all, able to stand up to sensible scrutiny. The remainder are at best only partial explanations, poorly substantiated conjectures, or mere descriptions of physical processes which are perhaps correct in themselves but with little real explanatory content. Not only do these limitations on credibility relate to much of the research material not entered into in this article. They also apply to the hypotheses that will be mentioned in the next few pages. On the other hand, not all should be automatically or totally abandoned, since it is only by systematic and open-minded gathering and recording of ideas and observations that the fundamental understandings of science are ultimately achieved.

Even the very development of electroplexy occurred on the basis of an incorrect proposition. It was initiated in the belief that epileptic convulsions occurred with exceptional rarity in schizophrenic patients; and a 'biological antagonism' was consequently assumed to exist between these two illnesses. Convulsions were therefore induced in schizophrenic patients in the hope that they might have a beneficial effect on the schizophrenia. The convulsions produced in the treatment, which later was re-directed mainly to depressive patients, were for some years elicited by drugs injected into a vein. In 1938, however, Professor Cerletti working in Rome introduced electricity for this purpose.

This original hypothesis failed to withstand the test of time and has been abandoned, in spite of the fact that the treatment itself has remained within the mainstream of management of depressive illness because of its continuously observed value.

Among other early concepts were those based on the principles of certain schools of psychoanalysis. These concepts postulated that the treatment fulfilled patients' unconscious desires for punishment, or that it symbolized their supposed wishes for death and rebirth. Hypotheses of this nature are not generally accepted by clinicians in the context of electroplexy. As will be recalled from the description of the means by which it is conducted, the discomfort is so minimal that a punitive quality can hardly be ascribed to it, at least on a rational basis, as a clinical measure.

Another hypothesis—also one in which an erroneous assumption of clinical punishment may prevent correct understanding—is the idea that the concept of 'negative reinforcement' is an explanation of the effectiveness of electroplexy. In contrast to psychoanalytical thinking, this hypothesis is based on teachings concerned with 'conditioning'.

It is a matter of commonsense and ordinary observation that as a broad and general statement those actions whose consequences are pleasant become more likely to occur, and those associated with unpleasant results are more likely to become eliminated. This principle is also integral to various scientific procedures based on 'conditioning', such as experiments in which animals are 'taught' that by pressing a pedal, food may be obtained (positive reinforcement) or in which they find that certain actions lead to unpleasant effects (negative reinforcement).

Among clinical psychiatrists, the rewarding of new behaviour to be learnt (positive reinforcement) and the punishing of undesirable behaviour to be eliminated (negative reinforcement—in this instance it is the depression which needs to be eliminated) are not generally regarded as concepts applicable to electroplexy.

Among laymen, a degree of misunderstanding about the

principles of conditioning is apt to arise when scientific thinking concerning negative reinforcement becomes compounded with the moral connotation contained within the word 'punishment'. But whatever areas of discussion may be opened out by the principles and practice of conditioning in general, as a basis for the clinical benefits derived from electroplexy most psychiatrists consider the explanation as fundamentally misconceived.

It is often observed that after one or two treatments the patient discovers that the initial fear (a supposed element of negative reinforcement) has little basis. The anxiety often subsides, but the clinical improvement increases as the course of electroplexy proceeds.

A still further hypothesis holds that it is an amnesia that produces the therapeutic results, claiming that memory erasure of the pathological feelings and thinking is the effective element. This hypothesis too receives comparatively little acceptance. Often for example the treatment confers benefit without any notable amnesia. And very commonly even those patients who develop amnesia continue, both during treatment and after recovery, to recall their earlier symptoms with an obvious clarity that heavily rebuts this supposition.

A theory that was widely held throughout those decades that preceded the virtual abolition of the convulsions was that the muscular convulsions themselves in some ill-understood way relieved the depression, perhaps by dissipation of psychological tension and its accompanying disturbed thinking through this particular medium of muscular activity. However this may be, it has been found that even since the strong muscular movements have become eliminated the treatment has remained equally effective. It should be added, however, that the changes in the electrical rhythms in the brain necessary to produce the very slight muscular movements that occur in the present form of treatment remain essential for its effectiveness.

There is a particularly important area of work which, though nebulous and arguable in some of its content, has received a great deal of useful research effort over the years. It is one that seems likely to supply us eventually with a fundamental type of understanding. This is the sphere of biochemistry. Within this biochemical group a wide range of highly technical research has been carried out in relation to many biochemical states found within the body in association with electroplexy, largely incomprehensible to those without professional training in this field. Only one biochemical example will be mentioned, but it seems to contain some of the most tangible factors and has attracted considerable interest. It concerns the biochemical compound known as noradrenaline.

To understand this hypothesis it must be appreciated that the passage of impulses along any nerve cell is an electrical process, whereas the impulses are transmitted across the gaps between the cells (termed the synapses) by a chemical process. On the far side of each gap is a membrane. This membrane, or at least part of it, is stimulated by the chemical carrying out the transmission, this chemical being known as the neurotransmitter.

The significance of these facts to this particular explanation of electroplexy is that in the crossing of the gaps in certain nerve pathways in some of those areas of the brain known to be involved in changes of emotional states, the transmission is carried out by noradrenaline.

Naturally, human brains in depression are not available for research purposes. However, decreased concentrations of noradrenaline in certain relevant areas of the brain have been suspected in cases of depression. Hence although by no means a watertight assumption—only indirect hints and animal comparisons being available—it is not unreasonable to postulate that electroplexy may increase the sensitivity of the 'receptor site' (the membrane previously mentioned) to noradrenaline, thus in some way perhaps increasing the effectiveness of noradrenaline. In experimental animals electroplexy has been followed by an increase in the noradrenaline in the brain. Also, the tricyclic antidepressive drugs have been found to increase the noradrenaline at the synapses in experimental animals.

It has also been found that reserpine, a drug which has been used for the treatment of raised blood pressure, sometimes produces undoubted depression as a side-effect—a point that can limit its clinical value. Indeed the interest in noradrenaline began when it was noticed that the administration of reserpine was associated with a decreased concentration of noradrenaline in the brain.

Finally, but far from exhaustively, emphasis has been placed on the temporary changes in the patterns of electrical activity observed after electroplexy by recording them with the technique of electroencephalography—a sort of photographing of the brain's electrical rhythms. It is thought by some workers that electrical changes in the deep structures of the brain, as well as in its surface cells, are produced by electroplexy and are of therapeutic significance. For instance, in one of these deeper areas—the hypothalamus—there are centres involved in the control of appetite and sleeping. Both these functions, as we have seen, are commonly impaired in the depressions that respond to electroplexy. But, as always, the factors are inconclusive.

In what types of depression is electroplexy to be preferred to tricyclics or monoamine oxidase inhibitors?

For the most useful understanding of this question (the tricyclics and the monoamine oxidase inhibitors are the two major groups of antidepressive drugs), it should be broadened out to include at least two other groups of factors in addition to the types of depressive illnesses themselves, namely the types of individuals suffering from them (people naturally vary in their personal reactions to any side-effects) and the wider circumstances of the environment (for instance the nature of a client's employment and social responsibilities, and the degree of supervision available from relatives and others).

A usefully all-embracing definitive answer therefore cannot be given if it confines itself entirely to the clinical features of the types of depression for which electroplexy is to be preferred. But clinically the predominant indication for electroplexy is a continuous depression of the 'biological' or 'endogenous' type as described. Reactive depressions or the volatile and relatively short-lived though sometimes frequently recurring depressions of hysteria (particularly the latter) should usually be dealt with by other means—which may include Samaritans' befriending. In the biological depressions, however, severe intensity of symptoms, or in less severe cases an unduly protracted depressive illness responding inadequately to suitable doses of the relevant drugs, usually point to a preference for electroplexy.

Commonly electroplexy acts more quickly than drugs, but it is likely to cause more inconvenience by requiring loss of working time, whether given on an in-patient or out-patient basis. And often this need for rapid relief may be the over-riding consideration. If the distress caused by depressive symptoms is unendurable to the sufferer or relatives, if suicidal risk is high, if loss of employment, serious damage to reputation, deterioration in family relationships or impairment of children's emotional development are likely to occur in the event of the illness proving prolonged, then electroplexy is likely to be the preferable treatment.

Another element that may occasionally render electroplexy the preferable treatment is the occurrence of drug side-effects unacceptable to the client or dangerous to the community—for instance drowsiness or blurring of vision in spite of re-adjustment of dosage by the doctor. Side-effects vary according to the particular medication. But even if they occur and require medical review for possible readjusting they do not usually require its discontinuation.

Some general conclusions

Like any other treatment in medicine, electroplexy is right for some people and wrong for others. Careful selection of patients by an experienced psychiatrist is always necessary, to ensure that it is not inappropriate for the person concerned. Moreover either too few or too many treatments may be given unless the patient's response is understood clearly enough.

Sometimes Samaritans are the people best placed to observe the progress and reactions of their clients' psychiatric illnesses. Indeed they may even be the ones most closely aware of undesirable developments or significant lack of response to whichever treatment is being given, perhaps at a time when a client's comparatively infrequent visits to the doctor may be inadequate for rapid enough detection of any pointers to the need for alterations in the management of the case.

Various pointers of this sort may be found. There may for example be a worsening rather than the anticipated improvement in the severity of the illness, occasionally indicating a need for change from drugs to electroplexy which would otherwise be overlooked. Alternatively the Samaritan's involvement may lead to a closer appreciation of the physical or social significance of side-effects—be they from electroplexy or drugs—which again may call for some modification of the treatment. Discontinuation of electroplexy may be required; or the need for a change from one drug to another, or for the substitution of drug treatment by electroplexy, may come to light in this way.

Hence no two sets of circumstances on which are based a decision about the preferable form of treatment are alike. No two groups of explanations to account for the action of electroplexy are alike. No two individuals in need of help are alike.

Any knowledge of changes for the worse noted by Samaritans during a depressive illness of the type described, whether or not they prove associated with a particular treatment, may be very helpful to those responsible for the clinical management. If the client agrees to their disclosure, such information may well forestall unhappiness, personal tragedy or even death by suicide.

A final aspect: well meaning people, rightly concerned to ensure that this treatment is not abused, may sometimes inadvertently disseminate unnecessary anxieties about it. Psychiatrists, non-medical people whose support can be of great benefit to those in need, and even reputable practitioners of other branches of medicine, are all groups apt to contain a minority of individuals expressing fears or criticisms of electroplexy which are out of balance with good psychiatric practice.

Perhaps therefore the following quotation from a leading article published in the *British Medical Journal* in October 1975— by which time thirty years of experience of widespread use of this treatment had accumulated—will be of interest:

ECT is safe—safer still with the now almost universal modification by muscle relaxants and brief anaesthesia—quick in producing a response and remarkably free from serious side effects; any alternative would have to be very good to rival it.

Definition of suicide
Suicide is the intentional act of taking one's life either as a result of mental illness, these illnesses frequently though not always causing distress to the individual carrying out the act, or as a result of various motivations which are not necessarily part of any designated mental illness but which outweigh the instinct to continue to live.

C. B.

17. What is the effect on the incidence of suicide of the removal of the most popular methods of committing it?

DR JEAN-PIERRE SOUBRIER*   (FRANCE)

This question has been discussed for many years throughout the world of suicidology right up to the last Congress of the International Association for Suicide Prevention (Congress VIII Helsinki, June 1977). I remember encountering this important topic at Congress III, held in Basle in 1965. This was the city in which the most prevalent method of suicide was by coal gas, and where at fantastic expense the gas had been de-toxicated—i.e., gas was supplied to households without any carbon monoxide content. For six months the suicide rate declined, and then returned to its previous level, and then gradually made up the deficit: the net result was no decrease in suicides, but the substitution of drowning (the Rhine flows conveniently through Basle) for gassing as the commonest means of suicide.

I should like to give my own experience in this matter after surveying nearly 10,000 patients interviewed on recovery from a severe overdose of drugs or gas. This may help the question of how to prevent suicide and enable us to understand exactly what suicide means. I shall break down the question under four headings.

* Dr Soubrier is head of a Psychiatric Department at the University of Paris; Secretary General of the Groupement d'Etudes et de Prévention du Suicide; French Representative, the International Association for Suicide Prevention (IASP); and temporary adviser and expert at the World Health Organization. He is author of many publications on suicide, and in 1973 produced an award-winning film with The Samaritans: *Prevention of Suicide—Myths and Realities.*

1. Lethality and suicidal methods: evolution over the years

Fifteen years ago over 50% of overdoses of barbiturates and tranquillisers were lethal. The treatment of these intoxications has been progressively improved and now, in 1978, only 0·5% of overdoses by those chemical compounds are followed by death.

Alongside this improvement in the techniques of detoxication and resuscitation, the medical emergency system was reorganized and faster transfer to detoxication centres by special ambulance and staff was arranged. It was not only the therapy itself, but the swiftness with which this could be brought into play, which was responsible for so dramatically decreasing the number of fatalities.

During the same period, new drugs were developed and many forms of anti-depressant became available. It was known from the time of their discovery that many of these marvellous drugs were dangerous if large quantities of them were swallowed, and some doctors were nervous about prescribing them because of this. A physician was often on the horns of a dilemma: he could give to a depressed, suicidal patient an efficient drug to treat the depression, which at the same time gave to the suicidal patient an efficient drug with which to kill himself by overdose.

The drugs which are sometimes called mood-relievers or mood-modifiers have the major effect of fighting inhibition caused by the depression, and thus could increase the patient's anxiety, thereby provoking or favouring reactions such as a definite suicidal act.

It took some time to arrive at the technique, now in the main confirmed, for prescribing such medication safely. The conditions were (a) that these drugs should be given in association with a tranquilliser; (b) that the prescription should always be explained as something additional to the psychotherapy which must be the preponderant part of the consultation; and (c) that it is remembered that maximum benefit from this medication can only be expected if the patient's environment is warm and understanding.

2. Other unsolved questions of suicide and depression

At Congress VII of the IASP held in Amsterdam in 1973, I discussed this matter on the basis of a piece of personal research. This was based on a study of 400 patients interviewed after a severe suicide attempt by overdose; or, it would be more accurate to say, an act of self-injury by drug overdose which was not followed by death.

Only 29% of the cases needed treatment with anti-depressants. 56% of them were simply given mild tranquillisers during the period of their hospitalization. 15%, mainly psychotics, were given major tranquillisers such as phenotiazines.

Three observations were then made:

(a) Not all suicidal patients need anti-depressants.

(b) A distinction should therefore be made between a suicidal act and depression.

(c) A suicidal act can represent a simple gesture, a cry for help, which will sometimes bring secondary benefits to the patient such as relief of anxiety and anguish, and liberation of inner tensions unconsciously related to the death wish.

Therefore we adhered once again to the theory of suicide being primarily a cry for help, the 'acting out' behaviour being an attempt to express or to verbalize the person's anguish.

Furthermore, in a context of a psychoanalytical concept of repetitive compulsion mechanism, most of these people, by not 'succeeding' in their suicide, were in fact achieving a certain success in what they were really (if not always consciously) attempting.

(In this connexion it is worth remembering the words of the late Professor Erwin Stengel, a former President of The Samaritans and also of the IASP, who compared the suicidal patient to Janus, with one face turned towards death, and the other to life.)

The conclusion of this research, reported at Amsterdam, was short and precise: medical compounds by their specific strong anti-depressant action will reduce the number of deaths by suicide, but have not so far decreased, and probably will not decrease, the number of non-fatal suicidal acts.

But how could we verify such conclusions?

3. The evidence of statistics and epidemiology

A good example is the controversy which seems to exist about the influence of The Samaritans in decreasing the number of suicides in the UK, in view of the fact that North Sea gas, which is non-toxic (though it can be used for asphyxiation) has gradually been replacing coal gas (rich in carbon monoxide) in that country. In fact, a careful study of the figures shows that the steady decline in the number of fatal suicides in England and Wales long preceded the beginning, let alone the completion, of the changeover, so that as far as I am concerned this is an example of what we call in French a *faux problème*.

Nevertheless, it may be quite interesting to discuss the subject, which has come up at all the IASP Congresses I have attended, including the most recent one in Helsinki. At the latter, Dr Richard Fox demolished the idea that a dramatic reduction, unique in the world, could be explained by a tinkering with the available weapons of suicide which began after the start of the decline. In the December 1977 issue of VITA, the IASP bulletin, Dr J. Brown of Canada refers to Dr Fox's contention that the only factor which is unique to the country with the unique reduction in the suicide rate is the constantly-expanding network of branches of The Samaritans, so that suicidal and lonely persons, 92% of whom are found to know about the organization, are able to find a listening ear, sympathy and 'befriending' at any hour of the day or night, from one of 20,000 volunteers in 170 centres. (All other factors, such as better diagnosis and treatment, are common to the entire developed world.)

Dr Brown replies to Dr Fox's praise of The Samaritans' befriending and scorn for the sea-gas theory as follows: 'The main argument of the opponents of the domestic gas hypothesis is that as soon as gas becomes non-lethal, suicide attempters at once switch to other methods—presumably methods which are almost equal in lethality to carbon monoxide. If this argument is correct, it should be possible to find a country in which the following developments occur in parallel:

'(a) a progressive reduction in the carbon monoxide content of domestic gas;

'(b) a progressive reduction in suicidal deaths from gas;

'(c) a progressive increase in suicidal deaths from other (equally lethal) causes that matches (b) and so keeps the total number of suicides roughly the same.'

It may well be that France is the country Dr Brown is looking for!

In 1975 the Groupement d'Etudes et de Prévention du Suicide helped the National Institute of Health & Medical Research (INSERM) with a study of death by suicide in France.

It must first be said that non-toxic gas from the region of Lacq in the south-west of France has been progressively replacing gas containing toxic carbon monoxide.

There was then observed a progressive reduction in suicidal deaths from gas. It was well known that the method of gassing was mainly fatal for elderly patients in a poorer physical condition and with less recuperative power than the young.

Next, the number of suicidal acts using drugs tremendously increased—although, as has been previously noted, emergency resuscitation techniques have been enormously improved.

The statistics of death by completed suicide have not changed, but have remained surprisingly stable.

Some years ago, most statistics of poisoning included toxic gas and drugs together under the same heading. However, it seems from the available statistics that people do still commit suicide by domestic gas in France: about 120 persons a year. This figure, which includes more men than women, officially represents 1·5% of deaths in which the verdict was suicide.

The method of suicide which is now officially considered the most frequent is *hanging*, which accounts for about 49% of male suicides and 30% of female suicides in France. (It is interesting to note that in the USA, hanging is consistently the second method of suicide, after firearms and explosives.)

A realistic point of view is that removal of toxicity from domestic gas plus the improvement of resuscitation techniques must save a certain number of lives, so the stability of the numbers of deaths by suicide must be restored by suicidal people turning to other methods less susceptible to neutralization even by the finest intensive care. We cannot usually resuscitate someone who has blown off the top of his head with a gun.

What seems to me to be of most importance is the improvement of our therapeutic methods in psychiatry and psychology. I have observed a growth in the understanding of the suicidal person and the depressed patient. The whole suicide prevention movement, with its many different organizations and approaches, has been active in this, and exchanges of views at national and international congresses have been most valuable. The amount of published work, much of it in the form of papers presented at these various congresses, which is available to the serious student of suicide, is now immense.

Better techniques are important, but are not by themselves sufficient. The emotional problems leading to a crisis have to be studied, sensitively and imaginatively. That is why I, as a psychiatrist, am concerned to encourage those engaged in crisis intervention and the care of distressed and despairing human beings. We must never give up our discussion of the mystery of man, of his conscious and unconscious mind, or his needs, ambitions, fears and hopes.

We must also never lose sight of the setting in which he has to live—as the sociologist Emile Durkheim pointed out 80 years ago, everything we have so far discussed will depend more or less on the culture of the society in which the individual is badly or sufficiently well integrated.

In any case, the death wish will remain amongst many persons, suicidal or not, and whether consciously or not.

We have been looking forward to the 'anti-suicide pill'. This could well be the magic minor tranquilliser which does not kill (except occasionally in unusual circumstances) but can be used as a cry for help, an often unconscious calling for understanding and care. Most of the resuscitated patients I have seen during the researches outlined in this chapter were not clinically depressed, but every single one of them was wanting, not to die, but to live better.

So the final answer to the question with which I have been trying to deal is suicide prevention at every stage—before the act, during the act, and after the act, and even after that.

4. Popular methods of suicide other than poisons or gas

Even though, as the old saying has it, *'impossible n'est pas français'*, it would be difficult to remove the Eiffel Tower, as was at one time humorously discussed. But since many suicides were committed from it, a study was undertaken some years ago of ways of preventing these. Its conclusion was that barriers must be made adequate and the watch by the guards doubled.

It was confirmed that after press reports of some unhappy person precipitating himself to his death from the Eiffel Tower, other persons would try to do the same thing the very next day. The fact that nowadays there are very seldom further suicides following a publicized one is accounted for by the fact that during the dangerous subsequent days the watch is always increased. Similar anecdotes could be related about such places as the Golden Gate bridge in San Francisco.

Conclusion

The most important conclusion is this: despairing people, some of them very ill, will be liable to commit suicide, but we have learned from many survivors (who could not have known that they would survive) that their feelings about suicide, about death and dying, were ambivalent.

It is true that action can be taken to obstruct suicide during the final act when the mechanism is triggered. Removal of toxicity from gas, provision of barriers on high monuments and bridges, and also regulation of firearms and the packaging of smaller amounts of pills, will help to slow down the suicidal act, giving time for a change of mind or for some form of benign intervention. This will increase the likelihood of a decrease in the rate of completed suicide. But these precautions will be most successful if they are designed not merely to prevent the body from being fatally injured, but also to enable the soul to be comforted and understood, and the unconscious mind to blossom.

In that regard, befriending is a better method, a better rope . . .

Definition of suicide*

Suicide is a final act of despair of which the result is not known, occurring after a battle between an unconscious death-wish, and a desire to live better, to love and be loved.

J.–P. S.

* The writer stresses that his definition may change from day to day.

18. How important is imitation in suicidal acts?

J. P. WATSON, MA, MD, FRCP, FRCPsych, DPM, DCh* (UK)

This is an important question, to which I cannot presume to give a definite answer. My aim here can only be to clarify.

Its importance is easily established. Suicidal acts comprise a major health and human problem of increasing magnitude. Suicidal acts are things people do, or behaviours; and when behaviour catches our attention, for whatever reason, we tend to seek ways of explaining or accounting for it. (This seems to be because we feel better able to predict and perhaps, where necessary, control behaviour which we can explain to ourselves in a personally meaningful way.) Knowledge about how people learn things is one possible source of explanation of behaviour; and imitation—as a technical psychological notion—comes under the general heading of 'learning'.

To take the matter further we shall need to consider the activities or processes which might possibly count as 'imitation'. Also, it will be necessary to examine the notion of 'suicidal acts' to see if this is likely to be a heterogeneous class with various kinds of 'imitation' differentially important in particular instances. We shall consider 'suicidal acts' and 'imitation' separately and then note some possible relations between them.

Suicidal acts

We know that there are important differences between people who commit suicide and the much larger group of people variously called 'attempted suicide', 'parasuicide', 'deliberate self-harm', or 'self-poisoning'. Naturally there is overlap between

* Professor Watson is Professor of Psychiatry at Guy's Hospital Medical School, London.

'suicide' and 'attempted suicide', some suicides having previously been attempted suicides and some attempted suicides subsequently killing themselves. One difference between these two groups is that the incidence of various psychiatric illnesses is much higher among suicides than among parasuicides.

In any classification of 'suicidal acts', we would naturally distinguish suicide from attempted suicide. Clinical experience suggests that attempted suicide is also a heterogeneous class. For instance, many would differentiate attempted suicide accompanying depression or alcoholism (or other 'mental illness') from attempted suicide labelled, perhaps pejoratively, 'manipulative' or 'attention-seeking'. Research has been sparse in the area of the typology of attempted suicide and so research findings do not greatly inform clinical classifications such as these. In one recent study* three main varieties of parasuicide were distinguished. Two seem to resemble the familiar depressive and 'manipulative' varieties of attempted suicide; but the third type did not seem to the authors to represent any familiar clinical grouping.

In our survey of various kinds of suicidal acts, then, we have only distinguished (a) suicide, often associated with mental illness, (b) attempted suicide (i) associated with mental illness, especially depression, (ii) 'manipulative', and (iii) other.

This might suggest that one 'cause' of suicide and attempted suicide is mental illness, especially depression. But this is a complicated notion and can be misleading, and we shall return to it later. Some people have listed motives for suicidal behaviour, or tried to classify suicidal acts in terms of motives; but no such activity has provided any generally accepted typology. This is because motives are hypothetical constructs inferred from observations and are not the observations themselves, so that their properties are not readily amenable to empirical confirmation. Also subjects themselves, and others concerned with their conduct, often say very different things about the 'motivation' for suicidal behaviour. (For instance, some psychiatrists, but very few patients indeed,

---

* Henderson, A. S., Hartigan, J., Davidson, J., Lance, G. N., Duncan-Jones, P., Koller, K. M., Ritchie, K., McAuley, H., Williams, C. L., and Scaghuis, W., 'A typology of parasuicide', *British Journal of Psychiatry*, 131 (1977), 631–41.

say that overdoses were manipulative or 'in order to gain attention'.) We shall return to this matter also.

Imitation

To start with, let us remind ourselves of ordinary language. *The Oxford English Dictionary* says: 'Imitate—"follow example of", "mimic", or "be (consciously or not) like"; imitation—"copy", "counterfeit"; imitative—"following model or example of".' Two ideas seem to be involved. One is similarity, resemblance, or sameness; and the other has to do with context, or meaning, perhaps intention or motivation. Me imitating you is not just a matter of certain similarities between us; it is also that I may wish to emulate you and am modelling myself on you, perhaps deliberately (although my intention could be dishonourable, as I promote a deception by trying to be mistaken for you), while I remain myself, my imitation remaining me and not being 'really' you.

These notions persist in 'imitation' as it has been developed as a technical term within psychology. So far as I am aware, its interest is as a variety of learning. As such, it was discussed by Thorndike more than 50 years ago but largely ignored for many years thereafter as learning theorists focused upon conditioning processes. Interest in imitation has revived with the development of behaviour therapists, 'modelling' now having a generally accepted place in the list of treatment techniques. Modelling seems to be pretty well synonymous with imitation.

A typical statement is 'another way to establish new behaviours is to have the person observe someone else perform a behaviour'.*
Bandura,† who has devoted a great deal of attention to modelling techniques says 'complex behaviours are often acquired by imitation'. Both these authors (and others) imply that contingent reinforcements, positive and negative, affect the effects of imitation. What this means is simply that imitating someone else may be

---

* Gambrill, E. D., 'Behavior modification', in *Handbook of Assessment Interaction and Evaluation* (San Francisco, Jossey-Bass, 1977), p. 51.

† Bandura, A., *Principles of Behavior Modification* (New York, Holt, Rinehart & Winston, 1969), p. 307.

followed by personally gratifying subsequent events, or by disagreeable ones; and if the former then more imitation is likely, while imitative behaviour is less likely to be repeated if it is followed by unpleasant events.

All these formulations refer to people actually imitating real behaviour seen by them in others—ways of talking or gesticulating to other people, for instance. Clearly, seeing others do suicidal acts gives opportunities for imitation with, one supposes, positive or negative consequences. Relatively few people have opportunity of this kind of imitation which only rarely seems to occur in clinical situations. Doctors have a tendency to kill themselves, however, and presumably this could be determined by previous contact with suicidal 'models'. But this should affect nurses, who have no such increased tendency to suicide.

Here we should ask if imitation can cover anything besides actual visual perception of a model's behaviour. Bugelski* notes that reinforcement may not always apply in imitative learning and notes that images (and presumably other sorts of mental events) are intervening variables operating between model and imitator, who presumably has to elaborate upon his perceptions before he can behave in a complex way. Hence it makes sense to suppose that people may obtain ideas about complex behaviours from others, but without seeing others do them. A representation of a behaviour as in a sentence or picture can evoke ideas contributing to intentions to adopt the behaviour. Hence, we can begin to accumulate a list of varieties of imitation of possible relevance for an understanding of suicidal acts.

For completeness we note (a) the modelling *in vivo*, which has already been referred to. This refers to seeing someone else engage in suicidal activity, and could increase or decrease the tendency to imitate the behaviour (positive or negative modelling).

(b) Ideation imitation of social origin. I have coined this phrase to refer to a range of occurrences in people's social environments which have in common that they may affect people's behavioural

---

* Bugelski, B. R., 'Human learning', ch. 26 in *The Handbook of General Psychology*, ed. Wolman, B. B. (Englewood Cliffs, Prentice-Hall, 1973), p. 526.

repertoires. That is, people read or hear about the behaviour of others, or see it reported in films or on television. The behaviour in question may be actual or fictional. It is presented in some sort of context, usually with meaning implicitly if not explicitly attached to it. This may include statements or suggestions about the effects or consequences of the behaviour, evaluated explicitly or implicitly as good or bad. All this may affect the observer's view of circumstances in which particular behaviour is appropriate.

For example, a person's tendency to violence (rather than some other behaviour) in response to unprovoked attack is likely to be affected one way or the other by exposure to reports concerning such violence. Or, awareness that it is sometimes said that people take overdoses of tablets in response to stress or because of difficulties of coping with life, tends to increase the likelihood that the person will himself respond to life difficulties by self-poisoning. Nowadays many people are aware of self-poisoning (in particular) as a thing people do; and this may contribute to the recent increased incidence in this activity.

(c) Imitation of biographical origin. This term refers to the possibility that imitation of suicidal acts (or whatever) may be determined at least in part by certain past personal experiences. This contrasts with the previous category where the influence of social rather than individual factors is emphasized.

Clinical experience suggests several possible candidates for this group of phenomena. Parental suicide, for instance, seems to increase the probability of suicidal behaviour in the children. Or, restated, suicidal behaviour occurs more frequently in groups of people who have previously lost a parent by suicide than where there is no such history. Of course, any interpretation of such a finding in terms of causation would need to explain how an event like parental suicide can cause effects like child suicidal behaviour some—even many—years later. One possible explanation would be in terms of parental suicide giving the child an early experience of personal loss and thereby creating vulnerability to subsequent loss experiences. This formulation might be developed to propose that any parental or even other significant personal loss during childhood—not just loss of someone by suicide—would increase later liability to maladaptive behaviour— perhaps not exclusively suicidal behaviours—in response to loss experience. In this sort of case, there would be a relation of sameness between cause and effect, but the similarities might be derivative, not immediately apparent. The imitative relation might be general, concerned with say 'capacity to cope with stress', or 'ability to tolerate frustration of personal desires', rather than specific, concerned with 'suicidal acts', for instance.

Imitation and suicidal acts

We have outlined some of what may be included under 'imitation' and 'suicidal acts', and can now seek to bring the two areas together.

We might try to assess the contribution of any variety of imitation in any suicidal act of concern to us. This would assign imitation a potential role in the causation of the behaviour, as playing some part in answering questions like 'why did this person take this overdose?' we would at once come across an interesting fact. This is that people who have taken overdoses often give explanations for their overdoses which differ from time to time, and from the explanations of their doctors, other professional helpers and relatives.

The importance of this is that suicidal acts comprise complex behavioural sequences potentially subject, like all such sequences, to intentional and conscious decision-making processes, so that suicidal acts are not fully understandable without reference to the subject's own accounts of his behaviour. Many suicidal acts seem to involve impaired intention and decision-making capacity, and the importance of any imitation must be assessed in the light of disturbances in these areas.

Any list of factors thought by patients or observers to cause suicidal behaviour would include depression; various manifestations of hostility; feeling tense, lonely, unwanted or in some other variety of intolerable subjective state; seeking to alter the behaviour of others; and modelling. Ambivalence would figure prominently in any exposition of these factors. In my experience persons who have taken overdoses usually emphasize subjective states in their own accounts of their behaviour. Observers are relatively more likely to relate the behaviour to external circumstances. (For instance, a patient whose recurrent self-mutilant behaviour was explained by staff as 'manipulative' described herself as behaving in this way to relieve intolerable tension associated with unpleasant thoughts which kept coming into her head).

One interesting aspect of this is that people ordinarily ascribe their feeling states to events or environmental characteristics, a process which assists in personal control of and desired change in relation to the environment. Hence self-poisoning often implies a sense of diminished control of self in relation to the environment. The suicidal person's normal strategies for behaving in relation to other people, events and things (to achieve goals, promote personal satisfaction, and so on) have broken down and in many instances the person has or has the sense that he has, become unable to affect his environment affectively.

Focusing on helplessness of this kind is a useful aspect of treatment of the suicidal person. Psychological approaches like this complement the medical psychiatric contribution typically expressed in terms of making a diagnosis. This is a useful approach in as much as it will draw attention to the presence of certain illness-syndromes. But no medically treatable illness-syndrome is present in the majority of attempted suicides, and a medical treatment approach can then be harmful, as it espouses medical solutions rather than the person's own responsibility for past conduct, present situation, and future actions, thereby doing nothing to alleviate the person's helplessness in relation to his environment. Helpnessness is sometimes learned by imitation.

The first kind of imitation in our list was modelling based on first-hand experience of others who have committed or attempted suicide. This occurs, but is relatively uncommon. Perhaps its least unfamiliar variant is what is sometimes called epidemic self-mutilation, typically involving recurrent superficial wrist scratching among groups of adolescent or young adult female psychiatric in-patients treated together. In these circumstances imitation is sometimes obvious, conscious, and directed towards particular kinds of response from others (such as staff).

Suicidal acts not infrequently imply some conscious or unconscious awareness of social norms about how people deal with difficult life problems, suicidal behaviour being part of the cultural repertoire of things people do when they cannot cope.

Unhappily this state of affairs has partly to be laid at the door of the medical services, which have often seemed more responsive to self-poisoning than to any distress or life difficulty associated with it. A person attending a hospital accident and emergency department remains likely to receive much more attention after an overdose than if (s)he attends complaining of distress or coping problems.

Related attitudes probably also contribute to cultural tendencies to suicidal acts in response to life or coping problems. There is the widely promoted notion that medicines are the answer to health and *inter alia* psychological problems; even a cursory glance at television advertising indicates the value of this particular currency. Still, Sir William Oster did wonder, half a century ago, if it was not the capacity to take medicine which distinguished man from the animals.

There is also abroad in some quarters the notion that distress is bad or undesirable, and should be prevented, eliminated, or treated. This increases the tendency to act in such a way as to reduce distress; and it is instructive to note how effectively suicidal behaviour can do this. Several mechanisms are involved including pharmacological tranquillization or oblivion, obviously, but also the changes evoked in others, including relatives and health professionals, exemplifying the fact that the involved concern of another or of others has a substantial and predictable distress-reducing power.

So far as one can judge, people contemplating or engaging in suicidal acts do not usually intentionally decide on suicidal activity in order to affect others. They are not attention-seeking in the sense that they (consciously) decide to attempt suicide primarily, deliberately, intentionally to obtain the attention of others. Many know or guess that attention may follow suicidal activity, but altering a disagreeable subjective state is usually experienced as the motivation for the act. The notion that knowledge of possible consequences of acts mediates itself by ideas about one's current emotional state is an interesting one, requiring further attention elsewhere.

I think that social imitation of the kind outlined here is relevant in those many cases of attempted suicide occurring in relation to distress and coping problems associated with life circumstances. These imitative pressures are presumably greater for women, especially young women, than for men, as attempted suicide is particularly common among young women. Perhaps another set of imitative pressures leads adult males in our culture toward antisocial activity, especially involving violence.

Our third category of imitation was that associated with derivatives of past personal experience. This may well occur in many instances of suicidal behaviour. Certain themes recur—one is the loss of loved ones, previously mentioned. Loss of close relatives during early life predisposes to later sensitivity to similar losses. A past history of such loss is not uncommon in suicidal patients; depression of mood is marked in some of these cases, and previous experience of loss predisposes to this also. But depression is not necessarily present in a person who is vulnerable to the loss of loved persons and who has a restricted repertoire of coping responses to such events.

Imitation may thus apply in a general area such as 'vulnerability to loss' as well as to specific acts, including self-destructive ones. The exact form of a response to stress may differ in model and imitator.

Themes other than loss which regularly appear important in understanding suicidal acts are a sense of personal insecurity, and problems in trusting others, giving and receiving affection, or tolerating frustration of instinctual wishes. These problems have vital roots in early childhood experience and a history of dis-organized parenting, generating later difficulties in these areas, is found in a proportion of patients who have attempted suicide. In some instances the sense of insecurity and problems of trust and affection seem to be present in the parent(s) as they are in the patient(s). The importance of these themes in determining suicidal acts is matched by their relevance for those who seek to help suicidal persons. Suicidal acts can usually be understood in part at least as messages about personal needs for affection, a trusting relationship with another human being, and a sense of personal security.

Definition of suicide

Suicide is acute self-inflicted death. This can be distinguished from potentially confusing phenomena such as chronic self-destructive behaviour and so-called 'accidental' death, by careful definition of 'acute' and 'self-inflicted'.

J. P. W.

19. What, in addition to our normal service, needs to be done to meet the needs of those in their (a) first or (b) second childhood?

(a) ANTHONY LAWTON, BA (Oxon), Cert. Ed.*

(b) GEORGE DAY, MA, MD†   (UK)

(a) The needs of those in their first childhood

It occurs to me that I might have been asked this question because someone thought I was still in my first childhood, and so I may be! But I am going to make myself feel more adult by taking first childhood to end at the same time as compulsory schooling. I am only going to talk about 'what ... needs to be done' by The Samaritans. The interests of society and the interests of those in their first childhood do not necessarily coincide in our society at present; I am going to concentrate on what needs to be done in the interest of those in their childhood. This may seem a bit serious but when we talk in terms of 'what needs to be done' we must ask ourselves from whose point of view. The interests of society might be adequately served by preventing suicide full-stop; the interests of those in their first childhood are rather more subtle. Finally I am going to concentrate on the needs of those in emotional difficulties, particularly those who are suicidal.

For many in that first childhood, especially in times of trouble, the prime need is for 'someone to talk to'. So often adults, even caring parents, do not stop to listen. Young people need time and space to express their feelings in a relationship where they feel safe. They need someone who has the insight to help them

* Anthony Lawton, who works at the National Youth Bureau, is a member of the Leicester Branch and of Festival Branch, and a co-opted member of the National Executive Committee. In 1976 he was awarded a Winston Churchill Travelling Scholarship to study emergency services for young people.

† Dr George Day is Honorary Consultant to The Samaritans.

explore their feelings and situation from various points of view, without having advice and solutions thrust upon them. They need relationships where they find limits against which they can establish where they are and where they are going.

What they often get however is very different: adults who think they know best; adults who have forgotten what being young was like for them and anyway have no idea what it is like for someone else; adults who say 'you'll grow out of it'; adults who confuse young people's needs for firm limits against which they can test out who they are with their own need to set standards (their standards of course); adults who lecture instead of listening.

The emotions of first childhood are very intense and very changeable. It is a truism that young people go up and down like yo-yos, a dangerous truism that leads to a devaluing of the downs. The end of a two-week relationship is every bit as real and as devastating for a young person as the end of a long affair for someone older. These emotions, though they may indeed be changed by the next day, can be quite strong enough to lead to a suicide gesture today. Young people, to the great exasperation of their elders, want things NOW, including someone to talk to 'now'.

The young, however, mistrust authority and bureaucracy; they are intimidated and deterred by many professional services with their defensive rituals of appointment-making and form-filling. They will not always approach establishment and established sources of support for these reasons, and also because they are less than confident that their confidentiality will be respected. But when it comes to talking, confidentiality is essential.

One fourteen-year old girl said in a study of teenage girls: 'I don't know why. I just don't feel I can go out and tell adults my problems because a lot of them have big mouths . . .' Another wrote: 'You can't talk to social workers and people like that, they go back and they tell people about your problems, your parents and things like that. And that's most why I don't talk to 'em about it. 'Cause I don't want 'em to go back and tell. So I just keep it to myself.'

So the relevance of an immediately available, confidential, informal service alongside other services is evident. That relevance is evident too from the increasing number of young people, including under-sixteens and some pre-teenagers, who contact The Samaritans, in fact who use the 'normal service'.

But what indeed is our 'normal service'? At a minimum it is the provision of a 24-hour telephone, and daytime/evening drop-in 'befriending' service, based in an easily accessible Centre, manned by carefully selected, prepared and supported volunteers of all ages and backgrounds. The service is free and confidential, based on principles of listening and supporting, of respecting callers' responsibility over their own lives and actions. Some would call this a counselling service, or at least a service based on Rogerian non-directive ideals; but the term 'befriending' indicates that the sort of relationship offered is not one that is the preserve of a select group called 'counsellors', rather a way of being that all can offer to 'friends' and others.

This 'normal' covers a multitude of sins. Some services are not manned for 24 hours; too many volunteers are not selected as carefully as they should be, nor as effectively trained and supported as one would hope. Too many Branch doors are locked in the day; too many Centres in the relative affluence the Samaritan institution now has risk losing their informality and availability. I mention all this because one thing those in their first childhood need is simply our 'normal service'. But that 'normal service' has to be as good as we can make it; and the young have always had an uncomfortable knack of touching the raw spots in society and its institutions.

The young not only make us ask questions of our real accessibility and availability. They highlight our ability to provide the listening care we offer. Those in their first childhood, when they present themselves, pose us problems to do with ourselves as much as their own difficulties. They quite naturally awaken parental feelings, tempting us to feel for the parent rather than the young person who has come in or telephoned. Anxieties that stem from our attitudes to the young and our lack of knowledge about their world may lead us to be controlling rather than supportive, to take away their responsibility rather than help them exercise it. Above all in our anxiety we may fail to listen.

Those in their first childhood lack the words to tell how they feel, so they try to communicate non-verbally by running away, or by becoming involved in activities society calls 'delinquent', or by a 'suicide attempt'. Most commonly difficulties centre around relationship problems, with parents, with family, with school, with friends, or lack of any secure relationship at all. If in our anxiety we concentrate on the way the young present their feelings, and for example are preoccupied with what to DO since the caller has run away and has nowhere to go, we may fail to help them sort out how they feel, and why. Preparation or training is about learning to cope with the anxieties that prevent us from listening in an accepting and non-directive way.

Too much of our training however, being 'talk' based, fails to touch the real feelings and attitudes of volunteers and does not confront them in experiential situations like role-play with what they really do or do not do. There is not always the support that will help volunteers cope with the feelings they have in the face of confused, depressed, suicidal youths and children; the support that will help them identify the all too easy flights to action to 'help' the 'poor child'; the support that will help them cope with the aggressive feelings that may be expressed to them or about them. Branches need 'young' volunteers around so that the service becomes sensitized to these issues, not least by learning to cope with the 'young' people in its midst. Sadly some services 'reject' young volunteers, and cannot cope with the anxieties they raise in the branch, so what hope have the callers? In short, our 'normal service' has much to offer those in their first childhood but we need to improve it.

There are however things we might do in addition, or in a redefinition of the 'normal', things that some branches are already trying. What is unchangeable in the Samaritan approach is the idea of 'ordinary' people befriending others in crisis, in confidence if the caller wants it and always respecting the caller's responsibility for herself. What should not be unchangeable is the context in which such support is made available, since the circumstances of various groups, including age groups, may vary and since the total cultural context in which we work may have greatly altered in the last 25 years.

We should be developing our activities in schools and youth clubs, not just responding to requests for talks but taking initiatives in approaches to schools. Sadly our relevance to those in their first childhood is threatening to many adults and many professional adults. Even a superb school pastoral system leaves room for a few who find it too difficult or too threatening to use that system of care and certainly room for many who are in a crisis in the school holidays. One of the things that might show we were out of our first childhood and well on the way to our second might be our ability to accept such painful realities.

Our role in schools could be wider than straight publicity. For a start there is nothing more ridiculous in telling people in a talk that you 'listen'! We need to show what we do by setting up situations where we are actively listening to what the 'children' want to tell us, showing we are accepting. Apart from knowing how and when they can contact us, what matters is that they see me and therefore the service as something 'OK' and 'for them'. But in such a situation we can begin to extend our function. We can try to get young people to recognize that talking about feelings, not bottling them up, in a safe relationship is a way of preventing and resolving crises. We can get them to learn a little about suicide, about how they should listen to others who talk about it because they may mean they feel bad enough to try it. Finally we may do a little 'befriending' in that school situation.

In the early 1970s the 'Festival Branch' of The Samaritans was developed. A branch that offers the 'normal service' from a tent at Pop and Folk Festivals has become one of the busiest in the country. The implication for so-called static branches seems to me to be that if we can find the courage to give up the comfortable (for us) surroundings of a centre, we can make ourselves more available to people where *they* are, instead of where *we* are. One branch has worked alongside youth-club workers, running group sessions on a weekly basis for anyone interested. The Festival Branch is now preparing a Bus Project which will include taking a mobile centre along the south coast in summer when many young people gather there.

Another area we might consider is an involvement in the care of hospital ward overdose admissions, which are increasing for young teenagers. Reference is made to 'epidemic levels' of attempted suicide, but the implication that this is a disease is unhelpful. Often a 'suicide' attempt, however seriously death was intended, is a form of communication, a particularly powerful one for the young who cannot articulate their feelings or who cannot change their life situation or who cannot get anyone to listen. Just because the fact that a person's life is difficult comes to light in a medical way after an overdose, we should not act as if medical solutions are needed. An on-going 'befriending' relationship providing insightful human support is of a value we should not underestimate for those in their first childhood who are suicidal. Should we be making ourselves available to all who are admitted after an overdose *in person*?

However we need to be aware of our responsibilities to young people going through crises which may affect their whole future development. The 'befriending' relationship at this age, and the learning that may come from this about coping with emotional crises, may have a significance for future growth that does not exist for other age groups. Any volunteer should reach minimum standards since in a crisis organization we cannot 'organize' who receives which sort of call. But there is a case for the development of a group with special responsibility for befriending young people in an on-going sense. Some would object that this is to take the road to professional specialists, a road that any good Samaritan should pass by. This is not to take that road, although I am not convinced of its evils if professional implies doing a job well. On-going befrienders are usually carefully matched to callers anyway, which is a recognition of what might be made more explicit for the young. We need to learn from some of the insights of 'professional' people, adapting their insights to our befriending. So fervently do we pursue our non-professional status, indeed as fervently as some other people pursue professional status, that we sometimes fail to consider what we should learn from others working with young people. I am thinking in particular of what a group of youth befrienders might learn about development.

We should not lose sight of the fact that The Samaritans are about suicide, and crises that might lead to suicide attempts. One thing we should be doing to meet the needs of those in their first childhood is to tell society what we have learnt about their suicidal behaviour. We know that many of the young who try suicide or think about it are not mentally ill, or starting a mental illness, but living in situations that have become intolerable for them. We know that given time and support most young people can resolve their crises for themselves if only we let them decide things including who should know about their situation. We should be telling society that the punitive and dismissive attitudes we take to young people's suicide gestures at times, especially in overworked, understaffed casualty wards, are at best unhelpful. As a society we seem so much more sympathetic to those with the 'misfortune' to succumb to a coronary in the rush for wealth and power, than to those who 'cause themselves' to be casualties, especially those young who have it all before them.

We need to be telling society that suicide 'gestures' and other 'deviant' youth behaviours are as often as not communications. They tell us as much about the world we create for young people as they do about individuals, and we should be attempting to change that world.

The Samaritans, and individuals within that service, act according to a principle which affirms the right of anyone of any age to responsibility over their own lives. Presumably then we should commit ourselves to creating a society where people actually have room to exercise such responsibility. Clearly our society does not allow such room to many people, particularly those in their first childhood who are an oppressed and exploited minority. We should be serving the needs of such young people, particularly those who are suicidal, if we started pointing this out. The Samaritans however, consider this is not their role, that this smacks of politics, that we must be neutral in such areas. This is to abdicate our responsibilities to suicidal young people.

If we do not side with the young in their collective distress, as we do in their individual despair, if we do not help them articulate their collective feelings and point of view as we do their individual position, if we do not befriend them collectively in society as we befriend and support them in the family or school, we are finally not neutral but against them. As Paolo Freire wrote: 'Washing one's hands of the conflict between the powerful and the powerless means to side with the powerful, not to be neutral.'

Definition of suicide
Suicide is saying Enough.

A. L.

(b) The needs of those in their second childhood

The decline into second childhood is insidious: so insidious that its traveller may be unaware of it. After the age of 40 degeneration begins in all bodily organs, with unacceptable deterioration of the faculties: 'I can hear perfectly well, but people do mumble so'; 'Nothing wrong with my eyesight, but they use such small print these days'. Two changes are inescapable: 'I'm not so spry as I used to be' and 'My memory is shocking these days. I find I'm doing the stupidest things'.

The brain cells die and disappear, never to be replaced. Thought processes are slowed. Concentration becomes more difficult. The memory becomes more and more capricious, and the vocabulary shrinks. If in addition the arteries to the brain become hardened and occluded, the brain receives insufficient nutriment and 'softens', and senile dementia ('second childhood') supervenes.

The Samaritans can do nothing for the demented; but they can do much for those burdened by a once-loved one, who is now impatient, petulant, unpredictable, and needing constant care and attention. It does such relatives a power of good occasionally to be able to voice their near-murderous feelings to a non-judgmental sympathetic listener.

It is safe to say that all sensations, pleasurable or otherwise, are blunted in old age. Pain from accident or surgery is not so excruciating for the elderly as it is for youngsters; and it may well be that emotions do not run so high. What deeply upsets the adolescent to the verge of suicidal despair may be shrugged off philosophically by those of riper years.

Much has been written about retirement and its dangers, and perhaps too little about bereavement. Both the senior citizen and the bereaved face the same dispiriting situation: loneliness and rejection by society.

Bereavement at any time of life is an icy sea into which the bereft are suddenly plunged and through which they must painfully struggle. For them there can be no turning back, and all sense of direction is lost. To survive they must keep afloat until they emerge, weeks, months, even years later, on the far shore: as second-class citizens in an unfeeling world. At first, while numbed and paralysed by the initial shock, they may have friends to buoy them up in a business-like way when practical matters have to be tackled. But these friends drift away, the numbness passes, giving way to aching pain and a thawing awareness of the full extent of their losses: loss of companionship, sense of purpose, standard of living, social status; of their inadequacy to cope with problems they have never met before, and dusk-to-dawn solitude.

Bereavement in the elderly, although less unexpected, is even more pitiless for the survivor, whose independence—his very sense of identity—is taxed to the uttermost. Moreover the change in life-style lowers resistance to disease-processes. The incidence of coronary thrombosis ('broken heart') is proverbially high.

Their suicide rate is also high and shows no signs of diminishing; but they do not elicit our help, and why not? There are several reasons. They are not habituated to using the telephone and are not mobile enough to call at the centre; attacks of endogenous depression, to which they are increasingly prone, render them apathetic and lacking in initiative. Above all, they 'have their pride': the same pride that prevents their applying for National Assistance and Supplementary Benefits. Too often they resent being beholden to anyone—even their next-door neighbour, let alone a charitable organization.

It is an impasse. We cannot go abroad ferreting them out: indeed it would be an impertinence to do so. They, or some neighbours concerned about their plight, have to make contact with us before we can help them. And then what? We are a crisis organization, geared to befriend the despairing through their darkest hours, and to steer those whom we suspect of suffering from endogenous depression towards proper medical treatment. Like innumerable individuals of good-will who do not happen to be Samaritans, we may each have our own 'little pensioners', for whose welfare we feel concerned, and with whom we find it rewarding to keep in touch; but as an organization we cannot possibly befriend the millions of lonely people for the rest of their lives. We would never have the necessary manpower.

A guilt-ridden conclusion, but commonsense must allay our consciences.

Definition of suicide
Suicide is the act of self-ending precipitated when future existence appears unendurable.

G. D.

20. What can and should a Samaritan-type service do to help high-risk people in, e.g., hospitals and prisons, or in the community (such as the handicapped or socially isolated)?

MONICA DICKENS*   (USA)

Since I have had no experience of a 'Samaritan-type service', I shall relate this question specifically to the Samaritans. Besides directing our publicity towards suicidal people and assuring 24-hour availability and complete confidentiality, what can and should The Samaritans be doing to reach out to people who represent a high suicide risk?

A lot more than we are doing at the moment, undoubtedly. Secure within our principle of not bothering unless they bother us, we tend to sit back in our comfortably shabby—sorry, unthreatening—centres and say, 'We are here if you need us'. That's good. That's how it should be. To feel safe, the caller has to be in charge. Doctors, social workers, priests can give people our number. Families and friends can urge them to get in touch with us. But they do not need to come unless they want to. It has got to be their choice.

This assumes that everybody knows the Samaritans and what we do and—more trustworthily—do not do, and that everyone who needs us has the energy and the courage to initiate a contact, or the physical means to telephone or come in. That could eliminate people in prison or a hospital, people who are bedridden or handicapped, and especially the old, who even if they have a telephone or are able to get to the Samaritan centre, may be too

* Monica Dickens has been a Samaritan since 1968 (and has devoted one of her novels to the work of Samaritans: *The Listeners*, Heinemann, 1970). In 1974 she founded the first Samaritan Branch in the USA at Boston, where she is Director; she is also Director of The Samaritans of Cape Cod.

proud or too accustomed to rejection to risk making that first appeal: 'I need someone to talk to'.

Prisons

Samaritans get very few calls from prison, since inmates cannot often make calls out. A call might be made through a social worker or prison officer, but it is not likely. Problems are usually dealt with internally, or referred to the prison psychiatrist. But because of all the circumstances surrounding a jail term, suicide and suicide attempts may be numerous.

Since inmates cannot reach out to be befriended, why not bring the befriending to them? Samaritans might get permission to visit, but they cannot remain in a prison 24 hours a day. Why not have the befriending done by those who are already inside?

In 1976, the Samaritans in Boston, Massachusetts, helped to start a programme called Lifeline in the Middlesex County Jail and House of Correction in Billerica, Mass. Soon after, Samaritan volunteers helped to start another Lifeline group in the Charles Street Jail, the oldest occupied prison in the United States, where men wait for trial in uncomfortable and hideously depressing surroundings for anywhere from two weeks to two and a half years.

Lifeline: what it is
It is a befriending service offered by selected inmates and prison staff to anyone who needs someone to talk to in confidence. Sounds like The Samaritans? It is, within the limits imposed by confinement.

From the Lifeline manual, issued to all who work in the programme: The purpose of Lifeline is to prevent suicide whenever and wherever possible. This manual has been prepared for one purpose: to assist you to recognize the potential suicide and to take the steps necessary to prevent it occurring .... Our purpose is to get to people before they become suicide risks.

Much of the manual is about befriending and listening, and recognizing changes in behaviour and signs of risk. There is a lot of important detail about prison situations, such as drug and alcohol withdrawal and sex deprivation, and instructions for emergencies:

> When a guy is jumpy and starts to curse and blow off steam, that may be healthy. But if he doesn't, he may decide to take it out on himself—cut up or hang up.
> CUTS:
> Stay put. Shout, 'Man cutting up, CELL NUMBER. . . .'

Lifeline: how it works

In the Charles Street Jail, the Lifeline workers include some staff and a changing number of inmates who are expected to be there for some time. Any of the inmate volunteers or the Samaritans who attend the weekly consultations at the jail can give examples of how befriending has helped dozens of anxious, angry and despondent men to hang on.

A Lifeliner reported to the prison psychiatrist that he was concerned about a man he had been talking to in the intake shower-room. After seeing the man, the doctor reported back, 'You're right, he did need attention, but by the time I got to him, you'd already given him what he needed'.

Kurt, a Lifeline volunteer had been trying to help a confused, distressed man awaiting trial. When he started to bash about in his cell, breaking furniture and banging his head, the tier officer said, 'Let's send in Kurt first to calm him down before we have to go in with force'. It worked. There was no violence and bruising, and no need for disciplinary action.

Lifeline volunteers try to see each man admitted to the jail and establish some kind of relationship so that he knows who he can talk to if he is in trouble. The 250-bed prison has a turnover of 5,000 men a year, most of them young, recidivist 'amateurs' from hopeless backgrounds. The confusion and uncertainty of awaiting trial and sentencing makes many men desperate enough for suicide.

At a national conference on suicide in Boston, a few of the Lifeline workers got furlough for the day to present the programme. They staged a role-play of a young man in prison for the first time after years of trouble, angry, scared, lost, hopeless about the future. The Lifeline worker did not say much. The talk was prison slang, inarticulate, real, very moving. At the end, a professional suicide expert got up to point out in orotund phrases how the Lifeline volunteer missed all his opportunities to counsel this unfortunate man in how his wasted life might be redirected. The young black volunteer stared, frowned, scratched his hands and raised his bony shoulders to his ears.

'Jesus, man,' he said. 'I was just trying to make friends with the guy.'

Lifeline workers get no concessions or benefits in the jail, but the personal gains are enormous. Sally, a Boston volunteer who has worked closely with the programme says, 'It forces the Samaritans to think of our work in a less narrow way. It's a humbling experience to see a man under stress growing into the work, getting self-confidence, feeling worthwhile on a level not otherwise possible in jail. All they have to give is time—and themselves'.

The Sheriff and the prison authorities place growing confidence in the service. Befriending makes many suicide attempts unnecessary. 'I see the Lifeline programme,' the Chaplain of the prison says, 'as the single most habilitative instrument to have arrived at the jail in my tenure here'.

This befriending programme initiated by The Samaritans in a United States jail is described here in the hope that other countries and other Samaritan branches might see it as some kind of workable model. There may be objections and obstacles to the idea elsewhere. There were at first in America. It was worth surmounting them.

Hospitals

The too frequent experience of someone brought to a hospital after an overdose is to be pumped out, cleaned up, given a long wait and a short session with a psychiatrist or social worker, and sent home. At home, there may be family or friends to help. There may be nothing but the same loneliness, mess and misery, and some more pills.

It used to be common procedure for anyone who made a suicide attempt to be admitted to a hospital from four to fourteen days, committed if necessary. Although committal is a breach of human rights which doctors are reluctant to enforce unless there is danger, it did at least give distressed people a few days away from the pressures that caused the attempt, a chance to sleep, a brief limbo of security in which some strength might be mustered to go on again. Now there are not enough hospital beds for this. As every Samaritan knows, it is hard to get a 'pre-suicidal' person admitted.

'I'm afraid I'm going to kill myself. Get me in somewhere quiet for a while.'

If you can pay for a private clinic, all right. If you can't, bad luck. No wonder people feel they must half-kill themselves to get some attention.

Casualty seems like a prime place for befriending. Samaritan volunteers might arrange with their local hospital to be called in to be with suicidal or distressed people.

'Casualty isn't the best place for anyone who's emotionally upset,' a doctor told me. 'No one can give him the attention he needs. I hesitate to start talking to him, because I know it will take time, and there's going to be someone coming through that door who needs medical help.'

Arrangements could also be made with the police, to make sure they know that Samaritans are not only willing to come to the station at any time, but willing to talk to suicidal people. Anxious, even. Imagine—they actually invite suicidal people to call!

In America, the Cape Cod Branch sometimes gets called out to people who have been taken off one of the two high soaring bridges over the canal, which seem, like the Golden Gate Bridge in California, to be a magnet for self-destruction. About seven people a year jump and die. But many stop their car on the bridge and while they are hesitating by the rail, a quick-witted driver will grab them, or get the police.

Driving up on to the bridge and stopping is more noticeable than leaving your car at the end and walking. Jumping on the side where the State Police barracks and the Coast Guard station are is another clue to ambivalence. On the Golden Gate Bridge, from which dozens of people jump every year, most choose the side where the houses are, in tune with the last-minute rescue fantasy.

In-patients
Samaritans often visit someone who has rung from a hospital. But ought we to wait to be asked? While negotiating with Casualty, could we not also talk to the people upstairs about asking patients who seem depressed and possibly suicidal whether they would like one of us to come? Most hospitals already have volunteers. Could they, prepared and supported by The Samaritans, be relieved of chair-wheeling and flower-watering to have time to sit and befriend patients?

The handicapped and the old
We should be in touch with spinal wards, acute and chronic, where depression goes in hand with injury and pain, and with our local homes for the handicapped, to see if we might help.

We should be more available for 'maintenance' calls for stuck, isolated people, confined to bed or a chair. Some of them do contact us, but perhaps we should make more effort, through social workers or doctors, to find out who and where the others are and whether they would like to hear from us. The call that we make is sometimes more effective than the one we receive. It shows that we are not kidding when we say we care. We care enough to remember and take trouble.

Survivors of suicide
It has been suggested that The Samaritans ought to run groups for people who have suffered a loss through suicide. But we are wary of groups, because we are not trained or qualified to lead them, and an unguided, uncontrolled group can get into more problems than it solves.

Do grieving people want to hear about someone else's unhappiness? What to do about the pale and shaking man who never speaks, or the woman who hogs the conversation until the others hate her, and then feel guilty because she is obviously so needy?

Individual befriending seems more useful. Suicide survivors are high risk people. How do we reach more of them? You can't ring somebody up: 'I say, I see in the papers that your son hanged himself. Would you like to talk about it?' But if you have good contacts with local doctors and clergy, they may steer to you lost, unhappy people who are not able to go on grieving to their friends for as long as it takes to grieve.

Could one send an unassuming card to people who have lost someone? Would that be intrusive, and against our policy of not pushing ourselves in where we are not invited? I don't know. How would it make you feel if you were mourning? Would it put you off The Samaritans, and lessen the chances that you might telephone on the next sleepless night of tears?

Schools and colleges

The suicide rate among college students and school children is rising. The Samaritans should be speaking in all local schools and colleges, both to classes and to groups of teachers and counsellors, and to parents too if they can be brought together. There is always a tremendous amount of anxiety that needs to be shared. Apart from individual needs for their own problems, students worry about friends. Parents and teachers feel responsible and guilty and inadequate. Everyone needs to be reminded that suicide prevention is a matter not for experts, but for every concerned human being with a pair of ears and the ability to shut up and use them.

Definition of suicide

Suicide is the chosen escape from pain, when there seems to be no other choice, nor hope of one.

M. D.

The twenty principles:
Comments on each by Samaritans

1. The Samaritans are a worldwide fellowship of volunteers
dedicated to the prevention of suicide and the
alleviation of the loneliness and depression that may
lead to it, by making their befriending immediately
available at any hour of the day or night to those who
feel they have no one else to turn to in their distress.

MICHAEL YORKE*

The remarkable development and growth of The Samaritans in
Great Britain over the past 25 years confirms three things: first,
the validity of the original insight of Chad Varah and his early
colleagues at St Stephen Walbrook on the value of befriending to
the suicidal and despairing; second, the considerable and increasing need of such a provision in contemporary society; third,
the quality of the practice of befriending over the years by
thousands of Samaritans.

From purely British beginnings, the organized use of befriending as typified by the Samaritans for the despairing first
spread through the Commonwealth. Now its progress can be
recorded in North and South America, Europe and Asia. This
spread is entirely natural, for befriending is not just a British
phenomenon, it is essentially something human. It is the free giving
of support, encouragement and love by one person for another
in need in a form and manner which helps the recipient to know
he is not alone; that he is wanted and respected for himself
regardless of his own attitudes and behaviour. It is an open-ended
and objective friendship which makes no demands on the recipient. While such an offering to another is of recognizable value,
it is often hindered by the giver's own problems, attitudes and
expectations. Thus befriending is undemanding on the client, but
can be challenging for the befriender.

* Canon Michael Yorke is Chairman of the Council of Management of
The Samaritans, and a former Director of the Chelmsford Branch.

189

Therefore it is not difficult to see why the organized use of befriending is being increasingly recognized as one impressive way to help the suicidal and despairing; those people who feel failures, who are broken by a sense of guilt, who are or feel isolated and unwanted. They find themselves met, at last, person to person in total confidentiality without judgements being made. From such an experience, many have found the way to new hope and life.

The relevance of such an offering to the suicidal was first hinted at in the last century by Durkheim in his classic *Le suicide* when he noted one of the factors in suicidal behaviour to be social isolation. Upon this, and with his practical insights, Chad Varah built his original work in 1953 at St Stephen, Walbrook, which in turn has been the model for Samaritan work as we know it today.

Thus, The Samaritans are not primarily a suicide prevention agency. They are a befriending service. The two things are not mutually exclusive, but they represent a different approach. The one sets out to prevent suicide; the other to befriend, support and give respect to people so that they do not wish to kill themselves. It is the latter to which The Samaritans are fully committed.

The principle under discussion records that such a service is provided by volunteers 'who are immediately available at any hour of the day or night'. It is clear therefore that if the service is to be reliable, the volunteers have to be of a certain quality, and they need to be organized to enable their full potential to be realized.

It is the Samaritan tradition that their members are volunteers. There is nothing intrinsically wrong with a befriender being paid; but in practical terms, it is believed that something of the spontaneity and freedom of the relationship could be lost. Maybe it is those very things which differentiate the Samaritan approach to people and those of competent professional social and medical workers. The befriender works because he wants to: his time is freely given as an equal with the client. But the volunteer is also carefully selected and trained for the work. The Samaritans are a crisis organization, and it is imperative that their staff can cope with crises. Lives can be at stake. But above all they need to be accepting, open individuals who can work with a wide range of personal attitudes and experience. Samaritans are ordinary people; but they are also special in their gifts and capacities.

But they need to be organized so that the service is coherent and reliable. Thus it is the Samaritan tradition to form into branches of about 120 people with an elected leadership who take responsibility for the branch's operation. The members work from a centre, under discipline, in total confidentiality and indeed in anonymity to the outside world. They are prepared in training sessions for the work; and are supported by in-service training at national, regional and branch level. Each person participates in the branch's care for clients. In such work they are never alone. Always another Samaritan is involved behind the scenes.

The branches offer a fully manned 24-hour telephone service so that there is instant availability in times of stress. To organize volunteers to such a level is no easy task but it is the Samaritan imperative.

The clients' needs are always paramount; they are often ignored or underestimated in contemporary society. So the quality and reliability of Samaritan branches aim to make some contribution in the field of personal distress; and the trust afforded by clients confirms the validity of this hope and practice.

Definition of befriending

Befriending is the free giving of support, encouragement and love by one person for another in need in a form and manner which helps the recipient to know he is not alone and that he is respected and wanted for himself, regardless of his own attitudes and behaviour.

M. Y.

2. The befriending which the volunteer offers to the caller is the personal concern of a compassionate fellow human being who, like the Samaritan in the parable, seeks simply to love him as a friend in his time of deepest need.

NANCY KERR[*]

'He was lying in the gutter having a fit. No one stopped to help him, so I brought him along with me for a cup of tea'. This was how a Samaritan described a man she brought with her, when she arrived at our Centre for telephone duty. Samaritans rarely first meet with clients in this way, but the incident stands out because of its similarities to the parable of the Good Samaritan. In both circumstances, only one person showed a spontaneous understanding and compassion for the suffering of another. Not everyone is able to perceive someone else's desolation. Not everyone then is able to be a Samaritan, but anyone can experience the despair known to the client. Neither the injured man of the parable, nor the client, who found himself lying on the street, had done anything to bring about this plight. Can we understand the feeling of overwhelming relief, when each man realized that someone was there by his side? At that moment, the value of the presence of another person far outweighed any number of consoling words.

It was because of his awareness of people's need to know that someone cared for their welfare, that the Rev Chad Varah first began a Samaritan telephone service in 1953. At the outset, he saw his role as one of a counsellor, but, in time, he came to realize the healing force that a team of listeners could provide. Those first listeners, just as today's volunteers, had to possess the

[*] Nancy Kerr is Director of the Liverpool and Merseyside Branch, and a Vice-Chairman of the Council of Management of The Samaritans.

caring sensitivity that is of necessity a part of the Samaritan volunteer. This is a basic quality volunteers bring to the movement, for it is only in an atmosphere of sincere caring that clients feel they can uncover their innermost fears and anxieties. But caring is not all that goes into befriending, for many self-disciplines have to be learned by Samaritans. For example, the ability to listen comes more easily to some than to others. Similarly, to refrain from giving advice is something that can, at times, demand much self-control on the part of the volunteer. In addition, the suffering a client is passing through must never be intruded upon by the Samaritan wishing to make a comparison with others or with their own personal experiences. These are some of the qualities and disciplines of the Samaritan, who is there, at the end of the telephone line 'to love him [the client] as a friend in his time of deepest need'.

The befriending offered by the Samaritan is not a means of solving a client's problem. Befriending will not eradicate pain and suffering, but it will change that which was unbearable to that which can be endured, because of the presence of a friend.

That friend may well be a very ordinary person.

Definition of befriending
In befriending, it is the genuine caring of the Samaritans that helps the despairing client face life refreshed.

N. K.

3. The volunteers are carefully selected for their personal qualities and natural aptitude for the work, without regard to their creed, colour, politics, age, sex or status.

NALINI ELLAWALA*

'How do you select volunteers?' is a question frequently asked. We in Colombo explain that they are chosen for their natural aptitude for the type of work we do and that we are concerned only with their personal qualities; that race, religion, politics, sex and social status do not merit consideration. All this is easily understood. It is more difficult to elaborate on these personal qualities and on how we assess a prospective volunteer on these lines.

On completion of the application form—which, in Sri Lanka, is constantly being updated, as we find it necessary to scrutinize more carefully the potential of prospective volunteers—we interview only those who have shown that they might be Samaritan material. At this interview, the panel of selectors (composed of a Director and one or two Leaders), ask such questions as will help to determine whether these applicants are well-adjusted people with a wholesome outlook on life.

The volunteer must be a person of intelligence and compassion. The one quality is of no use without the other as many clients are emotional types and most need intelligent handling. It is dangerous to recruit clever people who may not feel compassionately towards the desperate and suicidal who need our help. Nor do we wish to have people of great compassion but who will go to pieces when confronted with a complicated situation. A volunteer must be a sagacious person with a caring attitude for people, tolerant, patient and not quick to judge or condemn.

* Nalina Ellawala is Director of Sumithrayo ('best friends'), The Samaritans of Colombo, Sri Lanka.

The volunteer must also have a natural ability to establish instant rapport with a troubled stranger. Nevertheless, this does not mean that all volunteers are extroverts. On the contrary, some of the best Samaritans are introverts, who have the inward perception and empathy to get close to the client. Extroverts are not always good listeners and the volunteer must have the capacity to restrain the urge to talk and to utter only such words as will help to establish rapport and encourage the client to unburden himself.

The volunteer must not have any overwhelming personal problems which might keep him preoccupied. After the preliminary classes, all volunteers are put on probation for three months, and it is during this time, while being watched by the Leaders, that it is discovered if the recruit is able to cope with his own problems; this can be evaluated only through personal association. Too often clients have sought to join as volunteers. We know there is only a thin line which divides the two categories. The volunteer today may become a client tomorrow. Naturally, a Samaritan has problems, but he must have the inner resources which prevent him from being overwhelmed by them.

Clients often come with gruesome, bizarre stories. Tales that are fantastic, but true. To remain unruffled and composed, to be able to accept the story and the client without condemnation, the volunteer must not only be tolerant, but also able to take an unbiased stand on any issue. He must be devoid of in-built prejudices.

Dedication, dependability and trustworthiness are essential qualities in volunteers. Confidentiality is of the essence and many a confidence is shared on the explicit understanding that it is a confidence, so the volunteer must be trustworthy. He must be dedicated and totally committed to whatever he undertakes; unless this is so, it is difficult to enforce basic disciplines such as attendance and punctuality, especially in the East where the pace of life is leisurely and these disciplines are not rated as very important. We know that non-attendance and unpunctuality might ultimately mean life or death to a client. To the volunteer who is a constant defaulter and undependable, it means instant dismissal. But it is better to select volunteers carefully than to have to dismiss them later.

Some people seem to conclude that the Samaritan is a superior breed or, worse, that he considers himself to be so. It is therefore of utmost importance to explain to prospective volunteers that a true Samaritan is aware of the virtue of humility. Those who are humbled by the knowledge and marvel at the luck that has come their way in being happy, well-adjusted people, will offer their services to the organization because they feel sincerely that 'to whom much is given . . . of him is much expected . . .'.

Although the volunteers are nameless, they all have warm loving personalities. They are people from all walks of life—bank clerks, company directors, housewives, lawyers, engineers, teachers, etc. But they all belong to one category of person: they are dependable people with an abundance of such personal qualities which stamp them as Samaritans. After a time, when you have worked in the organization, you can easily recognize a Samaritan when you meet him. Unless the prospective volunteer has already the requisite personal qualities they cannot be taught these—a Samaritan is born and can never be made.

Definition of befriending

Crisis isolates and in isolation the ability to cope is drastically reduced. Befriending breaks the isolation and may, therefore, open the way to the resolution of crisis.

D. M.

4. The volunteers in each Centre recognized as a Branch of The Samaritans work under the supervision of a Director (or Chairman) and other Leaders, who are advised by consultants with medical or other professional qualifications, so that the highest standards of caring may be achieved. Consultants may also assist in the selection and preparation of volunteers and give help to clients.

JOHN ELDRID*

As The Samaritans are concerned with helping people in crisis situations often involving suicide risk, it is essential for the welfare of the clients that volunteers work under supervision.

The role of the Director assisted by other Leaders is to provide a central point of reference for volunteers which is essential when befriending people in despair. The Director must be prepared to take the final decisions, as the one who is ultimately responsible for the care of the clients and volunteers. Whilst it is necessary for the Director to share, when possible, this responsibility with the Deputy Directors and Leaders appointed by the Branch, the Director is the one who must be able to direct the Branch. His function is also to enable the Leaders to assist in this task and also enable volunteers to participate in the general running of the Branch, e.g., selecting new volunteers, running preparation classes, tutor groups and promoting further education. This results in the best aspects of a shared leadership and maximum volunteer participation. It is not the Samaritan policy to have lots of rules, but only to have the minimum amount which experience has

* The Rev John Eldrid is Director of the London Branch. He is a former Director of the Portsmouth Branch, a former Co-Director of the Festival Branch, and a former Chairman of the Council of Management of The Samaritans.

proved to be necessary in the best interests of both clients and volunteers.

As the Samaritans attract people in crisis situations, there is a lot of emotional pain to be borne by volunteers and a practical need to assess each client's situation. Therefore it is the responsibility of the Director and Leaders to be in touch with all clients either directly or indirectly through the volunteers. In the great majority of situations it is not necessary for the Director or Leader to see the client but it is essential for the Duty Leader to be kept informed and be available for consultation. There will be times, especially with clients who are depressed and at serious suicide risk, when face-to-face assessment by Directors or a Leader is necessary. It is important to recognize that Leadership in The Samaritans involves being a 'resource person' rather than a figure of authority. Whilst Directors and Leaders have special responsibilities as resource persons, they also take their turn of duties on shifts like other volunteers.

Each Branch is supported and guided, as required, by psychiatric and other professional consultants. It is evident that good consultation and wise professional support enables volunteers to befriend clients more effectively.

In this way The Samaritans are helping to build up a relationship between volunteers and professionals, which is a very positive step towards attaining the late Professor Erwin Stengel's idea of mobilizing men and women of the community, as one of the effective means of reducing suicides.

Definition of befriending
Befriending is giving the warmth of human presence to those out in the cold.

J. E.

5. In countries where the telephone is generally available, an easily remembered telephone number is advertised by each Branch, in addition to its address, to enable swift (and if the caller desires, anonymous) contact to be made with the minimum of effort on the part of the caller.

SYDNEY CALLAGHAN*

The telephone is the world's greatest modern inconvenience—so somebody said and at times it seems like this when it rings incessantly and invades the privacy of one's home. For The Samaritans, however, it is often the initial essential link between the client and us. His ability to use a phone—and this for some is a problem—and the response he obtains when he does so may be that which stands between life and death. He or she is always encouraged to call in person or if necessary we can and do go to him or her, but if he wants the anonymity of the phone only, that is his choice and it is respected.

For us befriending begins in the way he is dealt with when he first gets in touch with us. Concern, warmth and sincerity can be conveyed by the way the phone is answered and the conversation maintained. We do not ask for standardized accents, but we do ask for standardized practice—'This is the Samaritans, can we help you?' (For some of us the choice of 'we' is deliberate in that we are part of a team and not working in individual isolation). This can be and often is the introduction to a relationship in which the client is helped to feel that there are folk who really care and are not just a phone answering service.

Ideally the number of the branch should be easy to remember. Generally it is found that the GPO is helpful in granting one, but it is not always possible. Fortunate are those branches which have

* The Rev Sydney Callaghan is Director of the Belfast Branch.

numbers like 55555 or 23456. Others have to accept something like 24635 (the Belfast number) which the numerate can see is the even numbers 246 and the odd numbers in between. If you are neither numerate nor literate this poses some extra problems, but one can always ask somebody to get the number. Telephone operators have also been known to be most helpful in putting people through.

It is one thing to have an easy to remember number but it is not much use if people do not know it. The advertising of the number and the address is therefore an essential feature of the service. It is not just sufficient to advertise in the telephone directory but to use all the modern means of communication to let it be known we are available 24 hours daily to offer unhurried friendship particularly to the suicidal and despairing but also to any who may need a listening ear and an understanding stranger who is willing to become a friend in need.

Definition of befriending

Befriending is unhurried, unselfish identification with another person for as long as required with a willingness to listen without advising, to care without cosseting, to give strength without sentimentality, and to enable a client to retain his dignity by knowing that you are simply doing for him what he might be able to do for somebody else sometime.

S. C.

6. The Samaritans receive callers in person at their Centre, and invite telephone callers who seem likely to benefit to meet a Samaritan face to face. Callers are free if they wish to have contact only by telephone or by letter.

DAVID ARTHUR*

Doctors, ministers and social workers know exactly what it means to be rung at home at any time of the day or night, to be expected to take action, to listen and to give good advice, at once, with confidence. The telephone is both an instrument of divine communication and of devilish interruption.

Prior to 1953, and also since, a number of individuals and groups have run telephone emergency services, usually from the person's home, often ill-supported and badly organized. Inevitably the pressure told, and all but a very few of these emergency services closed rapidly. The concept of emergency help, instantly available, is an attractive one with a considerable sense of romantic endeavour. It is an idea which offers a challenge, too easily ignoring the very real practical difficulties—continued manning (day and night), personal commitment, genuine support teams, and a proper office organization with files and records.

A key feature of Samaritan work, from the start, was that it should ally professional commitment and detachment with the wealth of voluntary love and devotion of the ordinary layman. The genuine involvement of the Samaritan, offering care and affection, has never been far detached from a very unsentimental awareness both of the humanity of the client—good and bad— and the very finite resources—emotional and physical—of the volunteer himself.

* David Arthur was a founding member of the Edinburgh Branch and of the Correspondence Branch at Stirling, and is a former Chairman of the Council of Management of The Samaritans.

And so another characteristic essential to Samaritan work is its sense of anonymity and its sense of privacy. Both Samaritan and client must have a real sense of such privacy which each must learn to respect.

This thin and tenuous thread of life which exists between Samaritan and client is founded in the anonymity which only an office can provide, not because the volunteer wishes to remain uninvolved, but because he or she must write upon a fresh slate unaffected by family circumstances, by the presence of others, by the raw emotion of despair. To attempt to lay this foundation, without privacy, without the supporting yet cooler air of the branch office may add unnecessary dimensions of stress to an already overloaded situation.

None of this is to suggest that the good volunteer does not meet both despair and intolerable grief, or that he fails to be aware of all the factors which have led to the situation of misery. But the centre is a haven, a refuge, unaffected by emotion, yet warm and welcoming to the would-be suicide, offering a fingerhold to sanity, a place apart from the client's own despairing circumstances. Not for nothing was the symbol of the Durham Conference in 1962, which set up the national body, the Sanctuary door knocker of Durham Cathedral.

Intellectually, there is a highly respectable view, held in a number of continental branches, that the supporting link between client and helper can only be kept anonymous and free from emotion if the one means of communication is by telephone, thus freeing both sides from any unnecessary overtones which might detract from the relationship. Fortunately, man is not only a creature of intellect, but also of blood and flesh and of emotion. Thus the rapport of client and Samaritan is built through tears and laughter, the touch of a hand, a look, a gesture. It is a bond between two human beings, not two exchanges, it is a link established through the totality of two people meeting in the most real sense, forged in reality and not in the copper tendrils of a telephone cable.

To restrict or to limit this relationship to one part of human life is to impose a constraint on the client's right to choose whether to remain anonymous, or to be known. To be a voice on the phone, or to be fully a human being.

The risk of Principles is that they will restrict and dehumanize. The remarkable aspect of Principle 6 is that it has both made flexible and yet created a structure for the organization. The Samaritans were often known, at first, as The Telephone Samaritans, today they are The Samaritans. Having pioneered a telephone emergency service, they also pioneered a postal service through PO Box 9, Stirling.

Today all Samaritan branches, apart from PO Box 9 and the Festival Branch have a permanent office to which callers can come, and most branches advertise either their address or a box number to potential letter writers.

Chad's original vision of The Samaritans has changed considerably in practice but not in spirit. The Samaritans offer a service, in modern terminology, which is client-orientated. Without the client the service has neither place nor purpose; without the opportunity to communicate the service would wither and die. Suicide is a death in isolation, a final and despairing appeal from the outcast, a last and fatal call to listen. For each the way out is different—it may be in the mumbled words on the telephone, or in the downcast interview face-to-face, or in the sprawling letters. Whatever the method, each appeal is an expression of need and a means of seeking help. The Samaritan method in turn offers a way of breaking through that wall—a method that is always there, is flexible in response, and is, above all, humanely compassionate, firmly founded in reality.

Definition of befriending

Samaritan work is as old as mankind. In historical terms, however, it began on a dusty road. On a dusty road where there was a body and flies, and blood, and heat. In that heat and that dust, that body which was nobody's business became somebody's business.

D. A.

7. The Samaritans' primary and overriding concern is for those who seem to be in immediate danger of taking their own lives.

ANDREW TU

It is the task of the Samaritan to identify the immediate cause of danger, and the method to be used in the suicide attempt. The means of suicide must be removed at once, whether it is sleeping pills, a knife, or proximity to a high building. For example, a client may claim to have poison or sleeping-pills in his pocket. The Samaritan must by any means possible persuade him to hand over the deadly object. In his bewildered state of mind, the potential suicide will often comply.

Having removed the death weapon, the Samaritan must then pay attention to the immediate cause of crisis. Many factors may be involved in generating a suicidal state of mind, but usually there is one over-riding reason that brought about the crisis. It is the job of the Samaritan to attempt to identify that reason and to relieve the tension. The immediate cause may simply be that the client has lost several nights' sleep while under stress, and lack of sleep has deepened and exaggerated his state of depression about other problems. Tension can be eased by inducing sleep. On awaking, the client will be in a better state of mind to discuss his other problems. Sometimes acute depression may be caused by hunger, and a good meal will help to disperse the immediate pressure. Once the immediate needs are satisfied, there is plenty of time to discuss the client's real problems in a more relaxed state of mind.

The human animal lives by hope. A person who plans suicide

* Andrew Tu is Director of The Samaritan Befrienders of Hong Kong, and Representative of East Asia on the Intercontinental Committee of Befrienders International.

must have lost that hope. It is the Samaritan's task to rebuild hope and confidence. Empty words will not suffice; nor will empty promises that cannot be fulfilled. Hope must be based upon facts that can be realized. If the client's problem is a very difficult one, it will not be easy to build up his hope of obtaining exactly what he wants, nor should the Samaritan attempt to do so. But at the moment of crisis, even the tiniest bit of hope may provide a ray of light in the darkness of despair. This ray of light may not dispel the real causes of depression, but it will have some bearing upon those causes and provide an alternative solution.

At the moment of crisis, the client is shocked and numbed. He may not be able to speak a word: his grief can find no words of expression. The Samaritan must by any possible means spur the client on to some overt expression of his grief. When the client becomes angry, when he shouts or weeps, when he finds some means of expressing his emotions, the immediate danger has been reduced.

It will help through the crisis if the Samaritan befriender can discover what things or what people the potential suicide loves most. Once identified, the knowledge will help in the treatment. For example, a lady who has just been widowed once brought a child to the Samaritan volunteer, and asked him to find a place for the child to stay, as she intended to take her own life. She wanted to make sure the child would be cared for first. The Samaritan realized at once that this child was precious to her. He did not try to deal with the woman's problem at this point, but merely asked the age of the child. Concentrating on the loved object, the child, he said, 'This is such a sweet child. You must have loved and cared for him very much. Of course, we can send him to an orphanage, but have you considered that the child will cry for his mother and miss her affection? Could you really leave this child to such grief?' At this point the mother began to cry. That is a normal reaction, and it relieves the immediate crisis of grief.

Even when the crisis is caused by hatred instead of love, the Samaritan may find it necessary to avert a tragedy by entering for a moment into the client's hatred by saying, 'But if you kill yourself you will be playing into the hands of your enemy. It won't solve your problem. Is that what you really want?'

Sometimes it helps during a crisis to solicit the assistance of another person trusted by the client. This must never be done, of course, without the agreement of the client, as his right to completely confidential treatment is paramount. But a trusted friend may be of considerable help in restoring hope to the client.

Finally, but very important, in time of crisis the Samaritan must never leave the client alone to face his grief.

Definition of befriending
Befriending means being continually aware of another's feelings, seeking his personal welfare, and respecting his human dignity.

A. T.

8. Samaritans engage in long-term as well as short-term prevention of suicide by befriending despairing and lonely people who do not seem to be suicidal at the time when they seek help, or who seem unlikely for conscientious or other reasons ever to commit suicide.

MONICA DICKENS*

'Suicide . . . despair. . . .' The message is seen in a newspaper, on a notice board, on a little card left lying on the table among the old magazines in a waiting-room. 'The Samaritans. Day or night.'

Well . . . perhaps. The number is scribbled down, or the card slipped in the pocket if nobody is looking. Later when the pocket is emptied at night, the card or scrap of paper gets into the drawer of the bedside table. 'Though I'd never think of killing myself.'

But it is three a.m., and he has been awake for what seems like three hours, though it may be only 30 minutes, with the reminders going round and round in his head like red-eyed mice in a cage, of all the mistakes and failures, the missed opportunities, the possible disasters ahead. If the money runs out . . . if it was easier to make friends with people . . . if the remission of Joan's cancer turns out, as he knows in this pit of the night that it will, to be only a temporary illusion.

Joan is asleep in the other room. If he doesn't talk to somebody he will go mad.

He takes out the card. 'I'm not thinking of suicide. Can I still talk to you?'

'Of course.'

'I would never kill myself. There are too many people who depend on me. I know what suicide does to families. I would never do that.'

* See p. 180.

No human being can make such a prediction. There is a breaking point, attainable by everyone. Thanks to our vulnerable sensibilites, we have a passport to that dark, restricted land of pain and nightmare, where death seems to be the only way out.

A great deal of Samaritan work is trying to keep people from entering that territory. Suicide prevention can sound like a too forceful, too didactic expression for the quiet thing Samaritans try to do. It conjures up images of tracing calls and sending the police to stop the caller forcibly from taking his life. But if you use it in the sense of preventive medicine, it does describe one major aspect of Samaritan work. Doctors inoculate people, so that their own chemistry can build up antibodies to increase their resistance to disease. Samaritans inoculate people with befriending, which builds up their strength and belief in themselves, so that they can resist the disease of despair.

There are callers who have the pills or the razor-blades or the loaded gun at hand. Some are at a stage earlier than that, where they are considering suicide, but have not yet planned how. But there are also many, many lonely, depressed and troubled people who, when the necessary question is asked: 'Have things ever been so bad that you've thought of suicide?', will answer, 'Thank God, no. I hope it never comes to that'.

If the Samaritan branch is working right, and the publicity is wide enough, there will be more and more of those calls. New volunteers, fresh from instruction in emergency procedures, see themselves sending ambulances all over the place, and listening to people pass out over the telephone. After a few weeks, they wonder, 'Am I on the wrong shift? I haven't had any crisis calls. Am I missing something?'

Now is the time to reaffirm that our major aim is to try to get to people *before* things get so bad that they have to make a suicide attempt to get the attention they need.

Definition of befriending
Befriending reassures: 'I'm on your side'.

M. D.

9. If a caller is concerned about another person, The Samaritans try to support him in his anxiety and to suggest ways of obtaining help for his friend. The Samaritans do not intrude upon persons who have not sought their help directly, unless an identified responsible person informs them of the need of someone who is too young or old or ill to ask in person, in which case they may make a tentative offer to help.

JOAN CARR*

To some it might seem dull to read that in 25 years the Twenty Principles of The Samaritans have changed very little. In a world of rapid change and progress (they may say), surely that smacks of a rather hidebound approach to things? On the contrary. It is a tribute to the vision and foresight of Chad Varah, who thought out those sensible and sensitive principles, that in 25 years most are still totally applicable; and that where change has called for adjustments, only a little flexibility has been needed.

Principle No 9 is one that has in fact been modified in response to the experience of branches and also because of changed circumstances in that the public's awareness of The Samaritans is becoming greater year by year. Accordingly, in June 1976, the Council of Management resolved as follows:

' . . . that consideration be given by branches to the acceptance of third party calls when the caller appears to be reasonably well informed and reliable, and the prospective client is said to be *depressed, distressed,* or *suicidal.*'

It still remains true that we cannot interfere or push ourselves in at the request of a third party, but a tentative and tactful offer of help can be made in the circumstances described in the original

* Joan Carr is Director of the Dublin Branch.

Principle and in the more recent resolution of the Council. It may well be that our offer of help will be rebuffed, and if so we must accept this, but at least the distressed person knows both that *someone* cares and also that The Samaritans are immediately available.

Of course such a rebuff may leave the branch, and especially the volunteers concerned, worried and anxious. But are not these anxieties a little arrogant? Maybe. After all, our whole organization is based on the principle of the dignity of a human being, and so what right have we, as ordinary people, to go where we have not been asked? Would you or I go to a neighbour's house, if we knew we were not wanted? I doubt it. Why then should we, as Samaritans, go out to someone again who we sense doesn't want us: to help ourselves? To allay our own anxieties? To tie up the end? Possibly so; but *if* so, then our whole reason for being in The Samaritans is surely wrong. Hard words, but think well on them.

Third party calls, and the approach they must adopt in relation to them, may be particularly frustrating for new volunteers fresh from their preparation classes. To them, especially, the Principle may seem exceptionally guarded. Perhaps a role-play with a short discussion in the course of the classes could help to explain more clearly what The Samaritans' role should be, and why. To caring, concerned people a very clear explanation obviously matters.

There is another side to our natural anxiety over such calls (should it be called 'referral frustration?'), in that the callers themselves, by reason of a too-intense and continuous concern for the other party, could themselves be in need of our help and concern. Or, going even further, a caller might be using the third party subconsciously as a means of discussing his or her own problem.

How often, in our quest to find 'a problem' when a caller makes contact, do we unwittingly become side-tracked by the fact that the caller appears to be ringing about a third party, and thus lose sight of the point that our first duty is to the caller himself, not to the person or persons who seem to be the source of their anxiety? 'I am very worried about my husband who is an alcoholic, he needs help but won't seek it. Where can I turn?' It is very easy and perhaps understandable that the volunteer, too anxious to 'help' or 'do' gets confused and starts to worry about the husband, rather than the caller's feelings and emotional state. One of the organization's basic principles is the acceptance of the caller in his or her own framework, and the necessity of listening with the 'third ear' in order to find out what that framework is and how we can best help *the caller* to cope.

The person who contacts us asking for help for a loved one in pain is obviously having difficulty coping with the situation himself, and where the volunteer, after consultation with the Leader, knows that the exceptions do not apply, he or she will explain why we cannot go to the third party but will, as the Principle states, continue to support the caller in his anxiety. Who knows—through this continued contact, we may in fact reach the third party after all.

Another case 'of mistaken identity' in this area may be when the caller presents a friend's dilemma as a means of testing our ability to accept it, before trusting us with his innermost emotions. This may often happen when a caller is in an emotional crisis, which is often when the volunteer too is most vulnerable. Emotions are not quite so tangible as, say, a job crisis, or other more concrete and defined difficulties. In short, it is important to probe the situation gently before making the supposition that a call is a third party referral: it may not be. In our natural wish to help the person who, but for the present caller's intervention, might not have access to the care he desperately needs, we must not overlook the messenger who may, in truth, be that person himself.

Definition of befriending
Not doing, not giving, not taking. Just being.

J. C.

10. The Samaritans do not permit their immediate availability in cases of a suicidal emergency to be impeded by attention to cases of long-term chronic inadequacy, though callers in this category may be accepted as clients during a crisis.

JOHN ROGERS[*]

A Samaritan branch, not 500 miles from London, had a classic case, which lasted nearly ten years, of almost total inadequacy. He 'joined' when the branch was started.

He was unfortunate to be born of an overpossessive mother who took charge of his every want, including taking him to the loo, at least into his early teens. Later he had a girl friend, and could well have married but Mum did not approve. He worked for a long time in semiskilled jobs but went to pieces when Mum died. Soon after, at about 38 years old, he became a Samaritan client, by which time he had become unemployable and was on Social Security permanently.

The branch, being new and underloaded, put in great and sustained efforts, but the more the volunteers did for him, the more he leaned. Much discussion, sometimes very heated, went on at SiC meetings. The writer was called hard-hearted and worse when he pointed out that we were doing more harm than good. However, after about five years, the hawks won the day and the client was strictly limited on listening time and visits. He accepted it quite cheerfully and subsequently was none the worse for our inattention.

Sadly or perhaps mercifully, some four years later he died, due to a physical, not mental, illness. In fact it is unlikely that he was ever mentally ill, but was mainly the victim of selfish mother

[*] John Rogers is a member of the London and Chelmsford Branches.

love. Perhaps there is a moral here for mums in general, as well as Samaritans.

Definition of befriending

To help a lame dog over a stile (but not too slowly) by providing guidance and 'moral support' (though not moralising). Also to be prepared to become temporarily slightly lame oneself.

J. R.

11. The Samaritans do not flatter themselves that what
they have to offer will be helpful to every caller.
Those in charge of each Branch are responsible for
using their human resources to the best advantage,
and protecting them from being wasted by the grossly
psychopathic or any others not capable of benefiting
from befriending.

RICHARD SHUTTLEWORTH*

If The Samaritans have achieved much during the quarter-
century they have been in existence—which is one of the themes
of this book—is it because they have aimed narrowly? They do
not aim to help the psychopathic—in fact it is a rule they do not.
Their help to the psychotic is to help the client towards a decision
(if he will) to seek medical help. They do not, except for a period
at crisis time, give extended help to the chronically inadequate, or
to alcoholics, or to drug addicts. They do not provide accommodation for clients trapped sans job, sans money, sans sometimes
clothing, in a big city in a biting February.

They do not, which gives volunteers no qualm, give money to
clients; they do not sit on committees (save their own); and they
do not much write letters to the papers on 'general topics' (though
the Founder does, from time to time, write letters to *The Times* of
London on particular subjects).

Partly, of course, it is a question of resources: we do not have
enough people to do what we have set ourselves to do.

Further, a Samaritan volunteer is not a professional. In fact,
avowedly she—or he—is not a professional. And if she suddenly
has a realization (it may be on a lunchtime when away from

* Richard Shuttleworth is a member of the London Branch and its legal
adviser. He was for some years Chairman of the Friends of the London
Samaritans.

either of her telephones) that the client she listened to for four hours last night and at the far end of the evening persuaded to hospital might now—she is thinking about him so much—have rung her, and she is not available, she does feel—an undetached unprofessional feeling—that she has let her friend down. And another feeling she has is that she never knows, going in once a fortnight Mondays, or only hardly ever knows, what happened to Louise who cried with her and then went back to her violent husband and tearaway daughter, whether she came in the next day, and whether the Welfare services could do anything to help, or if Albert did in fact take and profit by the advice given him on the approach to contact Helen the girl in the Spanish class he fancied and was shy about.

If the most interesting thing about the founding of The Samaritans is not that Chad set up a counselling service in the City of London, but that he perceived, when that counselling service was in its infancy, that as much was being done for clients outside his door as inside by untutored helpers passing coffee and kindness, and 'constructed' The Samaritans on that perception, then one of the most interesting things about the organization now is the self-discipline of the volunteers—in point of attendance and effective performance far exceeding any other voluntary organization I know (and also many non-voluntary organizations).

And in point of obedience? When told by the Director of your Branch that you were wrong in your assessment of the woman: she is a beguiling psychopath (whom incidentally you should by now have spotted, it being eighteen months since you emerged from preparation classes) and your offers to telephone her each evening (which you shouldn't have made without reference to the Leader on Call through your SiC) and to befriend her are void: you were wrong, you should not. Yes—such obedience is built in to the system, which in this particular is authoritarian in concept: the reason being that we are an emergency organization to serve clients, and clients need in an emergency clear and prompt decisions.

Does the Director (or Directorate) ever get it wrong? Yes. And, of course, sometimes you *feel* he—or she—is getting it wrong, because he hasn't seen the client and talked to her for three hours, and because perhaps (arrogant you) you have felt for some time that he doesn't have the wits and insight you and some others in the Branch have for this particular sort of client. But, in fact, where not arrogant, part of the explanation for this 'un-Samaritan' feeling is because we are apt to become involved, not remain detached. The saving is that Directors of Samaritan Branches, while on occasion capable of prejudice in relation to a number of things, are: (a) careful and non-judgmental when dealing with clients, (b) have been assessing more clients' problems longer than most volunteers and have often been advised by branch consultants, and (c) have inherited a body of tough-minded expertise, brought together over the last 25 years, on what The Samaritans are for and how experience has shown The Samaritans best do their job. Much of the tough-mindedness comes from Chad and others who have been helping The Samaritans for some considerable time. It is constantly at risk, for though it is for the benefit of those clients we can help, it is—or sounds to be—at odds with some of what impels a large number of volunteers to join, and it is at odds with a conventional cosy chummy life. And it is essential for the next 25 years.

Definition of Befriending
Befriending is being loving and calm and close to the client while he struggles through his crisis.

R. S.

12. The Samaritans' service is non-medical. Callers requesting medical treatment may be helped to obtain this, and each Branch has at least one medical consultant, usually a psychiatrist, to advise those in charge of the Branch about such cases.

JEAN RAINEY*

Many clients who come to The Samaritans are found to have problems needing medical help, so why should the service offered be a non-medical one? There are various reasons for this but the main one is that, if it were medically oriented, the organization would lose its whole value and *raison d'être*.

There are many centres where medical and other professional help is available but the uniqueness of the service offered by The Samaritans is the way in which they are able to utilize the best of human qualities unhampered by the need for professionalism which puts limits on the nature of the relationship offered.

This is not to say that members of the medical professions neither have these qualities nor are able to use them in their work, but their training is highly specialized and their approach, of necessity, more formal and mainly directed toward the diseased part of the patient's functioning. Although they can be friendly they do not, and should not, offer the kind of friendship which patients often so badly need.

The Samaritan approach, on the other hand, can be more flexible. They are enabled, through preparation and continuation classes, to recognize the disease but can concentrate on the healthier areas of the client's functioning, encouraging them, through patient friendship, to recognise abilities of which they

---

* Jean Rainey is a long-standing member of the London Branch, and one of its Consultants. She is a Senior Social Worker at the Maudsley Hospital.

may have been unaware, thought they had lost or were too lacking in confidence to develop.

However, there are pitfalls into which volunteers can (and do) fall. This is why it is essential that each branch should have at least one medical consultant to advise on, and perhaps see, clients who cause medical concern, and also to work closely with volunteers who befriend such clients.

Some of those very qualities which go to make a Samaritan can also be abused by the more personality-disordered (psychopathic-type) clients who, too often, pass through Samaritan doors. Both professionals and volunteers are familiar with clients who 'collect' agencies and abuse kind hearts and the more sentimental (and perhaps the more omnipotent) of us. If these clients are not recognized for what they are and for what they can do to any Branch because of their destructive (not necessarily aggressive) behaviour then crisis work cannot be undertaken. Samaritan Branches are now, on the whole, better able to deal with such clients. This has come about through a combination of experience, discipline and sound advice from professionals who also had to learn (and are still learning) the sad, hard lesson that there are some people who cannot be helped.

It is not just with the more grossly personality-disordered clients that volunteers need guidance. Recognizing the various forms of mental illness, especially depression which can be hidden, is essential. In my experience Samaritans are only too anxious to seek guidance and help with clients with whom they feel out of their depth and are sometimes overly modest in the estimation of their abilities in this respect. This is probably how it should be and if branches are sometimes thought of as over-cautious in their referrals to doctors it is better to risk possible irritation and patronage than to miss a crucial disorder.

There is little doubt that Samaritan Branches (particularly in larger towns) see some of the most acutely, often hitherto un-treated, psychiatrically ill clients. They can present a frightening picture and must cause anxiety to volunteers, and it is essential that they should be secure in the knowledge that their branch has sufficient acceptance and goodwill within medical circles to refer willing clients (through their Directors and Leaders) for urgent assessment. This goodwill depends largely on the energy of the Director and the commonsense shown by and the preparation given to volunteers.

The conflicts which sometimes arise between volunteers and professionals can be caused when a joint responsibility is felt for clients. Volunteers sometimes view professionals as 'cold', 'detached', and with their 'hearts' trained out of them. Professionals for their part sometimes regard volunteers with suspicion—as 'bungling amateurs' in their dealings with and assessments of such clients. Fortunately, these attitudes are rared and should not exist where there is good rapport between those concerned and where there is recognition that all have their unique and essential parts to play in the alleviation of distress.

Co-operation comes with confidence and trust and this has to be learned on both sides. Samaritans recognize and respect the medical profession's competence and expertise in their field. Although this is, increasingly, becoming a mutual recognition there could be more acceptance of the Samaritan expertise, gathered over 25 years, with more cross-referring of certain patients who need befriending as a supplement to, or even as a major part of, their treatment.

Definition of befriending
Giving love and friendship to the lonely and despairing with compassion in their hearts but with their feet on the ground.

J. R.

13. The Samaritans are not a trained case-work agency, and volunteers are not permitted to attempt to do in an amateur way what social workers are trained to do with professional competence.*

HUGH VARAH*

From our earliest days we have been encouraged to admire people who are always busy doing things: mountaineers, rally-drivers, explorers or other active people in our society. It was continually drummed into us that inactivity was to be avoided at all costs. Both boys and girls continue to be taught that athletics and games should be dominant factors in their lives. It is not surprising then that the accepted norm when helping someone is to be actively engaged in doing things. One of the precepts we have to learn when we become Samaritans is that this assumption is far from the truth. We have to grasp the fact that it is not necessary to be physically active to meet a client's needs. Nor do we accomplish anything by trying to organize other Samaritans to run, fetch or carry. I once heard it said, rather disparagingly, of a certain committee lady that she was of little use because all she could be trusted to do with any degree of efficiency was run, fetch or carry.

I was recently invited to speak to a group of senior boys in a grammar school and during the course of my time with them I followed my usual practice of encouraging questions. It is an interesting point that the various incidents of current gossip quite often set the tone of the questions in this kind of situation. This is all the truer if it happens to be a particularly juicy bit of gossip. I welcome this because the more shocking the incident the better I am able to project the way The Samaritans work. I was not

* Hugh Varah is a member and a former Director of the Scunthorpe Branch and is a brother of Chad Varah.

disappointed on this occasion. One of the boys eventually plucked up courage to ask, 'If a schoolgirl who was pregnant came to you would you help her to get an abortion?' The bated breath of expectancy assured me that I had everyone's attention. I told them that when a pregnant girl came to us, the question of whether her pregnancy should be terminated would in the main be decided between her and her medical consultant but that her primary need would be love, support and an understanding of all the difficulties that would press upon her and the hostility she would have to face from those who were less discerning of her real problems. The whole of our resources would therefore be geared to help her face those difficulties. It was not the answer they expected but it served my purpose and after that the questions came thick and fast.

We may have someone within our Branch who is trained and qualified to deal with specific human needs but this must not lead us to suppose that we have to call them into the Centre or hand over to them. In fact quite the contrary. An expert may be needed in due course but in the first place our role is that of a Samaritan and not that of an expert. Generally speaking, the client comes to us expecting to find an ordinary Samaritan, not a doctor, welfare-worker or what have you. It may turn out during the interview or at some subsequent date that the client needs expert help or assistance. Should this prove to be the case there are a whole range of professional people who have expressed themselves willing to help our clients. In addition in the UK and many other countries there are statutory or voluntary bodies or both with highly trained and competent staff with the facilities to meet the practical needs of those who require such help.

Let me reiterate that which all Samaritans know but which in the stress of the moment can so easily be lost sight of: the presenting problem is not necessarily the one with which the client is unable to cope. Take for instance a pregnant schoolgirl, an unmarried mother-to-be or for that matter many unwanted pregnancies. The conceiving of a new life by the female of the species is a natural and integral part of life itself, for without conception the species would die out. It is not the pregnancy that is her main problem, it is all the resulting connotations that she will have to face. In an entirely different situation she would be full of joy and excitement at the prospect of having her baby.

I could discuss from my own experience many a problem whose sense of urgency tended to mask the heart of the matter. For instance there was the widow with two small children, heavily in debt, with the electricity cut off and faced with an eviction order. What a wonderful opportunity to be busy doing things. After half an hour or so she let fall the remark that two years ago her mother had died leaving her to cope alone, bereft of loving husband and dearest mother. How on earth could my being busy doing something have helped her share those two infinitely sad years of solitary grieving?

Whatever the problem, presenting or subsequent, we must firmly resist all urges to run, fetch or carry. Such urges are born of our own neurosis and anxieties, they do nothing to help the client. We must do that for which we have been trained and prepared.

I said to a Samaritan who prided herself on her practical approach, 'Your practicality is simply a narrowness of understanding, get rid of it'.

Listen, listen and go on listening until both Samaritan and client begin to get things in correct perspective, by which time it will be obvious that to be up and doing is either unnecessary, irrelevant or quite secondary to the primary needs of the client.

Definition of befriending
Befriending provides love, concern and compassion for distressed and despairing clients at the moment of their greatest need.

H. V.

14. The Samaritans are not a social welfare agency. They refer those who request material aid to the appropriate welfare services, except in countries which lack these.

ROBERT WITHERS*

The offering of material aid, and any relevant decision about who should qualify for such aid, is very much the business of a Welfare State. This may be in the form of financial benefits for those who through unemployment, sickness, age or other special circumstances are unable to earn a living. Or it may mean the provision of housing or temporary shelter. The former is generally the responsibility of central government (the Department of Health and Social Security) and the latter of local authorities (Housing and Social Services or Social Work Departments).

Inevitably the 24-hour availability of The Samaritans attracts some calls for help from those whose immediate and practical needs fall within the scope of one of these services.

In such cases the skill required of the Samaritan volunteer (and, on consultation, the Samaritan Leader) will be to ensure that the problem as presented is the real reason for the caller having made an approach to the organization.

If insensitivity to the real problem results in an over-impulsive willingness to contact or recommend a statutory service, then the caller will have every right to feel rejected by us—even though seemingly having had a need met by the referral.

Perhaps there are two separate skills to develop in order not to fail this particular caller. First, the in-depth listening which will enable an assessment to be made by volunteer and Leader on whether this is an appropriate case for referral. Secondly, and almost paradoxically, not to over-play the listening role and

* Robert Withers is Director of the Lincoln Branch and a Vice-Chairman of the Council of Management of The Samaritans.

223

yet be deaf to the message of the caller who genuinely needs to find the appropriate statutory service as quickly as possible.

The Principle reminds us that we are NOT a substitute for professional services to which the caller has a statutory right. But if we assume that everyone who mentions a need for money or accommodation has, in approaching us, come to the wrong place, we fail many who are longing to reveal deeper needs and would benefit from befriending.

A fine point of balance, and a challenge to the volunteer to learn how best to help the caller.

Samaritan leadership has a responsibility to be knowledgeable about statutory services and to establish a happy relationship with the officers of such services, keeping them informed about the local Samaritan Branch, its aims and methods.

In return it is likely that we shall be told how to make the best use of such services for our callers, both in normal office hours and, by use of on-call telephone numbers, overnight and at weekends.

We have an important share in the partnership of social services and must see that volunteers are informed about what help is available to those in personal crisis, understanding both the substantial resources of professional and statutory services and our own limitations in the meeting of material needs.

Definition of befriending
Margery Allingham, in one of her books, describes unexpected harmony between two very different men 'as if a dog and a fish had mysteriously become friends and were proud each of the other's remarkable dissimilarity to himself'. Samaritan befriending assumes the possibility of affinity between persons who might never have chosen each other as friends, and that this can be a loving and supportive relationship.

R. W.

15. The Samaritans are not a Christian Organization, except in the origin of the concept. Volunteers, whatever their original beliefs, are strictly forbidden to make any attempt to convert the callers or to exploit a caller's distress by using the opportunity to witness to the volunteer's beliefs. Callers spontaneously requesting spiritual help of a particular kind are referred, with their permission, to a representative of the appropriate body, who may or may not be a member of the organization.

DAVID MOORE*

Compassion, care and love are not the prerogatives of Christians. A rich vein of compassion runs through many religious traditions other than the Christian one and is at the core of many non-religious philosophies of life. And the human response of love and self-sacrifice appears in some shape or form in most, if not all, human communities.

Despair, crisis and need are unique to the person who experiences them. No two crises are alike and, to the person in crisis, his experience is uniquely his own. It follows from this that the true resolution of his crisis (if such is possible), must be framed in his own terms. It follows further from this analysis that the introduction into the crisis situation of attitudes, values or structures of belief which are alien to the client can only complicate and confuse an already complicated and confused situation.

True caring, true compassion, true loving must be 'other'-centred, client-centred. Any approach which attempts to convert or persuade the client to the helper's point of view is less than client-centred. Moreover, because of this, the self-regarding

* The Rev David Moore is a former Deputy Director of the London Branch.

attitudes of the helper will obscure his ability truly to see the client's need. It follows too that solutions arrived at within a conversion context, because they are alien to the client, may well have little if any lasting value.

It is salutory to remember that a person in crisis will clutch at almost any straw and will often go out of his way to try to please someone who he knows is trying to help him. So, by introducing extraneous factors, such as his own beliefs, the helper may not only be laying extra burdens on the client (by making him cope with the helper's needs), but may also be making very poor converts! And in the end the client is not truly helped, or is not helped as fully as he should and could be.

Surely the goal of most religious and non-religious approaches to life is some concept of wholeness, integration, maturity or whatever. It is the goal of most of us, Christian or non-Christian, to be able to stand face to face with our God or ourselves, or both, and be at peace, to make the very most of what we have it in us to be. If we really care for the client then the only goal that we may properly have for him is that we may be instrumental in helping him to find his wholeness, his peace. Our goal for him must be that he should be able to live acceptably with his 'internal' and 'external' worlds. We, as helpers, may be able to help the client to discover peace within himself; we can never, I believe, give it to him however deeply we may believe that our own philosophy of life is the key to wholeness, happiness or fulfilment.

The preceding paragraphs perhaps appear to presuppose some religious conviction on the part of the helper and an absence of this in the client. The converse, however, is equally important. It may be crucial for the client's wholeness that his crisis should be resolved within the context of his personal faith or convictions. Therefore the helper must be willing and able to place the client who seeks pastoral or spiritual guidance within a specific ideological context in the hands of known, trusted and compassionate spiritual counsellors or their appropriate equivalent . . . hence the vital importance of the team of specialist consultants and counsellors behind every Samaritan branch.

Principle 15 is then crucial and goes to the heart of Samaritan help. The Samaritan helps the client where the client is, as the client is and in the way the client wishes. The Samaritan respects the client in his wholeness, both actual and potential. The Samaritan hopes that the client will emerge from Samaritan help more fully and effectively himself, a freer person, a captive neither of The Samaritans nor of the attitudes and beliefs of the individual volunteer.

Definition of befriending
Befriending is being willing to share the unshareable, bear the unbearable, accept the unacceptable, suffer the intolerable and be with the client at the point and in the situation where no one else will.

D. M.

16. Volunteers are normally known to callers only by their Christian names or forenames and their volunteer's identification number, unless continued befriending by a chosen volunteer is arranged, when one of the persons in charge of the branch decides what other information may be given to the client concerned and whether hospitality may be offered by the volunteer in his or her home.

GEORGE MILLINGTON*

The use of first names by volunteers is the beginning of an informal and personal relationship which is so important to the client and at the same time protects the identity of the volunteer. The volunteer's identification number reinforces the security aspect and provides the means of easy identification within the branch. Volunteers give up a proportion of their time to the service of clients, compatible with family and business commitments, and branches must safeguard them from the attention of over-demanding, unscrupulous and psychopathic clients at home and at places of work. The withholding of the volunteer's identity to a client is thus necessary until such time as the director decides there are sound reasons for doing otherwise. The rule not only protects the volunteer but also ensures his effectiveness as a member of the branch.

Definition of befriending
Befriending is a caring friendship.

G. M.

* George Millington has been a member of the London Branch since 1956, and Chairman of the Branch Committee since its inception.

17. The fact that a person has sought the help of The Samaritans, and everything he has confided in them, is confidential within the organization. All communications from callers which could reasonably be regarded as of a highly secret nature, and those relating to criminal acts, are received in the strictest confidence and are revealed neither to any person outside the organization without the caller's express permission, nor to persons within the organization who are not involved, except the Director. Volunteers are not permitted to accept confidences if a condition is made that not even the Director should be informed of them.

MICHAEL CHARMAN*

It is an absolute rule, without which The Samaritans could fail, that all confidences, secrets or other matters related by a caller to a Samaritan are disclosed to no person whatsoever outside the Branch unless express permission is given by the caller. This includes exchange of information even between Samaritan Branches.

There is no exception to this rule except that a volunteer cannot promise a caller not to disclose information to the Director or Chairman of the Branch.

Callers will not feel able to disclose their inmost secrets, fears, troubles, crises or disasters unless they can be assured they will go no further—hence the common fact that the 'presenting problem' is often not the real problem but a testing out of the

* Michael Charman is Honorary Solicitor to The Samaritans, and was formerly Director of the Leicester Branch.

volunteer to discover whether he or she can be trusted with something that has never before been disclosed or discussed.

Widespread publicity such as 'Talk to us in Confidence' must mean what it says and must mean that whatever is said, however shocking, however apparently criminal, cruel or anti-social is still treated not only with compassion but with respect and will not be divulged. It is not easy to befriend a caller who tells of some violence to another, unless the volunteer understands that the confidence is a privilege probably told to no one else, that such a caller is most in need of all the compassion and understanding the volunteer possesses, and that by such disclosure the client is beginning the process of coming to terms with himself and his problem and of thinking out, with the volunteer befriending, the action that is best for him to take.

It is essential that the caller knows and believes that the volunteer will understand and appreciate the caller's predicament and will not be shocked or criticize or condemn.

It is essential when volunteers are selected that they understand that they will be faced with such problems, and that they will be rejected in the early stages of training if they are unable to accept that without exception all confidences must be kept.

Disclosing any information to the police, social services or any other authority, for example, that a caller has battered his wife will not help the caller or the wife even if the caller discloses his name and address—even worse if it is not known who or where he is. An enquiry will be set in force—the caller will never approach The Samaritans again and the adverse publicity will do untold harm and could effectively mean that the public who need our help will never call.

To help the caller to move in the right direction as to the best step next to take must be the best befriending possible, however much concern the volunteer has for the possible victim of violence—and such concern he certainly will have. It does not help the victim to raise a hue and cry but it does help the victim if the perpetrator of the violence is beginning to consider that he needs help and is not wishful of continuing this course of action. The thoughtful volunteer asks himself the question as to why the caller phoned for help, and tries to give that help with all compassion possible.

Samaritans are not above the law and are compellable and competent witnesses where a crime has been committed, and should they be asked to visit a caller and suspect that they may see evidence of a crime, they must warn the caller that they would be obliged to report it. It is then better that two volunteers go and that they ensure the caller has expert advice before confessing to the crime or giving himself up.

The mere suspicion that a story told by a caller discloses a crime does not mean such crime has been committed and no disclosure should be made except to the Director. Fishing enquiries by 'authorities' do not require answering since facts are not known, even if a caller has said that he or she has committed a crime. The statement need not be true and it is no concern of The Samaritans to do anything except help the caller. Samaritans must never be a source of fishing enquiries by any outside body—particularly as any assistance would be useless except to start off further enquiries. It can never assist the caller.

Children and young persons under the age of seventeen call in ever-increasing numbers and they must be befriended in the same way as adults. There must be no panic information given to anyone, especially those from whom they may have run away. Volunteers' own anxieties must never outweigh the importance of callers coming to terms with their problems themselves with The Samaritans' aid. If any disclosure is to be made, it again can only be made with the caller's consent, however young, and then only by the Director or Chairman.

One of the great fears of callers is that if officialdom is called in it is they who are at a disadvantage, which is very often true. To talk to The Samaritans in confidence knowing their story will not be disclosed and that they will be befriended through their crisis is the greatest help anyone can be given. The law must take its course but everyone has the right to have the best advantage—one of which should be befriending by The Samaritans.

The twenty principles

We must always keep our clients' confidence as well as their confidences.

Definition of befriending
Befriending is love—the complete compassion and empathy of one human being for another in distress or despair.

M. C.

18. The caller remains at all times in charge of his own destiny and is free to reject the help that is offered and to break contact without fear of being sought out against his will, even if it is felt certain that he intends to take his own life or to commit some other act which The Samaritans would deprecate. A volunteer in contact (whether by telephone or face to face) with a caller judged to be in some danger of suicide is encouraged to seek the caller's permission for a discreet approach to be made to him subsequently to ask how he is, and to record the fact if permission is granted. In such cases, 'follow up' is clearly not against the client's will.

DICK BLACKWELL*

Initially I would like to make clear the following points. (i) That the Principles do not define befriending, they arise from it. (ii) That I use the term 'group' to refer to the collectivity of other persons, ultimately the human race as represented to any individual by those around him. (iii) That I frequently use 'we' or 'us' to refer to The Samaritans because I feel happier speaking from the inside rather than assuming detachment.

The tension between the individual and the group, the one and the many, is one of the fundamental problems of human existence; along with birth, where two individuals form a relationship (as distinct from a group or system which involves three or more) to produce a third, making a group; and death, where the individual leaves the group.

The case of the individual seriously contemplating suicide,

* Dick Blackwell is a member of the London Branch, was first Co-Director of the Festival Branch and is now its Consultant.

which is the primary *raison d'être* of The Samaritans, is an extreme case of alienation from the group. It is unsafe to generalize about this case, save to say that the reasons a person reaches this point are enormously complex and individual. However, it is clear that for the individual turning to The Samaritans for solace, the group has failed him. He comes to The Samaritans because he has no one else with whom he can communicate sufficiently to give his life meaning. He turns to The Samaritans as the last outpost of the human race before he quits it altogether. At this point he puts faith in The Samaritans, but it is *his* faith. To presume to advise, cajole, pressurize or indeed do anything other than attempt, as one isolated individual to another, to share his anguish, is to violate that faith.

It is often overlooked that the fundamental difference between our clients and the rest of the population is the decision they have taken to contact us. They have chosen to invest their faith in The Samaritans and to be befriended by us. The volunteers have made a similar choice, since they must befriend each other if they are to befriend the clients; one cannot give what one has no experience of receiving.

Man's capacity to choose is the essence of his humanity. Existentially he is free to choose, but in the context of his membership of the group or society his choice is socially, culturally and economically circumscribed: that is, I cannot choose a course of action unless I can conceptualize and value the act, and am not prevented from carrying it out by my own inhibitions, values or lack of material resources, nor by the restraint of others.

The person on the verge of suicide can be seen as having no options left. The group offers him no choice, and having lost the capacity to choose he has to that extent lost his humanity, which, paradoxically he can only then regain by losing his life; i.e., by regaining the power of choice in choosing not to live. The comparison with martyrdom is inevitable and calls to mind the character in Alan Paton's *Cry the Beloved Country*, who explains his readiness to face martyrdom in South Africa, not as a selfless sacrifice, merely the choice of death in preference to a way of life which violates his own humanity.

The Samaritan client seldom has this resolve, his choice is more uncertain, his autonomy more precarious. It thus becomes clear that only by maintaining his freedom to choose his own destiny can his essential humanity be preserved. To violate this choice by imposing our own views, values and opinions is to dehumanize him fundamentally. It is to represent again the group against the individual, the group that has already failed him. Only a group that can accept him as he is, and accept his right to choose for himself can help him now.

Some measure of the enormity of such dehumanization can be seen in the global arena. I joined The Samaritans at the height of the Vietnam war. This war was primarily the attempt by one nation, the USA, to prescribe or dictate what was best for another nation, Vietnam. (Even if one's political allegiance leads one to view the Russians or Chinese as the aggressors, the basic issue of one group imposing its will on others is hardly altered.) This involved a dehumanization of the Vietnamese to the point at which it became permissible in American eyes to wipe out villages, including women and children, by Napalm bombing and infantry assaults.

This perspective raises two further points of relevance to our own situation. First, American action was significantly influenced by self-interest or fear of the spread of Communism. Similarly, the urge to advise or take over the suicidal client is usually motivated by the volunteer's fear of the implications of the client's freedom. The volunteer who cannot to some extent enter the hinterland between life and death cannot reach the client there. Secondly, the resistance of the Vietnamese people indicates the unreadiness of people to abdicate their humanity and their choice. Thus our clients would not necessarily be at all influenced by our persuasions, more likely being strengthened in their resolve to go against us.

In taking this position which appears as being *for* the individual, against the group, we are in fact mediating between them and ultimately strengthening the group. In the group/individual tension is life—each depends upon the other. If the group dies, so do its members; if the individuals die, so ultimately does the group. As John Donne wrote, 'Never send to know for whom the bell tolls, It tolls for thee'.

Definition of befriending
Befriending is the attempt by two or more people to bridge the gap between life and death through the relationship between them.

D. B.

19. The various Branches of The Samaritans are banded together in a legally constituted Association whose Council of Management represents all the Branches and reserves to itself the appointment of the person in charge of each branch, responsible for seeing that the above-mentioned Principles are observed.

JEAN BURT*

The Council of Management is responsible for the Samaritan movement, especially its standards and development. Each Full Branch is represented by a member or an alternate on the Council who has a vote. Other branches send an observer to Council meetings who may speak but not vote. The Council elects the Chairman of The Samaritans and the Vice-Chairman; appoints Honorary Consultants, Honorary Solicitor and Honorary Bursar and the General Secretaries; co-opts those Regional Representatives who are not already members. It approves the opening of branches and has power to order the closure of a branch which persistently refuses to maintain an adequate service. It once had to close a branch. Just as no volunteer goes it alone, so no branch is allowed by the Council to do so.

The most important business of the Council each year is to appoint Directors/Chairmen of branches. For this reason no other business is undertaken at the September meeting. It normally meets on two other days in the year.

This vigilance, together with visits to each branch at least once every two and a half years by two members of the panel of visitors—experienced Samaritans—acting on behalf of the Council, endeavours to ensure uniformly high standards of service to clients throughout the British Isles.

* Jean Burt is Joint General Secretary of The Samaritans, and has for many years been a Leader of the London Branch.

The twenty principles

The Council delegates some of its powers to an Executive Committee but carefully considers all recommendations. It is no rubber stamp.

Definition of befriending

Befriending is loving, though not always liking, *really* listening in confidence and with an open mind, the giving of comfort and hope to a fellow human being who happens to be in a state of crisis.

J. B.

20. Only the Council may authorize departures from these Principles, for instance by permitting new Branches to offer a limited service for a period, and only the Council may from time to time revise these Principles.

DAVID EVANS*

This virtually continues Principle 19. In such a complicated matter as human relationships there is constant discussion within the movement about the work; for example, one alteration in the principles that the Council authorized in 1976 is the expansion of the circumstances under which we may, under Principle 9, respond to calls from a 'third party'. Another more formal change is that the responsibilities of the Council towards posts are now limited by a resolution passed in 1974 to the British Isles, though one hopes that nevertheless the Samaritans remains 'a world-wide fellowship'.

Two interesting branches in the movement are the Festival Branch and the Scottish Correspondence Branch. The first provides face-to-face befriending at pop and folk festivals. The second, working from PO Box 9 at Stirling, exists to befriend by letter those who live in the de-populated areas of the Highlands and islands. Both represent a positive departure from the Principles. Both have proved themselves and been recognized as Full Branches, i.e., as true and thorough agents of befriending.

Principle 20 actually mentions the example of 'new Branches' which may be authorized to offer a limited service. This remains a problem, but rather for old branches than for new ones which are almost without exception manned at the Centre 24 hours of

* The Rev David Evans is Joint General Secretary of The Samaritans, and a former Director of the Swansea and Birmingham Branches.

239

the day. Also custom has long dictated that Samaritans work only by phone or through the 'Flying Squad' during the night.

The Council of Management consists almost entirely of actual Samaritans, most of whom have responsibilities as Director or Leader in their branches and all of whom do regular telephone duty. Therefore one hopes and believes that the Council is close to the essentials of the work, making no change in the basic nature of the service unless pushed into it by their own experience of the depressed and suicidal caller.

Definition of befriending

Befriending is offered by a Samaritan as his attempt to stand in for the best friend or close relative whom the caller cannot call on for whatever reason during his current crisis.

D. E.

19. (International version). The various Branches of
    Befrienders International (The Samaritans Worldwide)
    are banded together in such manners as are agreeable
    to the laws of the countries in which they work and
    are entitled to be represented on their national,
    regional or Continental council and to vote for the
    representative of the appropriate Continent on the
    Intercontinental Committee, registered as an
    Association under Swiss law, responsible for the good
    order of the whole organization, and its faithfulness to
    these Principles.

JOHN MCKECHNIE[*]

The Samaritans have long been an international organization. In
1963, Bombay, Hong Kong and Karachi were founding members. In the years following, Branches were formed in Africa,
New Zealand, Australia, Malaysia, Singapore and the USA. But
distance and cost, together with the magnitude of work in each
Branch, prevented an early meeting of overseas Branches.

Then, in 1974, following an extremely busy world tour by
the Rev Chad Varah during which he visited most established
Branches, and encouraged the formation of many more, the
first conference of overseas Samaritan Branches was convened
in London. The fifteen delegates from eleven countries met just
prior to the Manchester Conference in September 1974.

As the pale autumn sunlight filtered through the stained glass
windows of St Stephen Walbrook, these Samaritans, of all races
and backgrounds, worked together to form a permanent body

[*] John McKechnie is the former Chairman of Directors, The Samaritans of
Western Australia, and now the Representative of Australasia on the Intercontinental Committee of Befrienders International.

to further the work of befriending throughout the world. Unanimously, the Rev Chad Varah was elected Chairman. In reply to his election, he said that he had devoted the past 21 years to the establishment of The Samaritans in the United Kingdom, and he intended to devote his next 21 years to the establishment of Samaritans world-wide. The name, Befrienders International, was agreed upon as signifying the aims of the new body.

The principles under which member branches would operate were drafted at that inaugural meeting. It is from that draft that Principle 19 has been drawn.

There are a multitude of agencies in the world, working in the area of crisis intervention and suicide counselling. Some are professional or religious; others use lay volunteers. A number have formed themselves into national or international bodies.

The concept of 'befriending' suicidal and despairing persons has been developed by The Samaritans and is believed to be effective in lowering national suidice rates. It is a concept which, among other things, ensures that a client always retains the right to decide his own destiny. A client contacting a Branch of The Samaritans or Befrienders International will not be manipulated. They will know that, however vulnerable they may be, their present distress will not be subverted against them and their confidences will be inviolate.

In the area of suicide prevention, where different methods, theories, and indeed, ideologies abound, Befrienders International has chosen to offer the integrity of The Samaritans' befriending to callers of every land. It does this by requiring of its members' adherence to the great Principles of The Samaritans, first enunciated, and later revised by the Rev Chad Varah.

The International Committee is charged by Principle 19 with the duty of causing all the branches to maintain those Principles.

The same difficulties which had, until 1974, prevented a full meeting of overseas Branches will hamper the work of the Intercontinental Committee for some time to come. But, despite this, the goal of Befrienders International is to provide world-wide coverage. Every person in the world, regardless of colour or creed, should have the opportunity to contact a befriender whenever they feel in despair or suicidal. The choice of contact remains theirs. The availability of the choice is the responsibility of Befrienders International.

As existing branches grow stronger within themselves, and national councils raise sufficient money to help Branches outside their own borders, this goal will come closer.

Since the first meeting in 1974, Befrienders International has been growing. Due almost entirely to the unflagging efforts of the Chairman, thousands more people in the world are today within reach of a listening ear. Principle 19 binds all the Branches together in law. Belief in the power of befriending binds the members together in spirit.

Definition of befriending
Befriending is creative listening.

J. M.

20. (International version). Only the Intercontinental Committee may authorize departures from these Principles or undertake revision of them if this should be necessary.

VIJAYAN PAVAMANI*

The Calcutta Samaritans were born of a deep sense of concern for heart-broken, despairing individuals who have no one or nowhere to turn to in their hour of crisis. So, armed with a surplus of caring love, and fortified with determination, without volunteers or any finance worth mentioning, with fear and trepidation we placed our first ad. in the local newspaper in December 1971, inviting anyone driven to suicide or desperate measures to talk to us in confidence or meet us in our tiny office (in fact a little verandah). The response was overwhelming. To those who came or contacted us it was made abundantly clear that the home at the back of the office was equally open for befriending and listening.

Soon our clientele grew and so did the number of friends and volunteers who came forward to involve and care and give of themselves. Within two years through the efforts of the late Rev Canon S. K. Biswas and the Rev Chad Varah, friends in the UK raised sufficient money to build a small office-cum-residence for the Director in the compound of St Paul's Cathedral.

In 1974 the Director and his wife were sponsored by Christian Aid to visit the UK to attend the annual conference in Manchester and visit some of the Samaritan centres. This study tour proved to be profitable and encouraging not only in establishing links

* Vijayan Pavamani is Director of The Samaritans of Calcutta and the Representative of West Asia on the Intercontinental Committee of Befrienders International.

and friendships in England but in stabilizing and strengthening the work and the office management in particular. In 1975, Chad Varah celebrated the 22nd anniversary of The Samaritans and the first of Befrienders International in Calcutta.

All Samaritans are familiar with the many faces of despair— loneliness, misfortunes, bereavements, broken marriages, sexual problems, feelings of intolerable guilt, depression, and so on. But here in Calcutta chief among these are unemployment and acute financial pressures which drive people to desperate measures. And since India is not a social welfare state the problem is vast. We have tried to solve this in a small way by working in co-operation with existing social agencies like Mother Theresa's work, Salvation Army, MCC, SEVA, Ladies Study Group and others. In addition to channelling clients who require material help to these organizations we have worked out a system of sponsoring clients for job-oriented courses, self-employment through business and so forth.

Soon our office, run on a 24-hour service, became too small to accommodate the increasing number of clients, so we began looking for larger premises. In November 1976 the Calcutta Samaritans became a registered society, and early in 1977 we moved to *No. 17, Royd Street, Calcutta 700 016*, a centrally located and a much bigger office.

We have on our panel doctors, psychiatrists and lawyers who offer professional service to those who require and request it. A faithful band of 23 volunteers and workers make themselves available for listening, befriending, interviewing, manning the telephone and counselling. Our clients come to us with every conceivable kind of human problem. They come from all walks of life, from different cultural and religious backgrounds, from different age groups, with their fears and hopes, their problems and pain, anguish and anxieties, their dreams and distress, and we consider it a great privilege to be available to them in their hour of need.

The funds for running the office, telephone, allowances, and aid (which comes to a substantial amount) are raised locally through donations and fund-raising projects. We have had to include financial aid in our programme of realistically rehabilitating and helping individuals. When a man comes to us driven to despair because his wife has to resort to prostitution to feed a starving family, mere counselling and befriending will not help. Immediate financial aid is necessary, followed up by seeing that the man is employed in some way so that they need not fall back in the same circumstances.

We can depart from Principle 13 and apply the last six words of Principle 14 to the Calcutta Branch because we have the approval of the International Committee for this.

Calcutta is a city of contradictions—a city of palaces and bustees, of sheer indifference and overwhelming warmth. Its people can be sensitive and callous at the same time and there is isolating loneliness in spite of its milling millions. The Samaritans are happy to be friends of the friendless and the only reward we wish for is a smile of joy and a light of hope on the many desperate faces of those who come to us.

Definition of befriending
The suicidal crisis is frequently a crisis of isolation and aloneness. Befriending saves lives because it introduces another, caring person into the situation. The client is no longer alone.

D. M.

Reminiscences of members of the
London branch of The Samaritans
with recollections of Edinburgh and Belfast

From Jill 1999

'As you've still got your coat on,' came the grave voice of the sic as I fell down the crypt steps into my first duty, 'would you mind if I asked you to go out again, now, right away?' He regarded me, calmly, yet plainly expecting an assent. Images of what, at that time of evening, I might have to be going out again now right away for, slid, not calmly, through my mind: of course, an emergency. But could I, so new and inexperienced, cope? Would I get there in time? Could I keep him from jumping?—or what if it was an overdose? Could I even remember any plausible resuscitation technique? How could I make them feel I cared? What had ever made me think I could help? 'I think a dozen should do it,' the compassionate voice went on. 'Wait—perhaps it had better be thirteen.' Thirteen! (Sticking-plasters? *Stomach-pumps?*)

For the first time, a doubt seemed to strike the sic. 'Are you sure you can manage?' He leaned forward, his chin on his clasped hands. 'Sausages,' he said. 'There's a caff at the end of the road.' Then with a grave, tender look, he added: 'Don't let them forget the mustard.'

From Suzan 1610

Six years ago when Preparation Classes comprised specialized lectures and the dreaded 'sensitivity testing' I missed the highlight of Chad's sex lecture and thereby missed the anticipated meeting with 'the boss' as he was then called; my first meeting didn't take place until a few months later.

I was standing by the coffee urn lighting a cigarette, feeling a little vulnerable after a difficult interview with a client, when I was approached by this sprightly figure who launched straight into a lecture about how one should never light a cigarette with a flaring match—that nicotine was bad enough without adding a dose of sulphur! Before I could reply, he observed that I wasn't wearing my badge with name and number and ticked me off for that! I was attempting to mumble a feeble excuse wishing I could quietly disappear when his face broke into smiles, he put his arm round my shoulder and introduced himself. Ten minutes later I was not only eating out of his hand, but had agreed to do some secretarial work for him. We began that evening, with Chad dictating an enlightened and compassionate article for *Forum* which immediately provoked an animated discussion and cut through all small talk and any preconceived notions I may have had about him and marked the beginnings of a devoted and long lasting friendship.

From Nadir 352

It is a very great privilege to be asked for my reminiscences of the Samaritans, although I am only too well aware that I lack any of the qualifications necessary for being a contributor to this *festschrift*. I have, however, been around for a long time and like so many other people I owe The Samaritans in general and the Rector in particular an enormous debt of gratitude.

Almost my first impression of The Samaritans when I joined in the autumn of 1959 was an engaging atmosphere of rather dotty scruffiness—we were herded together in the outer vestry which continued to retain a distinct air of the war damage it had sustained. This not over-large room had to contain the volunteers, the staff, the clients, an assortment of tables, desks and chairs of varying age, the all important telephones, one of which, contained in a cupboard in a corner, was sacred to John Eldrid and commonly known as 'John's kennel', and, almost as important, the tea and coffee making impedimenta.

Although we were totally untrained in any psychological or sociological disciplines we were soon made aware that there were certain cardinal principles to be observed, the breach of which would involve instant dismissal; absolute obedience to one's superiors in the branch, complete discretion, no false sentimentality and above all the knowledge that the client's needs were paramount.

Dominating the whole organization was the personality of the Founder whom we new boys and girls referred to in suitably respectful tones as 'The Rector' (it was only when one had graduated to the rank of Companion that one could call him Chad); and yet although in the early days The Samaritans and the person of their Founder were inextricably united there was none of the hagiographical reverence, none of the awed hero-worship or personality cult that so often surround the Founder of a great national organization. Indeed any effusions of this kind were severely discouraged by the man himself whose three dominant obsessions seemed clearly to be The Samaritans, the growing of dahlias and the University of Oxford in a somewhat variable order.

For although we were dealing in matters often literally of life and death, the prevailing atmosphere seemed primarily to be one of laughter, friendship and of a caring openness—none of us were saints, most of us had some maddening traits, a few were unquestionably holy but all of us were welded together by Chad's vision into a common purpose and desire.

Perhaps I might be allowed to give two illustrations which seem to me to epitomize the unchurchy yet deeply caring spirit of The Samaritans. After one of our weekly Monday lunchtime meetings where anything and everything could be discussed, our very Scottish psychiatric social worker said, 'Rector, I met John X (the extremely evangelical husband of one of our volunteers) the other day, and he said that The Samaritans weren't really doing their job properly as they didn't "convairrt" people —*he* had been at a party the other day and had "convairrted" seventeen people.' 'Really, Mary dear,' drawled Chad in reply. 'I was at a meeting last week where to my certain knowledge he alienated 21 others, so perhaps you'd tell him that at the moment his debit balance is four.' I have always thought of that remark as being a supreme example of a myth enshrining a deep truth.

The other very vivid recollection I have is of the visit made to The Samaritans by one of our early Presidents, the Metropolitan of the Church of India, Pakistan, Burma and Ceylon, the Most Rev. Lakdasa De Mel. Like the Rector, the Metropolitan was a man of great compassion and total dedication to Samaritan concepts, indeed almost the last act of his life when he was dying of cancer in 1976 was to sign the deed conveying some land of his which he had given to the Sri Lanka Samaritans for their headquarters. Like the Rector, too, he was endowed with an extremely sharp wit and an equal devotion to the University of Oxford. The shafts of humour were therefore flying fast and wide that evening until Chad asked him to tell the little group of people in the vestry something of his experiences as Primate of that vast Province of the Anglican Communion. Suddenly all the joking and laughter stopped as he perched on one of the tables and very simply told us of a visit he had made to a small village in Assam, where a young girl of about twenty was dying in childbirth. When she saw the Metropolitan, she summoned up her rapidly failing powers of concentration to entrust to him all her worldly possessions: a tiny pair of gold earrings and five rupees in cash, which she wanted him to have for Jerusalem, because 'that was where the dear Lord had suffered and died'. So the little gold earrings and the five rupees went into a tiny gold cross which the Metropolitan presented on a chalice to the Archbishop in Jerusalem as a twentieth-century example of the widow's mite. When the story was over—and strangely enough although it was a busy time of the evening none of the telephones had rung during the twenty minutes it had taken—I saw that Chad's eyes were full of tears. He was always happy to laugh, but he was never ashamed to weep.

When Chad was instituted to the living of St Stephen Walbrook 25 years ago, the then Parish Clerk, who was 97 at the time, chose a particularly inopportune moment during the service to call out with a loud and ancient cackle, 'Ha, ha, you will never be able to get rid of me, I've got a life freehold and I'm good for a long time yet.' He was right: he lived to be 102.

Perhaps the most eloquent tribute, that we who have been

privileged to have been associated with Chad for the past twenty years and more can pay him, is to say that we pray that his tenure of office will exceed even that of his somewhat venerable Parish Clerk, for he taught us to be human; he inspired us to care.

From Vivien 2

In 1953 I was working as an 'au pair' girl in Paris when Chad wrote to tell me he was going to become Rector of St Stephen Walbrook, and was looking for a secretary.

On my return to London, and our first day at St Stephen's, we entered the church through the little churchyard at the rear and found workmen everywhere. The building had been in ruins and closed up for thirteen years after it was bombed during the war. Chad and I found our way to the outer vestry. One outside wall was nothing but plywood and the room was full of builders' rubble and old organ pipes. However, the inner vestry, though covered with dust was largely undisturbed and pretty much the way it had been in the former Rector's time, I suppose. There was a large rolltop desk, some nondescript furniture, the vestment closets, a telephone and an old metal-lined sink with running water—tea, our first thought: I must have made countless cups in those early years—first for the workmen, and later for our clients and volunteers.

I hadn't been with Chad many weeks before The Samaritans got launched with a vengeance! Chad had lunch one day with a journalist friend and talked to him about his idea for an organization to combat suicide. However, he obviously didn't make it clear that it *was* only an idea because in next morning's paper in large headings was the information that people in any kind of trouble or distress should call MAN 9000 and help was at hand!

I can't remember if Chad was late that morning, or if he had a meeting somewhere else. All I do remember is the telephone ringing and a young man at the other end sobbing in distress because his wife had run out on him and he had no idea where she had gone. I remember feeling thoroughly inadequate for this, and the many subsequent calls that first day. I don't believe any of our early clients ever did know that the 'organization' was really only Chad at the beginning. We had plenty of telephone calls, and fortunately some were from those anxious to help as well as those in distress. Those first volunteers became our friends. Most of them had little or no experience in social work, but they gave up their lunchhours to come and discuss ways of helping the clients. One of our first 'lessons' was not to appear shockable, and luckily I remembered this the first time I got an 'obscene' phone call. The same man telephoned many times before he gained sufficient confidence to come round and talk.

I remember another occasion when I was alone in the vestry and there was a knock at the door. I was typing and called for them to come in. No one came so I called out more loudly and glanced up in time to see the doorknob being turned ever so slowly. I wondered what to expect and my heart beat a little faster when the head of a very tall man appeared slowly round the door and asked a question. At first I didn't understand, but suddenly it dawned on me that his speech was different because he was totally deaf and if I looked straight at him he was able to read my lips.

I worked for Chad for three and a half years and when I left in 1957 to come to the United States the Telephone Samaritans (as they were then called) still was not large enough to permit the telephone to be manned for 24 hours. Now when I visit England again from time to time I always get quite a thrill to see a poster in some remote railroad station giving the telephone number of the local branch and realize how The Samaritans has grown from such a humble beginning.

From Barry 13

On a Sunday afternoon in late December 1953 I was sitting by a good fire talking to our churchwarden, a great friend of mine, when he said quite casually, 'I suppose you wouldn't be interested in helping my brother-in-law, Chad Varah, would you? He has just started an organization called "The Telephone Samaritans" at his church, St Stephen Walbrook, right next to the Mansion House, and as you work fairly near I thought it worth mentioning to you.'

I was interested but undecided, even after Neville had explained that the organization was primarily to help those tempted to suicide or in despair of any kind.

The next morning in the office my telephone rang and a voice said, 'I am Vivien, Mr Varah's secretary, we are having a meeting at lunchtime today—bring your sandwiches with you. We are looking forward to seeing you. Goodbye.' I was in!

I remember the first meetings well—the church which had only recently been rededicated after the extensive war damage had been beautifully and lovingly repaired, but the vestries were still in a blitzed condition. The outer one was barely weatherproof at one end, and there was a layer of fine dust over everything. The inner vestry (Chad's office to start with) was only a little better.

When I arrived there were about half a dozen people sitting around on old boxes and rickety chairs. Vivien talked to us about what was happening, and informed me I should be known as No 13. Then Chad came in. He talked to us about the vision he had, and he inspired me with the idea that ordinary people with a little help and sanctified commonsense could help many different people by befriending.

Being nearby I was able to pop in at lunchtimes, and often before going home I would look in to see what was going on. In those days the only way you were trained was by doing the work, meeting the clients and learning from your mistakes.

Every Monday lunchtime we had a meeting to consider the problems that had occurred that week and to ask Chad questions about our clients—however to begin with Chad and Vivien were the only ones who knew what should be done! The rest of us played it by ear and by prayer. Gradually order came and the outline of the organization began to appear.

We had our crises and our long hours when nothing much happened when we were on evening duty. We shut up at 10 p.m.

in those days. There were also the lighter moments and a great sense of fun. I wonder if anyone remembers the time the coffee tasted revolting, which upon investigation was traced to a drowned rat in the water supply tank over the little washing-up pantry off Chad's office. The consumption of coffee dropped off dramatically for a few days after that incident!

Always there was the 'togetherness', the trust that builds up between a small group of people who are involved in a new and experimental venture.

In the early days only about one in four of the volunteers stuck. I was looking down the list of the first 50 helpers and many were names that had come and gone, but a few were those who had formed the core of The Samaritans—who had become friends and colleagues to rely upon in any emergency.

Over the months and years various ways of keeping records, passing messages, contacting each other were tried. Some ideas succeeded, other just faded away, but the organization was growing all the time. Some article in a paper would bring in a flood of clients and with them would come the needed extra help in the shape of new volunteers.

Chad and others went out to various meetings to sow the seed. I remember going to a meeting in Harrow where I was expecting to talk to a small group only to find a packed hall with over 200 people present. The subject always got people going and the questions after the talk went on as long as the chairman allowed.

I was with Chad for seven very hectic, happy years and when I left it was to go to Theological College to be trained for the ministry. That was over seventeen years ago and I look back on those early days with the knowledge that I was in on the beginnings of an organization which now spans the world and is one of the best known of all agencies, dedicated to helping those in distress of any kind.

From Roger 44

I saw an article in the *Observer*. Easy conscience-saving work sitting by the phone? I did nothing. I queued to see the Temple of Mithras excavations and saw the notice on the church door. I did nothing. I saw an article in the *Evening News*. I phoned—'Come and have a chat,' said Chad.

I arrived and found a dirty dilapidated vestry with Chad on the phone. I waited twenty minutes then, cupping his hand over the receiver, Chad turned round and gazed at me. I explained who I was and a long silence ensued. Then—'There's a man in distress at Wimbledon Station. Do you think you could go and see him?' I went, listened to the extraordinary story which was unfolded and believed every word. Next day I returned to the vestry to find out what should be done and thus I became a Samaritan. One day I must go through the selection and training procedures to see if I am suitable!

Although The Samaritans had been in existence for two years when I joined, we had not the slightest idea that it would grow in the way which it has. Chad was in every sense the leader and the teacher. Not merely were we vague about what we were doing and how we should do it, but we were still groping for what our aims should be. At that time the medical world, the police and the Establishment generally were exceedingly suspicious about us. What could we properly do as untrained amateurs and where should we draw the line? What was our policy about confidentiality; about psychotic and unhelpable clients; about the non-suicidal, lonely person? Should we ever go to see a client or accept a reference from someone else? What hours should we be available? Who should we ask or accept to help and what were the criteria? Should we adopt the Fleet Street nickname of Samaritans or call ourselves the Telephone Samaritans or The Company of Samaritans or what? We did not call ourselves Samaritans but 'Rector's Assistant No oo'. There was so much to work out and develop, mainly on an *ad hoc* basis with thoughts only of a small group and a limited horizon.

'The Rector', or his secretary, the ever-cheerful, supportive and sensible Vivien Prosser answered the phone during the day and we took it in turns informally to come in during the evenings.

On Monday lunchtimes we gathered to eat our sandwiches and discuss what ought to be done and, I suppose, to give ourselves some group therapy. Chad was inspiration and backbone, helping, supporting and guiding us and somehow he always seemed to be around. Often he was around in the evening and he was readily available to give advice and guidance on the phone at home. Only now do I realize how hard he worked and how much responsibility he bore. He gave us and everyone confidence, although I now suspect that sometimes he was only just ahead of us. That was not surprising as there was no precedent for a group of tolerant, understanding and unshockable people, who had no common background of race or religion or class, who did not attempt to convert or redeem and who worked in the field of mental suffering which, at that time, was a willing mystery to most people who felt that it was evil, possibly recalling ancestral memories of witchcraft.

We grew from being a parish organization to being a wider Christian group which accepted those of other faiths, or of no faith, but the inner group, The Company of Samaritans, held special dedication and admission services which I found intensely moving. In accordance with the spirit of the period, and of the Parable, the specifically Christian aspect faded out for the organization, although not for many members.

The accommodation was cramped and unsuitable. If Chad's study was occupied, and the vestry was in use, we had to use the church to interview clients. Sometimes an organist would be practising with maximum power and we were forced to shout louder and louder until the music finished or, worse, stopped suddenly in the middle of a bar to try a passage again while our voices rang out in the sudden silence. Yet, somehow, the many inconveniences were not the subject of any real complaints, although often there was good-humoured grumbling. There was a wonderful close, caring, friendly and stimulating spirit—and we knew no other conditions.

The first experimental Night Duty was on New Year's Eve, about 1956. I stayed in the evening on my own until the early hours but no one seemed to think it worth phoning at such a time and nothing whatever happened, apart from other members ringing to see what was happening.

Gradually our organization became more formal, culminating in a Certificate of Incorporation being granted (and was it only a coincidence?) on Maundy Thursday 1963.

From David Arthur, on Edinburgh

Nothing could be more boring than to describe in patient detail the history of the foundation of a branch even if it was the first outside London, so this is not to recount the founding of the Edinburgh Branch in 1958–9.

It is twenty years ago now and all but myself of the original cast have left the Samaritan stage, but it is of people rather than places that I would like to write. Indeed this is true of the Samaritans as a whole. I suppose I have visited almost half of the branches throughout these islands and while I would find it difficult to recall details of any of the Centres, in most I can remember faces and friends.

What then from twenty years of Samaritan memories stands out from that first year in Edinburgh? My first meeting with Chad. I expected an aged cleric with beatific vision and an oriental cast of features. I got an energetic young man (same age as me now), chain smoker, non-stop talker about almost anything, astonishingly realistic and practical about what could or could not be achieved. More than my first meeting with Chad, I remember Chad's first meeting with the branch. All keyed up for the Kingdom of Heaven, we got Chad on sex, and in Edinburgh sex is something in which the coal is delivered. In our cold climate, we didn't have problems of sex, at least not until Chad arrived!

Our first sex caller. He hung up our emergency line for weeks shouting obscenities and was finally tracked to a phone box immediately outside the magnificent Usher Hall. (Perhaps it was the enormous organ that inspired him.) The heavy squad went out, and were in the midst of hanging the unfortunate client by the coat-collar from a meaty fist, when a little man in a dirty raincoat pushed through the crowd to announce—'I'm the GPO engineer, are you the Good Samaritans?'

Our first premises were in the basement of a church. After three weeks I had a call from the session clerk to ask us to move. 'You are,' he said, 'attracting all the wrong kind of people. The sort of people we wouldn't want in our church!'

Looking back on those twenty years ago, I tremble at what had to be done. There were no models on which to build, except St Stephen, and London was so different. There were no run-down city churches in which a base could be built; no dynamic leader with the time to give; no clear knowledge of what we faced; no Council, no Executive, no region, no regional rep., no general secretary. It is interesting to note, first, that Chad even let us start being so different, indicative perhaps of the Samaritan spirit to improvize and to be flexible, and secondly the warmth and commitment of ordinary people who worked for hours—cleaning, scrubbing, painting, training, fixing rotas, doing duties. To a school-teacher, sadly accepting so many of the restrictive practices of that profession, finding kindred spirits—bus-drivers, university lecturers, chars, housewives—ready, willing to get stuck in and try to do something for other people, was an eye-opener.

That first 48 hours. We opened at 9 a.m. on the glorious 1st of June—the phone rang at 8.20 a.m. with the words 'Happy Birthday, Samaritans—I don't really feel like saying that because . . .'. The phone literally never stopped that first day and night and for most of that week. And to the best of my knowledge it has gone on ringing ever since.

My first client. Even before the branch opened Chad rang to ask me to help a client whose husband had just committed suicide in London. I know who was more nervous and I also discovered my first Samaritan lesson—that you soon forget yourself and your fears in the despair of another human being.

The Samaritans have come a long way since that autumn of 1958–9; you don't have to hand-write cards and summary sheets. There are cassettes, books, papers on Samaritan work until they come out of our ears (and I have contributed my share to them), but I don't think that we are greatly different—human, people before places and things. Harry Whitley, who was Edinburgh's first Chairman, wrote a book called *Laughter in Heaven*. Bill Thompson, our first National Chairman once preached a sermon—'Look up, and laugh and live'. I have a feeling that a lot of those happy warriors who helped to start the Samaritans—Christopher Pepys, Bill Thompson, Harry Whitley, Jim Blackie—will be looking down on us with a laugh on their lips, and a lot of satisfaction.

From Sydney Callaghan, on Belfast

Maybe it was necessary and workable in the vast anonymity of a place like London. It could possibly fill a need in the cultured cosmopolitan atmosphere of Edinburgh, but was it really needed in Belfast? After all we are a closely knit island community very conscious of the cultural and religious backgrounds from which we come. People are not so isolated. Everybody belongs to something and we are part of the Welfare State with all sorts of folk doing good both openly and stealthily.

Chad Varah we had heard of—as had many others. Wasn't he the Church of England vicar who had been on 'This is Your Life' and was very knowledgeable about sex?

That is how it all seemed to me in August 1961 when along with about 50 other clerics (for we were not afraid of them in those days!) I went to a meeting in the Chapter House of the Belfast Cathedral. I went with many questions and even more reservations. Did we really need The Samaritans here? Haven't we enough people busy looking after others without adding yet another organization which had nothing new to offer? So I thought. But I went because it is always important if you are to be critical of anything to know what you are talking about—even for an Irishman!

It was evident from what was said that day some thought The Samaritans had something to offer. One was Bill Thompson, a much respected Presbyterian minister. He was asked to be the first Director, a position he occupied till he died in 1974. He was joined by Jim Musgrave, a Church of Ireland minister, and then somebody felt they ought to involve the Methodists, and that is how I got involved.

Along with Joyce and Lorna we met that day and decided we must have a Catholic as part of our team. We were much enriched by Father Hugh Murphy, a very highly thought of priest. From then to today we have always been an organization working right across the different religious, political and cultural divisions, and to do and be that is no mean achievement in our broken and fragmented society.

We were operational by the 1st November, about ten weeks after the first meeting. This was due to Bill's leadership, in that he had a remarkable combination of organizing ability and compassion. It was possibly also due to our not being encumbered by a committee—save one that looked after finance! It was chaired then and since by a noted public servant—Sir Robin Kinahan, a former Lord Mayor of Belfast.

When Chad Varah came for our opening meeting he said few other Branches had got off to such an auspicious start. The reason for the good start was to be found in the presence of the Founder, the business acumen of the Chairman and the leadership qualities of the first Director. The fact that we were the thirteenth Branch did not seem to do us any harm. Some would say that luck was bound to change and have wondered if it has in the present Director, who is also Chairman of the Irish Region, which now has thirteen Branches altogether.

I was wrong, of course The Samaritans were necessary and have obviously met a need. Accepted by other voluntary agencies, respected by statutory bodies (possibly because we know our terms of reference and do not exceed them) and relied on by thousands of people throughout the island who re-echo the comments of a client—'Thank you for caring enough to listen. If it wasn't for you I wouldn't be alive today.'

Chad said if it could work in Belfast, it could anywhere. He is right about the former for it does work here. We trust his confidence will be equally fulfilled elsewhere.

From Rosamund 1630

I remember Night Watch duties soon after I joined in 1972. At that time we were entertaining large numbers of mice in the crypt. The diet of biscuits, candles and volunteers' forgotten sandwiches produced fat and friendly rodents, much to the distress of certain Samaritans. A campaign was waged to rid the crypt of its amiable visitors. Two delightful but ineffectual kittens were imported. While they were marvellous value for soothing upset clients the mice population thrived, and yet another health hazard was added to the crypt. Mice, it was decreed, were better than cats and mice. So the mice reigned supreme until the Rentokil men came . . . Night Watch was never quite the same bereft of the inquisitive eyes and greedy scratchings of the little animals.

From Pat 400

I joined the Samaritans in the fairly early days (though not right at the beginning) when I was quite young, had just acquired a professional qualification and thought I had some time and energy and skill to spare. I offered these things to my local church and was a little mortified to find that they did not seem to have any use for them. Just at that time I heard of The Samaritans from several different sources. I volunteered and was surprised and pleased when I was invited to join preparation classes.

In the preparation classes I remember a young man who seemed to ask all the right questions and who knew all the right answers. In comparing myself with him I felt very inadequate and I was extremely surprised when I was invited to join the Samaritans and to go on duty. I am amused to find that twenty years later new volunteers recount similar experiences.

In those days we did night duty up in the tower of St Stephen's Church. There were two of us on duty for the whole night. Every effort was made to see that we were as comfortable as resources would permit. Our bunk room in the tower was equipped with two iron bunks (one on top of the other) rather like the ones I had slept on in youth hostels. One cannot move without disturbing the other person. We took it in turns to get up and answer the telephone. The telephones were on a shelf on the other side of the bunk room at some distance from the bunks. There was lino on the floor which was very cold to the bare feet in winter. By the time one had jumped out of bed and padded across the lino to the telephone, the shock of the cold floor had dispelled all sleepiness!

I remember a joker who used to ring us in the small hours of the morning to ask if we were awake. I also remember a lady telephoning to explain that she had ejected her cat from the window of her fifth-storey flat. She said the body was lying on the pavement below and she asked us what she should do with it!

From John 506

One evening duty in 1965, a new volunteer, or helper as they were then called, talked a client, reluctant to come to a church, into agreeing to meet her outside the Mansion House. She was given permission and, being a keen Samaritan, waited for a very long time. Sadly, but not unusually, the client stood her up.

She finally gave it up and fled back to the crypt, very red-faced and in considerable confusion. Seemingly, a city policeman had spotted her and asked her why she was hanging about for so long. In her innocence, she told him she was waiting for a client.

Then the penny dropped!

From Alison 335

For night watch, when I joined in about 1960, we slept in a room up in the church tower. There were two of us, two bunk beds, and two telephones. We decided which of us was to take calls on 9000, and who was to answer 2277 (you could tell which phone it was by the ringing tone). To answer them we had to get out of bed.

I remember that one night—I was in bed—2277 rang, and I sprang out—expecting a client needing to talk. It wasn't a client, it was Chad. He wanted to know the time of a train which he proposed catching—and I must go and get the railway time-table! The time-table was downstairs in the vestry, so, not over-pleased, I made my way down the stairs, collected it, and went back upstairs with it. I half suspected that he wanted to find out if his volunteers understood how to read a railway time-table. If so, he soon discovered that I couldn't.

From Jean 219

I *think* I became a volunteer of the London Branch in 1957. In those bad old days we were few in numbers and resources. We saw the clients in the beautiful but bitterly cold church and went out several times a week on 'flying squad'—sometimes more than once a night. When we had no money at all Chad used to go into the church and say a prayer and someone would die and leave us a small legacy! Not that he meant anyone any harm as he would say. One thing we had which was worth more than all the material things in the world and that was firm and constant support.

It was Chad's vision and brilliance that led to the concept of befriending, his humility in recognizing that this could be done by ordinary lay volunteers, and his wisdom in realizing that he would have to teach, direct and support us. This he did mainly through a lunch hour meeting each Monday at which there was usually 100% attendance. All too scared to go it alone! At this meeting we were able to off-load our anxieties and to learn how better to help our clients. Incidentally, some of us learned more about ourselves than we had done in a lifetime, often not a comfortable experience. However busy Chad was, he was always available in his study to a volunteer who was particularly worried about a client. What toll all this took of our Founder can only be imagined but it laid the foundations of direction of volunteers in work with clients.

From George 75

I remember Monday, 4th February 1957, when the Samaritans were featured on BBC radio in Stephen Grenfell's 'Our Day and Age' series. Six of us were on duty with Chad that evening and others stood by at home in case they were needed. We had no idea at the time that we were about to have our first experience of dealing with clients *en masse*. The first call came through before the programme went off the air, the first client arrived shortly afterwards and for 36 hours it seemed as if the telephone never stopped ringing. Over 300 clients sought our aid in that time. Few in numbers, we were hard pressed during that week but, unasked, volunteers appeared on duty whenever they could spare the time. Some took time off from work as leave to help out and others came straight from work and stayed on duty to the early hours of the morning. I remember the long hours spent by Chad interviewing in his study with frequent interruptions from volunteers seeking advice in dealing with clients they were seeing. Not until he was assured that all the clients had been seen and arrangements made for their on-going welfare did Chad let up.

From Patricia 916

As 916, I am a half-way vintage Samaritan but I think the greatest changes in our work have come in the second half of our existence. I joined in 1965 at the age of 50 plus, when suicide had ceased to be a crime but was still barely discussed and the verdict 'while temporarily of unsound mind' was used as a way round the horror of it.

Chad, 'The Rector' to us newcomers, took several of the training classes particularly the fourth one on sexual deviations —elsewhere still called perversions. He told us that we must never show that we were shocked at anything we were told for if we so much as raised an eyebrow the client might feel doubly guilty and go away in fourfold misery. I brightly thought I was a woman of the world and would manage it all right but I found myself holding my eyebrows down by force as he tested us with case histories while many in the class around me turned green with nausea and were never seen again, which was the point of the exercise. Nowadays we hear worse any day on the media. . . .

We had no sensitivity testing (I hope my dearly loved shift are not saying 'anyone can see that') but were flung in at the deep end. I remember being completely bewildered by my first masturbatory client who went straight into action on the phone and asking Chad, after, what I ought to have said—I'll draw a veil over what I did say—being told to think how I would have felt in his place, while my poor mind boggled around with the problem. I think the present open-minded attitude and the willingness to discuss anything with the young and the efforts now made in so many quarters to try to alleviate distress in others, is one of the greatest advances of our time; for the hand which Chad held out to the despairing 25 years ago has inspired thousands the world over to try to do the same, 24 hours a day all the year round.

From Tony 1277

I well remember joining the Samaritans in 1970 . . . and how nearly I did not get in.

I had done some work for a Methodist organization in Australia called 'Lifeline' and I was keen to pursue this when I settled in London in 1968, although I was not sure if 'Samaritans' was right for me. Anyway, I went along for a preliminary interview and, when I entered the old outer vestry where clients waited before being whisked downstairs, I was confronted by Eileen sitting at a desk looking for all the world like a friendly and reassuring hotel receptionist.

I was told to wait for a while and, while so doing, I noticed that one of the clients was sobbing quietly to himself in a corner and Eileen appeared to be taking no notice. So, presumptuously, I walked up to her, holding a copy of *Punch* on which I had scribbled a terse note, 'that man is getting rather distressed' and said in what I hoped was my brightest 'voluntary social worker voice', 'have you seen this joke in *Punch*?'

Eileen nodded sagely at my few written words, but, of course, she already had the situation well in hand. I have often wanted to ask her since what she thought of my youthful arrogance.

Despite that, I was selected for preparatory training and I found the classes very thought-provoking, although some of my antipodean sensibilities were somewhat stunned by Chad's forthright lecture on sex. I can still see him gazing around the room at the twenty or so of us huddled before him and emphasizing, 'Tonight, I'm going to talk about sex, about heterosexual sex, homosexual sex and abnormal sex. . . .'

After our preparatory course, some of us went on to the ordeal we most dreaded, 'sensitivity testing' whereby we were required to accept a 'rigged' problem call from one of our colleagues on a sort of makeshift telephone which was hooked up to a loudspeaker. I thought I sailed through mine, because of my past experience with telephone counselling and my own professional training as a broadcaster. There was no awkward gaps in the conversation, the distressed 'client' was treated to a superb and polished interview which would have done credit to my BBC employers, but which, I see with hindsight, lacked any trace of human warmth or involvement.

I went home quite convinced that I was to be God's gift to the London Branch and was surprised to be summoned to see Michael Butler, then Deputy Director, some days later only to be told, 'The position is this; we haven't accepted you, but we haven't rejected you either, will you do another sensitivity test?'

He went on to tell me that my very glibness and ease with the telephone, my ready flow of words, had made him feel that I was not a very caring or concerned person, but I might well have potential if I were not so glib.

My second 'sensitivity test' was held in Chad's own study with the great man himself looking after us. This time, there was little need for me to feign nervousness or hesitation; I was scared stiff! Luckily for me, I passed that test and, to my great joy, I was admitted to 'helper' status.

Since then, apart from countless shifts at the branch, I have done countless broadcasts and talks about Samaritans, and it is difficult to assess fully the tremendous change wrought in me personally by being given the sheer privilege to 'belong'. I shudder to think what would have happened to me as a developing human-being had I failed that second sensitivity test!

From Cynthia 961

In 1970 the London Centre asked me if I would contact the producer of a BBC Italian programme which was to broadcast about suicide. I was summoned to meet him about half an hour before the programme went out, only to find that it was part of a link-up with a studio in Rome where several other people would also talk to a suicidal client on the telephone. There would be three programmes in all, with a different caller each time. I had collected statistics and made some notes such as, 'The aim of the Samaritans is threefold: *ascoltare, accettare, amare*' (to listen, to accept, to love). But that epigram never got said. It was obvious that one just had to play the whole thing by ear. I was extremely nervous. Supposing one was called upon to advise rather than listen? Suppose my Italian went to pot? Supposing the client spoke in a strong Sicilian dialect which would be difficult to understand?

We sat in a large studio with a shrouded piano in one corner and, earphones adjusted, made contact with Rome. The producer gave a brief resumé of the work of The Samaritans. The caller on the first occasion was a girl who talked quite a lot about nothing very specific. The girl on the second programme a week later was in tears. I asked the producer if, for the last programme, I could invite an Italian client whom I was befriending to accompany me. So to that programme he came; it was very brave of him and, as he was rather apprehensive lest his sisters recognized his voice, just before going on the air we agreed to call him Franco instead of using his real name. Imagine our horror on discovering that the compère on that occasion in

Rome was also a Franco. Still worse was to come—the caller was yet another Franco from Milan!

When we said our farewells, the producer told me that the series had meant a great deal to him because a very close relation had committed suicide.

I had promised to reply to any listener who wanted to write. It was then that the really hard work began. Today I keep a drawer full of letters, and in some cases copies of replies, because even after several years I still receive a postcard saying, 'You will not remember me. I am Anna. Everything is all right now. *Tanti cari saluti.*' Her first distraught letter told of an unfaithful husband who neglected her and the children, driving her to the brink of a nervous breakdown. Many correspondents were sick, elderly, lonely or in financial straits; some were in all these categories. Other letters came from people with unusual requests. Could we put them in touch with two British soldiers whom the Italian family had befriended during the war and whose present whereabouts were unknown, having moved away from a Yorkshire village? Thanks to our Leeds Branch, the two brothers' new address was traced. A pregnant girl wanted to come to this country to have her baby so that it would be registered here. She was living with a married man and they wanted to avoid the stigma of illegitimacy that would follow the child all its days, for in Italy the letters 'N.N.' (father unnamed) would be stamped on all documents at birth, at school, at work and doubt-less at death. Everything was arranged with a Midlands nursing home. Telegrams were exchanged. I would take a day off to meet my correspondent and take her across London to catch her train. And then at the last moment the relative who had promised to lend her the money let her down. The child was born in Italy and photographs of my friend's son arrived. I hope that life will not be too hard for him. Then there was a girl who wrote frequently, lengthily, and almost illegibly over a period of five years. She was at loggerheads with her parents and brother and seemed to travel from relation to relation around the country because my replies were often returned marked 'Gone Away'. I became quite attached to her: every letter produced a new problem. She had, however, two great assets: a nice sense of humour and a faithful boyfriend. After a long silence I received news from her a few months ago to say that she would be getting married last October and would certainly inform me—and her family—as soon as the ceremony had taken place. I am still waiting for that card.

It was a long time before I felt I could relax in the evenings without having to hammer out on my typewriter a draft reply to one or other writer. As far as possible I tried to refer people to their nearest branch of 'Telefono Amico'. One had often to skate over thin ice. Supposing the bitter matrimonial row had cooled down by the time my reply reached the writer? One could not say 'What a brute your husband must be!' It could be that, having let off steam by throwing a few plates at each other, the couple were now reconciled or even deliriously happy.

Yes, it was a lonely and very humbling experience to think that a number of people took the trouble to write as they did to an unknown woman in another country.

From Violet 70

Many things spring to mind when I think of the early days of The Samaritans, or 'Chad's Gang' as we were known amongst ourselves. Most of all I wonder how we coped with the inadequacies of those days: though those who sought our help didn't seem to notice them. Perhaps the close proximity when sitting side by side in a dimly lit, often cold, church helped to generate warmth both physicially and otherwise. I remember vividly the Monday lunchtime lectures from various learned people, and the sharing of sandwiches and of course the inevitable cup of coffee. Many close friendships were forged which, because of the fellowship of concern for those who suffer, have withstood the passage of time, even over more than twenty years.

A Caller's Story

'CATHERINE'

I was not suicidal when I contacted The Samaritans. I did not wish to lose my life but to live a different kind of one. This new life was going to be difficult, I was fumbling in the dark and I needed someone to switch on a light and show me around.

It had taken me 24 years to finally come to terms with the fact that I was homosexual. A disastrous marriage and a recent visit to a psychiatrist had all confirmed my fears. And I was very frightened. My mother had reacted to the psychiatrist's report with tears, my father with disbelieving silence. There could be no guidance from them. They were as helpless about it as I was. But the psychiatrist was kind. 'Go and live in London,' he suggested. 'There are plenty of homosexual clubs there.'

I didn't particularly like this idea, although I knew that it would be impossible for me to carry on living at home, in a small town where my sexual eccentricities would have to be kept secret and I would be forced to live a kind of Jekyll and Hyde existence. I was anxious to try to become friends with homosexuality, not to be ashamed of it and if it could be accepted by others, I knew that this would help me enormously. But I was not sure where to start to find this acceptance. Certainly not from those closest to me and I couldn't find the courage to tell my friends, some of whom had known me for as long as fourteen years. I needed confidence in my new sexual self and I didn't see how I could find it in the homosexual clubs of London. I had frightening stories about these clubs—young girls being swallowed up by masculine-looking ladies. They sounded to me more like a battleground than a gentle introduction. Above all, I needed someone to talk to who was not a psychiatrist—for I was not in need of treatment, just a little support and encouragement.

It was in this frame of mind that I came across a newspaper article about The Samaritans. I had always imagined members of the Samaritan movement being busy talking people down off window ledges and I was surprised to learn about the 'befriending' aspect of their work. It seemed to be far too good to be true but I decided to make enquiries. Perhaps someone in The Samaritans would be willing to befriend a bewildered homosexual. While I was making preparations for moving to London, I wrote a tentative letter to Chad Varah at St Stephen Walbrook.

The prompt reply I received was full of encouragement, so much so that I had to read it six times before believing what it said. Chad Varah had made arrangements for an interview and even given me some helpful suggestions about the kind of accommodation I should look for in London.

A week later, I stood outside St Stephen Walbrook, in the City of London, plucking up enough courage to go in for my interview. It was rather like going to ten dental appointments at once. I stumbled down the steps into the warm cave-like interior of the Samaritan headquarters. There were several people about, sitting around on chairs and benches. A selection of teddy bears sat in one corner of the room and I began to feel better. Someone asked me if I would like a cup of tea—I could have been standing in a Lyons Corner Tea House, there were no inquisitive glances, no questions. I explained that I had an appointment with Chad Varah but they gave me a cup of tea anyway which was most welcome at that particular moment. I sat down beside the bears and waited. Would this man say very little like my father or would he burst into tears like my mother? Perhaps he would advise shock treatment or electroconvulsive therapy. I was about to leave my tea and run when a man with a gentle voice and twinkling eyes introduced himself as Chad Varah and asked me to come into his office.

There was something extremely comfortable about him, a feeling of having known him from somewhere before. Perhaps this was due to his attitude towards me—he seemed to be pleased to see me and as we walked along to his office, he introduced me to members of his staff as if I was already a friend.

I thought he was an incredible man. He sat in his office discussing homosexuality as easily as other people talk about yesterday's lunch. I must have looked a bit like a fish for the first part of the interview, as I gaped at him in wonder. He was so very easy to talk to—within an hour, I had described my childhood and adolescence to him, my uneasy relationship with my parents, their uneasy relationship with each other. And then I was able to describe to him, without any embarrassment, how I had always considered myself to be male, the way heterosexual love had kept going wrong, how I was very much attracted to a lady in my office. When he asked me what I felt about her, I was able to tell him with complete confidence. It was the most wonderful moment—to speak of longings that were so much part of me but couldn't be accepted by anyone who thought they knew me well.

It was a long, relaxed and intimate interview, which was an unusual experience in itself for me. I have never found intimate conversation relaxing and it was entirely due to Chad Varah's skill in handling my temperament.

The date and time for another interview were arranged. He told me that I was certainly homosexual, that he had had to ask me so many questions in order to be absolutely certain. And now that he was sure, he said that he would be pleased to help me to adjust in any way that he could and that he would like to feel that I could turn to him whenever I had any problems.

He had already helped me more than he would ever know. He had accepted me totally, had talked to me in a way that no one had before—man to 'man'. He had given me the kind of pep talk a young man needs from his father before he goes out into the world. I stepped out of the Samaritan headquarters with a feeling of inner strength. Whatever happened to me from then on, however many masculine ladies swallowed me up, I had a good friend to turn to and a broad shoulder to cry on.

After that first interview, I saw Chad Varah again several times. As I was virtually going through another period of adolescence, I was constantly in need of reassurance, and he helped me through the birth pains of my first lesbian relationship. In my lowest moments, he was always optimistic for me and when things were going well, he encouraged me along my way.

Six years later, I have settled happily in a small town where my lover and I are accepted by our employers and by our many friends. Perhaps we have just been lucky, but I believe that Chad Varah has a great deal to do with it. My attitude to my homosexuality, thanks to his help, is natural and open, and it seems to follow that other people adopt the same attitude towards it themselves.

So—thank you, Chad Varah and thank you, Samaritans.

Appendix

Note on organisation*

Local level

The Samaritans work in *Branches*, of which there are 167 in the United Kingdom and the Republic of Ireland. Each Branch provides a confidential telephone befriending service 24 hours a day, and befriending face to face at the *Centre* for those who seek it, except (in most Branches) during the night, when volunteers meet clients elsewhere. The Branch is controlled by a *Director* (called *Chairman* in Scotland), *Deputy Directors* and/or *Leaders*, with a Samaritan-in-charge (sic) for each shift. Branches have one or more *Consultants*, of whom the most important is the psychiatric consultant. The administrative and financial support for the Branch (as distinct from its work, which the Director controls) is the responsibility of the *Branch Committee*, elected by the Branch members at the AGM.

National level

The Samaritan Branches collectively are incorporated as a company limited by guarantee (the word 'Limited' being omitted from its title by licence), and known as 'The Samaritans Inc' with offices at 17 Uxbridge Road, Slough, Berks. It is governed by the Memorandum and Articles of Association.

The *Council of Management* of The Samaritans consists of a representative of each Branch. The Council's most important duty is to approve nominations for Branch Director appointments, and one of its three meetings a year is devoted almost exclusively to this task.

*For further background, see Chad Varah, *The Samaritans in the '70s*, 3rd revised ed., Constable (London), 1977.

The Council of Management also elects an *Executive Committee*. The Committee comprises a representative of each *Region* (of which there are twelve in the British Isles), who is responsible for maintaining contact between Branches in his or her area and The Samaritans as a whole; the *Chairman* of the Council, and its three *Vice-Chairmen*; the *Honorary Consultants* to The Samaritans; and members co-opted on account of special expertise. The Committee meets every other month, normally in London.

International level

The Samaritans have Branches in Africa, the Americas, Asia, Australasia and Europe. In 1974 the Council of Management agreed that these Branches should cease to be under the Overseas Committee of The Samaritans and should form an independent sister organization called *Befrienders International (The Samaritans Worldwide)*.

Chad Varah is the Chairman of Befrienders International, and each Continent has a Representative on the Intercontinental Committee which governs it.